Social Policy for Social Change

**BARBARA FAWCETT • SUSAN GOODWIN
GABRIELLE MEAGHER • RUTH PHILLIPS**

palgrave
macmillan

First edition published 2010

 PALGRAVE MACMILLAN
15–19 Claremont Street, South Yarra 3141

Visit our website at www.macmillan.com.au

Associated companies and representatives
throughout the world.

National Library of Australia cataloguing in publication data

Authors: Barbara Fawcett, Susan Goodwn, Gabrielle Meagher and Ruth Phillips
Title: Social Policy for Social Change
Publisher: Palgrave Macmillan
ISBN: 978 1 4202 56161 (pbk.)
Notes: Includes index
Subjects: Human services, Social policy
Dewey number: 361.61

Publisher: Elizabeth Vella
Project editor: Liz Spelman
Editor: Gail Tagarro
Cover designer: Dimitrios Frnagoulis
Text designer: Patrick Cannon
Permissions clearance: Wendy Duncan
Typeset in Bembo 14pt by Linda Hamley, Melbourne
Cover image: Shutterstock/Trutta
Indexer: Mary Russell

Printed in Malaysia

Internet addresses
At the time of printing, the internet addresses appearing in this book were correct. Owing to the dynamic nature of the
internet, however, we cannot guarantee that all these addresses will remain correct.

While every care has been taken to trace and acknowledge copyright, the publishers tender their apologies for any
accidental infringement where copyright has proved untraceable. They would be pleased to come to a suitable
arrangement with the rightful owner in each case.

CONTENTS

Acknowledgments

Many individuals provided support and input into the process of writing this book. Thanks go to Elizabeth Vella of Palgrave Macmillan for her enthusiasm for the book from the outset. We would also like to thank David Lilley, Eileen Fishwick and Shaun Wilson for reading and providing very helpful comments on different parts of the manuscript.

Barbara Fawcett would like to acknowledge the support given by family members, Maurice, Katie and Sophie and to recognise the positive and intellectually stimulating collaboration brought about by this project.

Susan Goodwin would like to acknowledge her colleagues, in various research projects over the years, who have deepened her knowledge and understanding of social policy and social change. These people include Amanda Elliot, Kate Huppatz, Jude Irwin and Robin Miles. She would also like to thank Bettina Cass, who introduced her to the discipline of social policy. Her family, Don, Luca and Billy have been very patient; thank you.

Gabrielle Meagher would like to thank her long-time collaborators, Shaun Wilson and Karen Healy, for their intellectual and personal companionship. She is also grateful to Natasha Cortis, who generously agreed to allow us to draw on work that she and Gabrielle had done on 'welfare-to-work' programs for chapter 9. She would like to say *Tack så jättemycket* to her colleagues at Stockholm University's Department of Social Work for providing a wonderfully hospitable working environment during the final stages of her work on the book. She is also extremely grateful to her husband David for his patient and loving support.

Ruth Phillips would like to thank her colleagues in the Social Work and Policy Studies Program, and especially members of the Social Policy Research Network for creating an innovative intellectual environment for social policy thinking and research. She also acknowledges the support and patience of her family, Michael, Eugene and Reuben.

Writing the book has been a wonderful opportunity for us to work together and share what we have learned in years of teaching and research in the fields of social policy, political economy and social work, and from direct interactions with people in the human services. We would like to acknowledge human services workers and recognise the very challenging and important work they do, regardless of the seismic shifts that sometimes occur in the availability of resources and in directions in social policy.

About the authors

Barbara Fawcett is Professor of Social Work and Policy Studies in the Faculty of Education and Social Work at the University of Sydney and an Honorary Research Professor at the University of Bradford.

Susan Goodwin is Senior Lecturer and Associate Director of the Doctoral Division in the Faculty of Education and Social Work at the University of Sydney.

Gabrielle Meagher is Professor of Social Policy in the Faculty of Education and Social Work at the University of Sydney.

Ruth Phillips is Senior Lecturer in the Faculty of Education and Social Work at the University of Sydney.

Barbara, Susan, Gabrielle and **Ruth** are all members of the Faculty's Social Policy Research Network.

Preface

How to understand and intervene in social policy as a human service professional is a perennial problem. This book directly engages with that strategic imperative, while also making clear links between the dynamic fields of theory, policy and practice. Throughout the book, we pay attention to the many ways in which strategic engagement with key political, social and economic frameworks and agendas can facilitate both policy development and policy change. We explore how social policy is made and implemented, how those working in the human service field can utilise knowledge to constructively engage in the production of social policy and how social policy can be framed in radical, reactionary and re-invigorated ways. We draw examples and ideas from a range of countries in order to provide comparative insights about the background, impact and effects of social policy.

The central project of this book is to establish meaning and perspectives around social policy as a tool for or facilitator of positive social change. We view the concepts of social policy and social change through a range of political, ideological, social and academic lenses. We emphasise how social policies are formulated under the influence of various, often conflicting, drivers and explore how different policy spaces can be flexibly utilised to bring about social change. As part of this process, we appraise both large-scale and localised policy frameworks in the human service practice environment. Throughout, the formulation of social policy is not viewed as a rational, linearly orchestrated process but rather as an ever-changing mix of interpretation, construction and the interplay of different interests, perspectives and orientations. As a result, social policy is portrayed as dynamic, engaging, flexible, provisional and often specific to its context. Our perspective on social policy seeks to highlight opportunities for human service professionals to achieve change in a variety of ways and situations.

A note on language

As will become clear, language is significant in social policy. At this point, then, we would like to say something about some of the choices about language we have made in writing this book. From an international perspective, various terms are used to describe the services involved in social provision. Common terms include 'welfare services', 'social services', 'public services', 'social care services' and 'social administration'. The meaning and usage of each of these terms varies from country to country, and even within nations local distinctions and ambiguities prevail. Thus, we use the term 'human services' as a catch-all category covering a broad range of services and facilities provided by public, non-profit and private agencies. The category includes the diversity of services provided to the public such as childcare and adult day care facilities, homeless and housing services, social security offices, adoption and foster care services, mental health services, family support services, education and health services and the range of forms of economic assistance. As this book concerns social policy in its broadest sense, the terms 'human services' and 'human service organisations' are used regularly, except where more specific terms are more appropriate.

The people who work in the human services sector of any given society are also identified—and they identify themselves—in a variety of ways. While the term 'human service worker' or 'human service professional' accurately describes workers in the sector, workers often refer to their professional or organisational affiliation or specific occupational field when describing themselves. So, for example, human service workers are also public servants, community workers, social service workers, social workers, health workers, nurses, youth workers and aged care workers. Again, we use a variety of terms in this book to acknowledge this diversity. Workers are variously referred to as human service workers, human service professionals and human service practitioners.

The preferred terms for individuals who use human services reflect meanings that have been attached to social provision, and these meanings position human service users in very specific ways. As Kristin Heffernan (2006) observes, the language used to describe individuals who use social services has shifted over the past 50 years, and these shifts can be associated with new ideas about the nature of provider-user relationships. So, for example, terms used in the 1960s such as 'client' and 'patient' were challenged on the basis that they suggested, and produced, a fundamental inequality between providers and users, making practitioners the 'experts' on the social needs or social problems of individuals. Similarly, the more recent language of 'consumers' can be related to the emergence of consumer rights movements wanting more say in the design and delivery of social provision. However, it is also associated with the reframing of human services in line with a market economy, whereby services are seen as commodities and recipients are regarded as customers. Even more recently, a language of 'service users' has begun to replace the language of consumers, both as a way of establishing individual rights to involvement in social provision *and* as a way of government's identifying and targeting groups of the population (Beresford and Croft, 2004; Clarke, 2006). In specific areas of social provision, language is just as politically charged. Labels such as 'pensioners', 'beneficiaries', 'recipients', 'cases', 'victims', '*the* disabled', '*the* aged', 'youth' and so forth, have all been subject to debates about how labels constitute people and position them in relation to others. This book is attentive to these debates, and seeks to refer to those who access social provisions in ways that emphasise the ubiquity of human service usage—all people receive social services at some point in their lives—and avoid stigmatising or marginalising particular groups of users.

The language we use to describe people who are active in social policy processes also varies. As will be discussed, social policy can be a relatively closed or open affair, involving specialised groups or entire communities. In this book, terms like 'decision-makers', 'players', 'stakeholders', 'actors', 'participants', 'policy networks', 'policy communities' and 'citizens' are used, depending on the context. Most significantly, the book is concerned with highlighting the range of social positions from which intervention in policy is possible.

Finally, we focus most of our attention on what we call, following Harold Wilensky (2002), 'rich democracies'. These are countries in which welfare states have developed over the twentieth century, and that have market-orientated economies, high per capita incomes and some variant on a parliamentary democratic system of government that gives citizens a meaningful voice in policy-making. Over the last 50 years, social scientists have used many terms to collect into a single category Western Europe, North America, the rich countries of east Asia and the Antipodes. These include the terms 'industrialised nations', 'advanced capitalist nations', 'advanced industrialised societies', 'post-industrial societies', 'stable democratic states', 'the First World', 'the North', 'liberal democracies', 'OECD countries', 'Western liberal democratic societies', and so on. Each term has its strengths and weaknesses and carries theoretical baggage.

Many have had some 'time in the sun' as the term of choice, or contention. We favour Wilensky's term because it is concretely descriptive and carries relatively little theoretical baggage.

By choosing a single collective term to stand for a large and internally diverse group, we are clearly assuming that it makes sense to talk about these countries *as a group*. How much the rich democracies have in common, how much they differ, and whether they are converging under the pressures of modernisation and globalisation is much debated among political economists, political sociologists and social policy analysts. We do not seek to contribute to this debate. Rather, our aim is to create an empirical and analytical boundary around the scope of the book. We breach this boundary only occasionally, when powerful examples from nations with different social and economic structures and levels of development serve to illustrate a point or provide a contrast. This boundary creates a universe within which policy comparison makes sense because other things, such as the level of economic resources and the openness of government, are more or less equal.

Overview of the book

In chapter 1, we focus on what social policy is, and on the significance of social policy and social change. We emphasise the centrality of human services in social policy, describing the ways in which social policy shapes the human services sector *and* the ways that human services shape and make social policy. The chapter presents key concepts and ideas related to defining and analysing social policy. This material provides a basis for the more detailed interrogation of social policy for social change undertaken throughout the book.

Chapter 2 explores the processes involved in making social policy. This chapter questions conventional depictions or 'maps', which suggest that the policy process follows a rational, linear format designed for solving social problems. We argue that human service workers often experience policy processes as a much messier means of naming, framing, interpretation and contestation. Social policy production can be seen as a set of discursive activities. However, the chapter is also interested in the institutional or organisational spaces available for human service workers to participate in such discursive activities. We therefore discuss how participation in policy processes can be opened up, and closed down, as a result of different approaches to governance.

In chapter 3, we look at the essentially political nature of social policy. We explore how history and context influence how social policy is formed, drawing on specific examples of struggles for power over meaning, ideology and resources. To communicate the political nature of social policy-making, and to explain why human service professionals need to understand this, we focus on some specific areas, such as healthcare and women's policy. The chapter also provides an overview of the range of players in policy processes and the interactions between them. These include those involved in social policy-making and delivery, and organised bodies that advocate on behalf of different interests in the policy process.

In chapter 4, we explore the relationship between values and policy processes. We begin by examining the connection between ethics, morality and values before reviewing the ways in which the addition of rights influences the discussion. We also consider the links between different political approaches—specifically, social democratic, neo-liberal and 'third way' orientations—and their underpinning value systems. Throughout, the 'taken for granted' assumptions are interrogated and the implications for human service professionals are appraised.

In chapter 5, we set out some key economic dimensions of social policy in order to demonstrate how and why understanding quantitative and monetary dimensions of social policy matters. Human service practitioners tend to think of themselves as orientated towards people and values, rather than towards numbers and money. Yet those who are able to understand and engage the economic dimensions of policy formation and policy analysis are better placed to participate in social policy and resist the inappropriate application of economic ideas. We examine different dimensions of social spending; in particular, what instruments governments use to reallocate social resources through the taxing and spending they undertake, what kinds of income support and social services governments in different rich democracies spend taxes on, and what impact different levels and patterns of social spending have on inequality and poverty. We also consider the role of private social spending, and assess the argument that social spending is a drain on economic growth.

In chapter 6, our focus is on organisations that implement social policy, with an emphasis on human services. Because human service provision always takes place in an organisational context, we need to understand how people and organisations interact in the process of social policy implementation. The chapter includes a systematic exploration of theoretical arguments for and against the involvement of different kinds of organisations—public, NGOs and for-profits—in human service provision. We also examine some evidence about the impact of diversifying the kinds of organisations involved in human services. From a policy perspective, we argue that it is crucial to recognise that the policy *context* in which different kinds of organisations operate is critical to the ability of organisations to pursue their own goals.

In chapter 7, we consider how people, as implementers of social policy, are enabled and constrained by their organisational environments and by broader social structures and discourses, such as gender and professionalism. We examine two key groups of people involved in social policy implementation—human service practitioners and volunteers—and consider some key debates about their identities, roles, relationships and motivations. We also include a brief discussion of the role of the service user in the social policy process, since important developments in both discourse and practice have changed their position in recent decades. Overall, the chapter aims to offer some concepts, arguments and evidence to support practitioners' reflections on their own participation in social policy for social change.

In chapter 8, we highlight that a purely rational scientific basis for social policy has proved elusive. The reasons are complex. They touch on some of the most fundamental issues in the philosophy of science and the nature of human institutions. We aim to give a sense of this complexity by examining the links between research, social policy and human service practice. We argue that although the idea of evidence is far more complex than is often portrayed, research does and should play a crucial role in the social policy arena, and that human service professionals can gain much by participating in research activity. To this end, we include an extended discussion of evaluation, which is the research activity that human service practitioners are most likely to engage in. However, we also argue that evidence does not, perhaps cannot, replace politics in defining and alleviating social problems.

Chapter 9 examines a key area of reorientation in social policy. 'Social inclusion' has become, or is emerging as, a core social policy framework in a number of rich democracies, often in association with a 'welfare-to-work' reorientation of income support systems. We analyse how such umbrella policies reorientate the objectives and goals of welfare states more broadly, and draw on this analysis to assess the application of broad social policy frameworks critically. The major aim of this chapter is to provide a critical insight for human service workers into how understandings of broad social policy frameworks can be utilised to improve, or perhaps to homogenise, the experience of service users. The chapter also encourages human service workers to retain a critical perspective while engaging, in productive ways, with the social inclusion agenda.

In chapter 10, two examples of radical interventions in social policy are used to explore the differences between reactionary entrenchment and significant advancement in social policy. The first is the 'shock and awe' campaign of the Howard Liberal-National Coalition Government (1996-2007) to take over Aboriginal policy in the Northern Territory in 2007. The second is the approach taken by the Labour Government in England towards 'looked after' children, or children in the care system, between 1997 and 2002. Although these two policies have very different underpinning rationales and consequences, we draw attention to the fact that both interventions were centrally directed, both had universal application and both were directed towards groups grappling with marginalisation and the consequences of social exclusion. We review how these radical interventions came about, the consequences for their target groups and the implications for human service professionals.

Chapter 11 explores the recent emphasis on the role of communities and community participation in a range of social policy areas. This shift has been heralded as an important element in the reinvigoration of social services and social protection, signifying a renewed commitment to social policy for positive social change. The chapter examines the emergence of new relationships between governments and civil society and discusses what these new relationships may mean for human services. In order to examine the traps and opportunities that the 'return to community' presents to human service organisations and human service practitioners, the focus is on the policies, projects and practices that emerge around the concept 'community capacity building'.

In the concluding chapter, we draw together the various themes of the book to demonstrate the importance of viewing social policy as a flexible instrument and strategy for achieving social change. This chapter encapsulates the fundamentally optimistic threads running through the book, which position social policy as a process that can be harnessed by human service practitioners in their work at the point of service delivery or through their advocacy with and for the groups, families or individuals they work with.

We acknowledge that this book has been written at a time, in the first decade of the twenty-first century, of great turmoil in the wider world.

Persistent poverty, enduring conflict over ethnic and religious identity and power, economic turmoil, and ongoing struggles over resources signify a world short of optimism. It is a world where solutions to big social policy problems seem as elusive as ever, while the issues of how to share the world's riches, and how to ensure the safety of the global environment, are becoming more acute. We hope, however, that our book embodies and engenders a feeling of optimism, of moving forward through a process of critical engagement, where both the failures and successes in the use of social policy are seen as a mechanism for social change. We are passionate about finding solutions to inequality and exclusion from participation in the rewards of our time, especially exclusion from the tremendous insight enabled by the rapid and ever-deepening exchange of knowledge about how things are working now.

CHAPTER 1

Social policy and social change

Introduction

The general aim of this book is to bring to light the dynamic links between policy, theory and practice in order to provide a new approach to understanding and intervening in social policy in rich democracies. This approach places human services at the centre of social policy development and analysis, as well as seeing human services as key sites of social change. In this approach, social policy and human services are considered inseparable: social policy makes (and breaks) human services and human services make (and break) social policy.

This chapter establishes understandings of the two key concepts of the book: *social policy* and *social change*.

Social policy is described in terms of different types of public interventions relating to social needs and social problems. These interventions have implications for four distinct spheres of society—the state, the market, the family and the community, which can be but are not always understood through welfare state analyses.

Social change is described in terms of global, national and community transformations as well as changes that occur at the individual level. Social policies are implicated in social change: the very idea of developing and implementing public interventions to address social problems or social needs involves a commitment to social change. As such, human service workers are also implicated in social change.

Our aim in this chapter is to present the themes and concepts that provide a basis for the more detailed interrogation of social policy for social change provided throughout the book.

Human services and social policies

Government provision for social welfare has a long history and the social services that have developed over time have increasingly become integral to people's lives. The systems that have been developed for maintaining and lifting standards of health and education and protecting citizens in old age, illness, incapacity, unemployment and poverty have become, in many countries, an expectation. In rich democracies, social provisions go well beyond basic health, education and poverty alleviation. For example, the Australian Institute of Health and Welfare (2007a) reports on social spending across more than 50 different areas of service provision, including services for children, families, people with disabilities, people caring for people with disabilities, aged people and people with specific illnesses, conditions or special needs. The report also identifies more than 20 different categories of cash transfers, including payments for parents, orphans, low-income tenants, older people, students and young people. Today, then, most individuals in countries like Australia encounter human services in their daily lives—in educational institutions, in healthcare settings, as parents, as residents and as workers. In one sense, government provisions for social welfare are often taken for granted. At the levels of policy and politics, however, they are hotly contested.

Contemporary social provisions have their origins in the nineteenth century, when rapid urbanisation and industrialisation in western societies dramatically transformed living conditions. Schemes for public sanitation, education, policing, prisons, juvenile detention, public workhouses and mental asylums, are all examples of early social services. Philanthropic agencies also began developing social services to work with the destitute, working alongside statutory agencies such as courts, asylums and workhouses. These new services accompanied legislation governing working conditions, health and safety standards and public and private behaviour, while new mechanisms for measuring populations and recording social change emerged, enabling further development in the role of government in social life.

During the twentieth century, human services became increasingly professionalised and institutionalised. Social services, rather than being seen as charitable actions or emergency measures, began to be regarded as an expression of state responsibility for the health and welfare of the citizenry. The period often referred to as the 'high tide' of the welfare state, the 1970s, witnessed the expansion of social provisions into yet new areas of social life. It was during this period that new social movements politicised a whole range of emergent social needs—domestic violence, sexual assault, disability rights, gay and lesbian issues—and made claims on the state for services and the funding of organisations to provide services (Goodwin, 2003). In the twenty-first century, despite the 'rolling back' of some aspects of the welfare state, western governments continue to be integrally involved in providing for social needs. These developments have resulted in a proliferation of diverse organisations and agencies engaged in social policy activities. Human service professionals are located in such organisations as these.

In this book, we argue that the fields of social policy and human services are inseparable. This is because social policy makes human services—social policy shapes the working lives of human service providers in real and significant ways. Because of this, human services need to be considered the objects of social policy—entities that are produced and reduced, reformed and transformed by social policies. At the same time, human services make social policy. Because human service workers are often fundamentally involved in providing services to people whose circumstances are directly and vitally affected by social policies, practitioners are expected to contribute to the monitoring, evaluation and development of social policies. As a result, human service providers are consistently required to interpret, enforce, circumvent, research, advocate and design social policies.

We turn first to the idea that social policy makes human services.

One of the most basic ways that social policies shape the working life of human service providers is by producing employment settings and sites and, indeed, creating human service occupations themselves. Social policy involves the allocation of resources to meet social needs; a significant proportion of these resources goes to services and the organisations that administer services. As a result, funds that flow from social policies are spent on the professionals, para-professionals and technical and administrative staff involved in the delivery of services. The beneficiaries of social policies, then, are not only the *recipients* of services, but human service *providers* as well. Social policies also create different categories of human service work—community care policies will require community care workers, family support policies require family support workers, child protection policies require child protection workers and so on. In this way, social policies can be seen to shape the very existence (or non-existence) of employment and occupational opportunities for a large cross-section of the community, well beyond those conventionally regarded as the objects of social policy—the sick, the poor or the disadvantaged.

As discussed in more detail throughout this book, employment and occupational positions in the human services are not limited to government or public sector jobs. Human services are predominantly funded publicly but they are provided by a mix of public sector, non-government, private and voluntary organisations (Bryson, 2001; Brown and Keast, 2005; Mendes, 2008). The distribution of jobs within this 'mixed economy' of welfare is also shaped by social policies. The sectoral locations, for example, of aged care nurses, childcare workers and family support workers have changed significantly as policies about how best to deliver these services have changed. In turn, the types of human service work undertaken and the financial rewards that flow from this work depend on sectoral location: for example, those employed in public sector organisations often receive higher incomes and more generous benefits than those working in non-government social service organisations. Again, these are basic ways in which social policies shape the working lives of human service workers.

In addition to providing human service employment opportunities, social policies govern the activities undertaken within human service agencies. Social policies provide the substantive frameworks for service provision—who gets what, when, in what form and under what conditions, and how provisions are financed (Chambers and Wedel, 2005). While only some human service workers will be primarily involved in designing these frameworks, they are an integral part of the work of all human service workers. Frameworks include those developed at the levels of national and sub-national government (state, provincial or local government) and at the level of 'small scale policy systems' (Flynn, 1992), such as professional associations and social service organisations. In this sense, social policies are involved in *making* the work of human service providers at the level of day-to-day practice.

We turn now to the idea of human service workers making social policy.

While policy frameworks and systems can set out the parameters for practice, it is also the case that individual practitioners are constantly making decisions in relation to the implementation of social policies. They are thus involved in the interpretative acts of deciphering, defining and applying social policies to fit specific circumstances. This is one sense in which social policies are 'made' at the level of individual practice. For example, many policies are implemented by what Michael Lipsky (1980) called 'street level bureaucrats'. According to Lipsky, street level bureaucrats actually create policy through the multitude of decisions they make when interacting with clients.

The many studies of police officers, firefighters, teachers, nurses, case workers and other front-line workers typically show that these groups of workers exercise considerable discretion in the implementation of policy. Stephen Maynard-Moody and Michael Mushena (2003) in *Cops, Teachers, Counselors: Stories from the Front Lines of Public Service* reiterate the significant role of front-line workers in making social policy and demonstrate the ways in which they make policy choices and influence the direction and outcome of policies. According to their research, workers do not tend to treat citizen-clients as 'abstractions … but as individuals with flaws and strengths who rarely fall within the one-size fits all approach of policies and laws' (Maynard-Moody and Mushena, 2003, p. 94).

Human service workers, through their contact with individuals, families and communities, encounter a great deal of information about social policy gaps and impacts. At times, this information is very stark: when a client loses a child or ends up in jail, or when a community disintegrates because social policy could not deal with the uniqueness or singularity of their circumstances. Social policies, by their very nature, are generalisations. They generalise about social issues, social problems and social relations in an attempt to produce patterned responses. So, for example, policies prescribing 'de-institutionalisation' of people with mental illness, 'capacity building' for disadvantaged communities or 'equal opportunities' for women are a general response to a whole set of diverse situations and circumstances. As such, social policies are not designed with the needs of *individuals* (or specific families or particular communities) in mind; rather, they are designed for *groups* (or categories) perceived to share common features (Bacchi, 1996; Fincher, 1995). Because of this, social policies will fail some, perhaps many, individuals on some occasions.

Despite or perhaps because of this inherent 'weakness', social policy is a vehicle for social change. The idea of developing general responses to recurring or patterned individual problems is particularly significant for human service workers. Much human service work is distinctive in its simultaneous focus on individuals and the social context of their lives. In some positions, this includes an expectation that workers will intervene beyond the individual level of experience. This means that where workers encounter issues or problems that require a generalised response, they are expected to contribute to program development, policy debate and policy development. This may involve participating in social action or activism or it may be confined to feeding information 'up' through the organisation, 'through the right channels' (Dalton et al., 1996, p. 20). In other organisations, workers will be limited to administering existing social policies. Yet they, too, contribute to program and policy development through data collection and record keeping. While these may appear formalised and constrained ways of imparting information about policy gaps and impacts, service data and records are often drawn upon in the evaluation, monitoring and review of social policies.

Human service professionals do not only participate in making social policy through their workplaces. They are often involved through membership of professional associations, unions, inter-agencies, peak bodies, social movements or lobby groups and in their private lives as individual citizens.

In order to participate in social policy for social change, this book provides a comprehensive discussion of the issues and debates relevant to making and delivering social policy and the knowledge, skills and resources related to social policy engagement. It also provides grounded examples of the pitfalls and dilemmas associated with social policy for social change in the contemporary context.

What is social policy?

Often, commentators on social policy begin with statements about the struggle to define social policy, resulting in what Alan Fenna (2004, p. 322) regards as 'conveniently vague definitions' in which 'virtually everything and anything "society" does is social policy'. Definitions of social policy vary, but there is general agreement that, in essence, social policy is concerned with the principles and practices of pursuit by government of social outcomes. For this reason, social policy discussion and analysis conventionally focus on government action in the fields of income support, healthcare, housing, education and training and the personal social services. Clearly, the boundaries of social policy extend into areas that are conventionally described as 'economic policy'—for example, employment, industrial, monetary and taxation policy, and other areas of 'public policy' such as immigration, law enforcement, industrial relations and criminal justice. But while public policy refers to all the policies of government, social policy focuses more on quality of life issues that affect the overall welfare of citizens. In this book, social policy is understood as *systematic public interventions relating to social needs and problems* (Fitzpatrick et al., 2006, p. 2).

Social policy: governments and public interventions

To speak of social policy in terms of systematic public interventions involves making a distinction between organisations in the private and public sectors. Public sector organisations are governments and their various agencies. A community group may have a 'policy' of charging fees for certain services; a commercial company might have a policy of affirmative action in the workplace; a religious organisation may have a policy of giving to people who are poor. However, these are not *public* policies because they are undertaken by private organisations, which have discretion over how and to whom they apply these policies. Also, individuals can opt out of the policies. Thus, the public–private distinction is fundamental to understanding social policy. In short, public interventions involve the exercise of authority over citizens within political jurisdictions, which can be backed up by the force of law (Fenna, 2004, p. 5).

In most countries, there are multiple levels of government; thus, social policy includes the activities of national, state/provincial and local/municipal governments. Indeed, many aspects of social provision are undertaken at lower levels of government, which often have significant powers of their own, including the power to raise finances independently of the central state. Often, however, the authority to raise the bulk of revenue through income taxes rests with the national government. Hence, responsibility for social policies is allocated to lower levels of government through power and resource sharing frameworks. In federal systems, such as Australia, the US, Canada and Germany, policymaking is complicated by the tensions of intergovernmental relations; gaps and overlaps between jurisdictions can emerge. In chapter 3, we discuss how this occurs in health policy in Australia.

The existence of multiple government centres also creates the potential for diversity in social policies within nations. For example, in Canada, sole parents may receive different benefits depending on the province they live in (Westhue,

2006); in Australia, education systems vary from state to state (Kenway, 2006). This kind of jurisdictional complexity can also occur in unitary states like Britain, France, Sweden and New Zealand, where local governments can have an important role in social policy. For human service professionals, understanding social policy requires knowledge of governmental roles and responsibilities. This involves being able to identify which levels of government are active in particular social policy areas and how power and authority to make decisions is distributed between levels of government. We sometimes refer to this as an understanding of the legal and administrative arrangements for social policy.

Forms of government action

In addition to understanding the legal and administrative arrangements for social policy, it is also useful to be able to distinguish between different types of public intervention, or forms of government action. In doing so, we are reminded that the field of social policy is concerned with much more than expenditure on pensions and benefits; it also comprises a broader set of instruments, each of which requires attention. There are three main forms of government action or public intervention used to address social problems and meet social needs. These are: cash benefits, provision of services and regulations (see Le Grand, 1993). Thus, social policy needs to be considered in terms of actions around money, services and rules.

Cash benefits

One form of government action to address social needs is the provision of cash benefits to individuals or households. Cash benefits can be paid directly, in the form of income support payments such as unemployment benefits, aged pensions, childcare assistance, rent assistance or family allowances. But they can also be paid indirectly by reducing the tax some people would otherwise have to pay, through tax exemptions, tax deductions or tax credits. The first form—direct cash benefits—are perhaps the best known, as social policy debates often centre on the cost and coverage of 'welfare payments'. The second type—where cash benefits are delivered through the taxation system—is, however, an increasingly significant social policy instrument. As we show in chapter 5, cash benefits make up the majority of social expenditure in rich democracies.

Services

The funding or direct provision of social services, such as healthcare, family support, education or housing, is another means by which governments meet social needs. Services may be offered universally, to all citizens; education is organised this way in most rich democracies, health in many. Other services are provided to meet specific needs, such as family support for isolated and at-risk families and home care services for frail older people. Some services, such as child protection, are non-voluntary, provided by agencies granted legal powers to intervene in the lives of individuals. These 'statutory services' are almost always provided by public organisations. The extent of publicly funded services and the kinds of organisations that offer them—public, non-government or for-profit—differ from country to country. We consider these variations in chapters 5 and 6.

Regulation

A third means by which governments take action in the social arena is through regulation, which is the implementation of rules governing what organisations and individuals can and cannot do. Theodore Lowi (1966) defined 'regulation' as governments' way of controlling, constraining or modifying the actions and behaviours of groups and individuals. Social policy is replete with examples of regulations associated with social needs and social problems. Legislation governing public health issues, workplace health and safety and housing and education standards has been introduced as a way of establishing universal standards in society. Anti-discrimination legislation in relation to race, gender and disability, and laws around the treatment of children and people with mental illnesses are mechanisms designed to establish and protect human rights. Organisations providing social services are regulated by governments, which may mandate the quality, standard, scope and nature of their activities. Similarly, individual behaviour is constrained and modified by government action—wearing seatbelts, taking drugs and having sex are all the subject of regulation. There are likely to be thousands of regulations in any one rich democracy that are designed to achieve broadly social goals.

Government regulatory activities, particularly where they concern the regulation of previously 'free' markets or aspects of family life deemed to be 'private or personal', have been at the centre of debates about the role of the state in society. In the field of social policy, however, regulation is often a preferred option. Manning and colleagues (2007, p. 17) suggest that this may be because 'it is generally the cheapest way to achieve a social policy goal'. In most modern societies, governmental regulatory activity has increased over the past few decades, particularly as the market has moved into social service provision. Regulation is seen as a crucial way of ensuring quality, accessibility, legitimacy and accountability of publicly funded or publicly mandated activities and services.

A fourth form? Government inaction

This section has focused on social policy as public interventions, which have been described as government *actions* (occurring at all levels of government) taking various forms: cash, service provision and regulation. However, to take into account the full range of government approaches to social intervention, the term social policy needs also to cover government *inaction* on social issues. In other words, government inaction and non-decision, particularly when consistently pursued against pressure to the contrary, can be considered social policy. One example of social policy as inaction in Australia would be the failure of public intervention in the area of dental healthcare (Lewis, 2006). Another example concerns paid maternity leave (Burgess and Strachan, 2005). Norman Ginsburg (1992) argued that social policy as inaction and non-decision are particularly apparent in areas such as family policy, where governments uphold the privacy of the family while inevitably, at the same time, intervening in many ways in family life.

The ability to recognise and distinguish between different types of government action (and inaction) enables human service workers to participate in debates about the diversity of options available to address social needs. So, for example, nurses and teachers confronted with poor health or educational outcomes in a given community are encouraged to explore the issues and solutions in terms of the distribution and impact of cash benefits, tax relief, service provision and the appropriateness of rules and regulations, as well as consider areas of government inaction. Similarly, analyses of the social policy agendas of different political parties or governments need to consider the ways in which they are orientated towards or away from different types of governmental action, either in particular areas of social life or as a general approach.

Social policy: states, markets, families and communities

Government action (and inaction) not only embraces the direct provision of cash benefits and services but also concerns regulation and subsidisation of a range of other actors and activities. For this reason, social policy analysts typically talk about four distinct spheres in society, namely the 'state' (discussed in detail in the previous section), the 'market', the 'family' and the 'community'. Within this schema, social policy is conceptualised as the state intersecting with the other three spheres. The schema allows us to understand public interventions as including the government actions which shape private, non-government and informal welfare. It also provides a basis for talking about a 'mixed economy of welfare' or 'welfare mix' (Healy, J. 1998), which includes government *and* non-government provision of welfare services and welfare benefits. Our aim in this section is to set out the broad contours of the way social policy analysts define and theorise the spheres and their interactions. In later chapters, we discuss their operation and interactions more concretely.

The market

The market is the domain where money talks. When conceptualised as an ideal type by sociologists and economists, the market is the domain of free exchange between individuals, and all three terms—'free', 'exchange' and 'individual'—are critical. In markets, individuals choose to exchange things they own (money, goods, services, their labour) for other things they want with other individuals who are assumed to be doing the same. Ideally, these exchanges are freely chosen and each party benefits, from his or her own perspective. More concretely, the 'market' is more or less synonymous with the economy, comprising businesses engaged in producing and circulating goods and services to people who have the money to buy them. The people who own or are employed by one business are the customers of other businesses, completing the circle. Markets, then, respond to *individual* preferences, not to *social* preferences (Ocampo, 2006), which is one reason why the market is often thought of as the 'private sector'.

In social policy terms, the intersection between government and the market is conceptualised as government action to compensate for the failure of the market to provide comprehensively for social needs or address social problems. From this perspective, the state steps in to provide benefits and services, either because it would be 'unprofitable' for the market to provide them or owing to the lack of allocative justice that arises because only those who are able to pay in markets receive services or benefits. In liberal capitalist democracies, the market is generally seen as being capable of providing for many individual needs; social policy is required when it does not. Public interventions are required, for example, in situations of market failure where the market excludes people who are considered 'bad risks' and have extreme needs. Public interventions are also needed when people do not have a choice of provider (in the case of monopolies) and when people are required by law to receive services (in the case of statutory services). Governments also become involved if people do not or cannot bear the costs of services considered necessary requirements of life in a particular social context. Thus, the inequitable or indiscriminate nature of market activities can be seen to shape the activities of government.

Government action can also shape the market domain, and it does this in a variety of ways. Indeed, economic historians have shown that governments actually establish markets by creating or removing and enforcing property rights and other rules to ensure that markets operate properly (Polanyi, 1944). Governments also support the market by providing incentives and subsidies to some private providers. In addition, they regulate markets, particularly through the regulation of the quality, nature or scope of products and services provided through the market. Some markets are regulated so that provision is made more universal or more equitable. Similarly, government can regulate the labour market by regulating the relationships between the buyers and sellers of labour. This has been one of the most important government interventions in relation to social welfare in the broad sense. The setting of wages and conditions through industrial relations institutions and legislation, such as the minimum wage in the US, the family wage in Australia and equal pay legislation in numerous countries, has been one of the key ways in which individuals secure their standard of living.

Social policies, then, can *privatise* social welfare and *commodify* goods, services and labour when they shift activity or responsibility from governments to the market, or they can *socialise* welfare and *decommodify* goods, services and labour when they shift activity or responsibility from the market to the state. As we shall see in later chapters, in recent decades the market sphere has had a resurgent role in social policy, as market institutions and ideas have been taken up by governments in the social policy field.

The family

As feminist social policy analysts such as Jane Lewis (1993; 2006) have pointed out, the family has always been the main provider of welfare. The continuing provision of informal welfare by family members, particularly women, is the backdrop to most social policies. In addition, many social policies, in effect, shift the boundaries between state and family by defining and re-defining the proper role of each, and this process of identifying state and family responsibilities is ongoing and contested (Naldini, 2003). Debates about the legitimacy of public intervention in family life have circulated around issues such as domestic violence, child-rearing practices, the roles of men and women, sexuality and reproduction, all of which have been regarded as 'private issues' that should be immune from government action. The balancing of responsibilities between the family and the state in the provision of social welfare is a key aspect of social policy.

There is a range of ways in which government action shapes family provision of welfare (see Fine and Shaver, 1995). Sometimes, family provision is enforced through the non-provision or withdrawal of public assistance. The lack of government provision of maternity benefits, childcare services or aged care services, for example, can be considered ways in which social policy enforces family provision of care and support for children and older people. Sometimes, family provision of welfare is relieved by government—childcare services, education, free healthcare and aged care services all 'relieve' families of these responsibilities. Finally, family provision of welfare can be 'supported' by government, through the development of partnerships between state, community and family. Here an example would be the 'shared care' arrangements put in place where families are expected to care for sick or disabled relatives, with assistance from government benefits and community service providers. Social policies, then, can *familialise* goods, services and labour by insisting that they be largely produced or supplied by families, or *de-familialise* goods, services and labour by enabling them to be provided through other institutions (Esping-Andersen, 1999).

The community

The sphere of society labelled 'community' has many names: 'the Third Sector', the 'not-for-profit sector', the 'voluntary sector', the 'social economy' and, increasingly in Australia, the 'non-government' or 'NGO sector' (Brown and Keast, 2005). This sphere consists of a variety of diverse organisations, associations and relationships. In international circles and the United Nations, it is called civil society. Civil society refers to the array of non-government organisations (NGOs), such as churches, Scouts groups, sporting clubs, veterans' groups, unions, book clubs and parents and citizens' associations. What is distinctive about these associations and organisations is that they freely organise themselves and engage in 'voluntary' activity (Deakin, 2001; Walzer, 1995). They may be involved in social, cultural or political activities and be self-fulfilling (providing benefits to members) or they may carry out activities primarily for the benefit of others. For example, they may be established for the specific purpose of providing welfare or other services to geographically defined local communities or to status-defined groups, such as members of an ethnic community. Benjamin Barber (1998, p. 4) described civil society as 'the realm we create ourselves'.

Historically, organisations in this sphere were the first to provide social services and assistance outside the family, through trade unions, professional associations and friendly societies. In many countries, organisations of this kind continue to be one of the main channels through which welfare is provided. As well as providing services such as childcare, family support, meals, counselling and sociability, community organisations have also been responsible for setting up voluntary insurance schemes (usually for income maintenance or healthcare), fundraising for social needs, establishing food and work co-operatives, developing self-help groups and undertaking social activism or pressure group activities (Powell, 2007).

The idea that civil society somehow exists *between* the market and the state has resulted in the community sector being regarded as a 'Third Sector'. The Third Way approach in social policy, in which government action is focused on forming partnerships with civil society, has come to be regarded as a means through which a raft of social and political problems can be addressed. This approach, discussed in more detail in later chapters of this book, leads to new intersections and overlaps between government and community-based organisations. Identifying all of these activities of the community sector alerts us to the ways in which social policies can both *formalise* and *informalise* social provisions. For example, social policies can informalise areas of social need by encouraging service provision by volunteers, philanthropists, charities or churches to take responsibility for resource re-distribution, through food security programs and emergency relief. On the other hand, social policies can formalise social provisions by funding activities previously undertaken by community groups or paying for work previously undertaken by volunteers or community groups.

Social policy involves the state intersecting with the spheres of the market, the family and the community, and as a result the overall welfare of citizens is enabled and constrained by a broad range of forces operating across these domains. Ideas and practices related to the impact of government actions and inactions on the realms of the market, the family and the community are much contested and they shift according to political and ideological preferences. Understanding government actions in terms of a series of approaches in the way goods, services and labour are arranged provides a useful set of questions that can be asked of any social policy approach. These include: to what extent does the approach decommmodify or commodify goods, services or labour? To what extent does the approach privatise or socialise goods, services or labour? To what extent does the approach familialise or de-familialise goods, services or labour? To what extent does the approach informalise or formalise goods, services or labour?

As will be seen throughout this book, policy analysis and policy development are thoroughly normative exercises based on ideas about what 'should' and 'ought' to be done about any given situation or issue. The approach described above makes it possible to think of social policies as impacting across social domains. They thus affect the economic situations, working lives, family lives and intra-familial relationships of individuals, and the nature of community and associational life.

Social policy and the welfare state

Although often used interchangeably, the terms 'social policy' and the 'welfare state' are distinct concepts. As Fenna (2004) points out, social policy is an umbrella concept describing a type of government action that has existed for centuries. The welfare state, by contrast, is a specific and quite recent phenomenon. A feature of twentieth century social and economic development, the welfare state promised to deliver economic security to people disadvantaged within the market economy of capitalist societies. It was argued that state intervention was required because the scale and complexity of modern social life exceeded the capacity of the family and community spheres to remedy social inequalities and problems. Welfare states are concerned with meeting social needs, primarily through the provision of social services and income support to its citizens. In welfare states, these supports are qualitatively distinct from those formerly (or concurrently) provided by philanthropic organisations based on a charity model of welfare. Instead, support flows to individuals on the basis of rights and entitlements, whereby citizens can expect the state to protect minimum standards of living (Mendes, 2008b).

Welfare states are distinguished by the distribution of social responsibilities and activities between the state, families, the market and other community and non-government providers, including the church. Some welfare states are based primarily on public funding and service provision; others less so (Alcock, 2001). A common approach to describing and analysing welfare systems in rich democracies has been to use Gøsta Esping-Andersen's typology of welfare regimes. Esping-Andersen's typology has been much criticised but remains an important point of departure when thinking about differences between welfare systems and welfare states (Arts and Gelissen, 2002; Bambra, 2005).

Esping-Andersen (1990) identified three regime types: the liberal, the conservative and the social-democratic. *Liberal welfare regimes* are typically found in Anglo-Saxon countries: the US, the UK, Australia, New Zealand and Canada. Although there are differences between them, these countries share some characteristics, such as residualism and an encouragement of market solutions in welfare. Residualism is the belief that state welfare institutions should come into play only when the family and the market break down, and so forms of state welfare are usually either highly targeted or restricted to people who are poor and disadvantaged.

Conservative welfare regime countries include Germany and France, Austria, Belgium and the Netherlands. The essence of the conservative regime type lies in its blend of status segmentation and familialism, or belief that families are predominantly responsible for social provision. In the conservative welfare regime countries, private for-profit solutions have generally played a marginal role in addressing social needs. Instead, non-state solutions to welfare issues mean extensive involvement by non-profit, voluntary organisations, often affiliated to the church.

Social-democratic welfare regimes are found in the Nordic countries. This model of welfare, according to Esping-Andersen, was largely constructed as a contrast to the other two regime types. The principles of universalism, comprehensive risk coverage, generous benefit levels, egalitarianism and full employment are its cornerstones. Universalism is coupled to citizens' rights; that is, social entitlements are attached to individuals and based on citizenship rather than on a demonstrated need or an employment relationship. This means that citizens have a basic right to a broad range of services and benefits regardless of income and position in the labour market. The social democratic welfare regime is characterised by a high degree of de-commodification—policies that lessen individuals' reliance on labour market participation, and de-familialisation—policies that lessen individuals' reliance on families (Esping-Andersen, 1999; 2002).

The inclusion of Australia as a liberal welfare regime has been criticised from a number of angles. Castles and Mitchell (1992), for example, argued that Australia belongs to a 'radical fourth world of welfare capitalism', achieved primarily through equality in pre-tax, pre-transfer income rather than through welfare rights. Other researchers have described the Australian welfare state as an 'exception' or as 'exceptional' in regards to the provision of social protection through wage protection and universal health insurance. Despite this, the Australian welfare state has always been regarded as a 'residual' welfare state because of the targeted nature of means-tested social security payments to the poor and disadvantaged (Frankel, 2001, pp. 76–77). Advocates of the residualism of the Australian welfare system argue that it ensures maximum services and benefits are received by those most in need at a minimum cost to the taxpayer. However, critics argue that targeting stigmatises and marginalises the recipients of welfare, causes poverty traps and is socially divisive (Mendes, 2008, pp. 49-50).

As described above, the residualist model contrasts with the universalist approach prevalent in social democratic countries, where welfare services are provided to all citizens regardless of gender, income or position. Advocates of universalism argue that it enhances gender equality, social solidarity and cohesiveness, reduces poverty traps and enables recipients of social services to receive services and benefits without discrimination. However, critics claim that universal benefits are costly, benefit the middle class more than the poor and do little to address inequalities in society (Healy, J. 1998). In chapter 5, we test some of these arguments against data about patterns of spending, poverty and inequality alleviation in the different regime types.

The field of welfare state analysis, including both theoretical conceptualisations and cross-national empirical studies, has predominantly focused on comparing and contrasting the structure and impact of social security (cash benefit) arrangements and, to a lesser extent, labour market policies. Indeed, one criticism of Esping-Andersen's typology is that he failed to acknowledge the significance of provisions other than cash in promoting welfare. These critics point out that policies concerned with services such as education, health, childcare, aged care and so forth are also critically important for well-being and are organised in quite different ways in different countries (Abrahamson, 1999; Alber, 1995; Anttonen and Sipilä, 1996; Bambra, 2005). Questions of whether services are targeted or universal and about the extent to which services enable de-commodification and de-familialisation are just as important as questions about income support arrangements in understanding how welfare regimes differ and how they work.

The welfare state research tradition that focuses on services rather than cash has been very concerned with questions about the sources or agents of provision. In particular, it has been concerned with the balance of provision of services by the state, market, family, non-government and voluntary services sectors. Welfare mixes in all countries have developed historically but have undergone quite similar changes in most countries in recent decades: the privatisation, de-centralisation, market orientation and introduction of purchaser-provider models in welfare services have been dominant trends. In addition, as discussed above, there has been growth in the informalisation of welfare services, where services previously provided by professionals are now provided by volunteers, families or 'communities'. These changes radically alter the nature of welfare states, but are dimensions that are missed in welfare state analyses that focus only on changes to income support policies. Such trends are analysed in several later chapters.

Social change

The central project of this book is to understand the scope and importance of social policy in facilitating social change. Like the concept social policy, social change can be viewed from a range of perspectives. Social change is sometimes an all-encompassing process brought about by big events or actions such as a political revolution or war. More often, it is a gradual process of evolution in values and social and economic structures over time.

Social change happens in various ways and at different paces. Its effects vary and its outcomes are experienced and evaluated divergently by people in different social positions. The impact of the World Wars, for example, was devastating on many levels; the general loss of life and communities, the loss of a generation of young men, the dividing of sovereignties, cultures and economic resources and the spectres of new tyrannies such as fascism or the atomic bomb. However, as a result of coping with the impact of such enormous events, some social groups made gains. After World War II, for example, the industrialised world witnessed a dramatic shift in the participation of women in work and education. The first systems of comprehensive welfare state provision across rich democracies also emerged during this period, as the reparation of societies and economies required means of rebuilding and strengthening social cohesion (Izuhara, 2003, p. 5). This was a period of significant economic growth and social change towards strengthened social provision in many countries. It should be seen in the light of the general acceptance of Keynesian economic policy framework, which, in contrast to the dominant neo-classical framework of today, promoted state intervention as a key to full employment and economic growth.

In recent decades, within rich democracies, social change is more likely to arise from a complex set of local and global or international forces. Some of the most obvious social changes during the last three decades are related to, for example: the constitution of families—sole parent families, one child families, blended families, families with same sex parents and so on; living arrangements—single person living, higher density living, living away from families, young people staying at home longer; the demographic characteristics of the population—related to low fertility rates and increased longevity; gender roles—in families, work, education and political participation; the growth and diversity in the number of refugees—from Sub-Saharan Africa and the Middle East, or climate change refugees from threatened Pacific Islands; and the advent of the internet—immediate global communications, internet paedophile networks, greater public scrutiny of the actions of big corporations.

These kinds of social change have occurred at the level of national populations, but social changes also occur at the level of individual and community values. Often it is at this level that social change has been seen as predominantly positive, where, for example, social justice has triumphed over racism, human rights have triumphed over exploitation or slavery and equality has triumphed over segregation or sexism. For human service professionals, social change achievement is often measured against a set of positive ideas and values about what a better state of being or living standard might be, often understood in terms of enhancing well-being. Defining what constitutes a better life is also a fundamental issue for contemporary democratic governments, whose social and economic agendas will be based on sets of espoused values in order to bring about social change. We discuss these issues in more detail in chapter 4.

While it is often assumed that the aim of social policy and the welfare state is positive social change, or change for the better, this is never guaranteed. Not all social policies aim to improve conditions for whole populations or for all time. Indeed, social change typically involves struggles over power and resources, and there are winners and losers. Further, even policies that are aimed at change for the better can have unintended negative consequences. Governments and human service providers are thus involved in social change with a variety of effects. Through their actions, governments and human service providers can both attend to and promote the things that enhance well-being, but they can also neglect and even undermine them. These themes will continue to be explored throughout this book as we examine the complex role that politics, values, economics, organisations and providers play in social policy.

Conclusion

In this chapter, we have emphasised the central place that human services and human service workers occupy in relation to social policy; human services are produced by social policy and are key players in the production of social policy. As such, human services are crucially implicated in social change. Social policy, as discussed above, is linked to social change through its mission to intervene in social life, particularly those aspects of social life that are understood as social needs or social problems. Although interventions are often attributed to objectives such as social development, improved standards of living or enhanced well-being, social policies can have wide-ranging, unintended and contradictory effects. Social policy *analysis* thus becomes important for those working in the human services field.

In this chapter, we have discussed some of the important ingredients of social policy analysis. The first relates to understanding the legal and administrative or governmental arrangements for social policy. The second concerns the identification of different forms of government action, including inaction, frequently employed as instruments of social policy. The third addresses the significance of understanding the intersections of social policy across the domains of society, described here in terms of the state, the market, the family and the community. The fourth is the utility of welfare state analysis for social policy analysis, particularly where welfare state analyses incorporate a focus on the depth and coverage of human and social services. These themes and the concepts and issues related to them reappear throughout the book, where they are discussed in detail or in relation to specific developments in social policy.

The next chapter, which focuses on social policy processes, follows up in more detail the idea that human service workers make social policy.

CHAPTER 2

Making social policy: maps and mechanisms

Introduction

Social policy is a crucial mechanism by which needs are identified and legitimated and public resources are allocated to address them. Understanding the processes involved in policy-making is therefore fundamental to any project that aspires to equity, social justice and social change. Throughout this book, we understand making social policy as a process through which social needs are produced, defined and addressed. Conventionally, this process has been depicted in terms of a number of phases, stages and moments. In this chapter, we discuss the usefulness of unpacking and mapping the social policy process in these ways. We describe making social policy as the work of a broad set of actors. Human service professionals are involved in policy-making in a range of ways—as public administrators, lobbyists or researchers, professionals or 'experts', service managers or service providers, advocates or activists, representatives of peak organisations or convenors of consumer and self-help groups and as local community members or citizens. But we also acknowledge that participation and influence in policy-making can be affected by modes of governance and institutional arrangements. As such, this chapter also provides a description of some of the key mechanisms available for human service workers and human service users to participate in policy processes.

Mapping the social policy process

It is tempting to think that making social policy is an orderly and rational process, characterised by a particular sequence of clear and identifiable steps and undertaken by people with significant expertise and authority. Often, retrospective accounts of how social policies were made reflect this ideal, depicting policy-making as a problem-solving process that was rational, balanced, objective and analytical. In such accounts, decisions are seen to have been made in a series of sequential phases, starting with the identification of a problem or issue and ending with a set of activities to solve or deal with the issue.

Public policy analysts Michael Howlett and M. Ramesh (1995), for example, suggest policy-making can be broken down into 'phases of applied problem solving'. The five *problem-solving* phases that they identify are: (1) problem recognition—recognition of an issue requiring policy action; (2) proposal solution—identification of a range of courses of action or options; (3) choice of solution—weighing up these alternatives and making a decision about the best solution; (4) putting solution into effect—implementing policy decision; (5) monitoring solution—in some cases, the outcomes of the decision are monitored.

However, making social policy cannot always be equated with problem solving. First, often no one single problem in need of a solution governs the process; rather, it is shaped by a complex intermeshing of related concerns. Second, social policy processes often bring problems into existence; in this sense, social policy creates problems that are seen to be worth solving or have some possibility of being solved. Third, the problem-solving approach assumes that it is possible to weigh up rationally the alternatives and their consequences so they can be fully understood in terms of both costs and benefits, for the present and the future, and for target groups and the rest of society. Finally, the problem-solving approach skims over the political nature of social policy-making and understates the way social policies arise out of conflicts over the nature of the problems confronting society. The issues relating to problem definition are discussed in more detail further in this chapter, and the political nature of social policy, including the key lines of conflict, will be covered in chapter 3.

Along with other policy analysts, Howlett and Ramesh (1995) also suggest that the phases of the problem-solving approach to policy-making can be connected to a number of distinct stages in a 'policy cycle'. The idea that policy-making is a cycle of specialised activities often appears in policy analysis texts and guidelines for policy practitioners. Representations of the policy cycle invariably break policy-making down into distinct types of activities. The five *policy cycle* stages that Howlett and Ramesh offer are: (1) agenda setting, (2) policy formulation, (3) decision-making, (4) implementation and (5) evaluation. Variations of the policy cycle abound, with some including more specific stages and others describing similar activities under quite different headings (Colebatch, 2006). What is common to policy cycle approaches, however, is the view that it is useful to disaggregate policy-making activities in this way. It is suggested that sequenced approaches can help policy-makers work out where they are up to and what to do next, and assist policy analysts to 'identify the factors that get in the way of policy delivering its intended outcomes' (Newman, 2002, p. 348).

Linear or cyclical depictions of the policy process are far from universally accepted, however, as adequate accounts of the nature of making social policy. Hal Colebatch (2000), for example, claims that participants in policy processes constantly complain about the lack of fit between official maps of policy-making and their own experience. He argues that in most policy participants' experience, policy-making is extremely contested and ambiguous. The specified stages often overlap in ways which preclude any neat systemic view of when or how policy is made. Drawing on the experiences of community service workers in Australia, Linda Hancock suggests that such constructions are 'at odds with the messy argy-bargy of the lived experience of policy work and tend to underestimate the politics of policy' (Hancock, 2006, p. 66). She argues, for example, that the policy cycle approach assumes a central governmental role in policy decision-making. In her experience, the notion that policy is 'made' by public officials does not take account of the increasingly complex and multi-layered relationships between government and NGOs in policy processes. Janet Newman (2002) and Anna Yeatman (1998) make the point that linear, rational approaches do not give enough attention to the significance of policy implementation or the operational aspects of policy. Newman (2002, p. 348) suggests, for example, that implementation cannot be considered a late 'stage' of the policy process but is integral to it. Similarly, Yeatman (1998, p. 28) argues that the 'street level' (that is, the level of direct service delivery) should be regarded as an inherent part of the policy process, involved in all that occurs from the point of policy formulation to the point of delivery. (We return to discuss these issues in more detail in chapter 7.)

Making social policy does involve, of course, a range of differentiated activities. For example, evaluation and agenda setting involve quite different objectives and tasks. Identifying these different objectives and tasks can be useful for practitioners seeking to intervene or advocate in particular processes. But it is also important for human service professionals to be able to recognise the more deep-seated aspects of the process, particularly the way in which making social policy involves contests over meaning as well as over authority and resources. Colebatch (2007), for example, argues that policy is best understood as a particular way of understanding the world, or a way of 'framing' and 're-framing' problems. From this perspective, social constructionist approaches to making social policy can shed light on policy processes. Before moving on to describe one such approach, it is useful to think about how social problems and social needs are understood from a constructionist perspective.

Constructing needs and 'social problems'

Over the past three decades, the constructionist approach to social problems and social needs has emerged and developed. This approach focuses attention not only on the social conditions themselves, but also on the definitional activities that facilitate such conditions becoming understood and reacted to as problematic, as 'social problems'. As such, it focuses on *how* certain phenomena and/or issues in society come to be defined and understood as problematic by some portion of the citizenry. From this point of view, social problems are not seen as distinct, given social arrangements to be studied and corrected. Rather, they involve 'interpretive processes that constitute what comes to be seen as oppressive, intolerable or unjust social conditions' (Holstein and Miller, 1993, p. 4). So, for example, writing about the relatively recent emergence of social action around the 'problem' of hate crimes—violence against lesbians and gay men—Gail Mason (2002) makes the important point that violence against lesbians and gay men is not a new phenomenon. To illustrate her point, she provides historical examples such as the systematic extermination of homosexuals in Nazi Germany. Until recently, however, violence against lesbians and gay men was not regarded as a social problem requiring systematic public interventions (laws, services, education campaigns and so forth), although it may have been understood, to use C. Wright Mills' famous distinction, as a 'personal trouble' for individual victims. It was only through the emergence and impact of anti–violence movements, community activism and community action that hate crimes became understood as a social problem. These shifts in understanding can therefore be seen as discursive accomplishments.

Another example of the social construction of social problems is the 'discovery' of domestic violence in western countries during the 1970s and 1980s, when feminist activists asserted that violence against women was not a personal problem, but a systemic, political one. This process of politicising domestic violence involved renaming practices and creating a new type of public discourse. A very different example of problem construction can be seen in the recent identification of 'childhood obesity' in rich democracies. Here, the previously personal problem of children's weight has come to be understood as a social problem requiring public interventions. The activities of health professionals, medical researchers and industry lobbies have all been important in the presentation of children's weight as a social problem, and organisations as diverse as media regulators, education departments, parent bodies, advertising companies and food manufacturers have all had a stake in defining the nature of this problem. From the constructionist perspective, then, there is no such thing as a discovery process that uncovers 'real social problems'. Abiding situations *become* social problems through shifts in understandings. Carol Bacchi explains: '(t)his is what is meant by the sometimes misunderstood phrase that people do not discover problems, they create them' (Bacchi, 1999, p. 9).

Through her depiction of three 'moments' in the process of turning social needs into social policy, Nancy Fraser, an American political philosopher, has provided social policy analysts with an alternative way of mapping the policy process. In her discussion of the 'politics of need interpretation', Fraser (1989) highlights the political nature of social policy (see also Dalton et al., 1996; Bertone, 2003; Albrecht and Seelman, 2003; Stein, 2004; Roman, 2008; Dean, 2006). The first moment is 'the struggle to establish or deny the political status of any given need' (Fraser, 1989, p. 165). Here, a range of actors including social movements, professionals, citizens, consumers and the media are involved in politicising what was a depoliticised or privatised phenomenon. Examples of establishing need in social policy abound, and human service workers often talk about this in terms of trying to get an issue 'on the agenda'.

Fraser's second moment involves contests over 'the interpretation of the need'—how it will be named and what solutions are put forward as desirable. So, in the example of hate crimes and domestic violence, a variety of 'solutions' has been posited, ranging from criminalisation of violence, community education, safety strategies, refuges and anti-discrimination legislation, to counselling for offenders and victims. Often at this stage, 'experts' and professionals become involved in decisions about how problems should be 'named' and how they are best dealt with. In some areas, human service workers can be positioned as experts for the purposes of interpreting needs. In other cases, human service workers will find their interpretations subjugated to other professional discourses such as legal, medical or economic discourses.

The third moment is the 'struggle over the satisfaction of the need, the struggle to secure or withhold provision' (Fraser, 1989, p. 166). This moment includes the struggles to ensure solutions are forthcoming and adequately resourced (or, in the case of regulations, enforced). Much social policy debate centres on this third moment—the adequacy, effectiveness and coverage of public interventions. Fraser's approach implicitly includes many of the phases of the problem-solving approach as well as of the policy cycle approach. It is distinctive, however, in the equal attention it gives to the different actors, organisations and discourses involved in the process, and to the different stages in the process. Most importantly, it reminds us that the way social needs and social problems are politicised and interpreted are just as important as the actions taken to address them.

Social policy analysts have begun to develop approaches to analysing government policy-making that go beyond taking social problems as given and that concentrate on the *meaning creation* involved in policy design (Colebatch, 2006; Marston 2004). Carol Bacchi (1999; 2000; 2008) provides a useful framework for analysing the discursive aspects of social policy. Her approach, which she refers to as 'What's the problem represented to be?' (Bacchi, 1999; 2008), has enabled policy analysts across a range of fields to move beyond arguments about the best way to address social problems or satisfy social needs. Instead, it probes the conceptual underpinnings of problem representations—the assumptions and presuppositions—and considers what is left unsaid. This approach makes it possible to think about the effects of policy proposals in terms of what is likely to change and who is likely to benefit. It also concentrates on how the subjects of particular policy approaches are constituted—who (or what) is held responsible for the problem and what may be the effects of the attribution of responsibility. In this approach, rather than seeing social policy as governments reacting to (and potentially 'solving') identifiable social problems, the focus is on how governments, and indeed all policy participants, give a particular shape to social 'problems' in the ways we speak about them and the proposals we advance to 'address' them (Bacchi, 2008).

For human service workers, frameworks for analysing and understanding the discursive aspects of social policy-making are valuable, but they too can be considered incomplete. This is because policy-making is generally undertaken within the boundaries of organisations and institutions which set out the rules of engagement between various stakeholders. These rules or conventions will largely determine who is able to participate in policy-making and how they participate. In contemporary modes of governance, not everyone who wants to participate in the making of social policy has the opportunity to do so. Those who can participate will find their policy capacity constrained or enabled by the participatory mechanisms available to them. In other words, institutional arrangements structure the interactions that take place and provide organisational locations or 'policy spaces' where these interactions can occur.

Mechanisms for participation in policy-making

In liberal democracies, there are a variety of mechanisms beyond the ballot box for citizens to participate in social policy development. Human service professionals therefore participate in policy development in a range of ways. As discussed in the previous chapter, social policy arenas in most rich democracies have evolved in a way that responsibility for policy development and service provision is spread across different levels of government, an extensive NGO sector and, increasingly, the private sector. While making social policy has come to occupy a core role for modern governments, governing has become a more complex process involving mobilising public authority through a range of distinct, overlapping and often conflicting organisations (Colebatch, 2007). In this context, contemporary discussions of the policy process rest on a useful distinction between 'governing' and 'governance'.

Government and governance

A raft of writers on the policy process (Rhodes, 1997; Pierre and Peters, 2000; Newman, 2001; Daly, 2003; Pierson, 2004; Nye et al., 2007) argue that governing, or the business of making binding decisions for a given political community, has become less and less the exclusive business of governments and government agencies. Instead, governing has become more a matter of negotiation between state actors at various levels and other interests in society. Pierre and Peters (2000, p. 68), for example, argue that 'the state no longer has a monopoly over the expertise, or over the economic or institutional resources necessary to govern'. As a result, in describing how social policy is made, it has become more appropriate to speak of 'governance' rather than governing.

In social policy arenas, discussions about the shift from governing to governance can be grouped into two main camps. First, there are those who see the new emphasis on collaboration as the product of an ideological shift towards neo-liberalism and a move away from the conception of the state as the provider of welfare. Second, there is a view that the informalisation of government functions can be seen as a move towards more participatory governance, where non-government actors are able to engage more in matters of social policy than they have in the past. Put simply, in the first view, changes in governance are seen as a shift towards less democracy, whereas the second view sees at least a potential for increased democracy and civic engagement in matters of policy and social development (Hasenfeld and Garrow, 2007).

Even in the context of governance, policy development can vary between centralised models operated by decision-making elites and participatory models in which government divests some level of authority for developing and implementing social policy and actors other than government are brought in (Brown and Keast, 2005). Policy-making can therefore be understood as existing on a continuum between very closed and more open systems, providing different opportunities for participation. In addition, policy processes vary over time, across different policy sectors and with different governments. Policy sectors have their own cast of players, their own policy community and their own institutional arrangements. In order to understand how social policy is made, it is therefore useful to be able to recognise a range of different models of policy-making and the institutional mechanisms for participation associated with each of these models.

Opening governance: new institutions, new actors

Up until the 1970s, a standard way of discussing social policy-making was in terms of the closed, unitary system of government of the Westminster traditions that derive from the parliamentary system of liberal democracy. According to these traditions, political parties, with the help of pressure groups, formulated alternative policy platforms and then presented them to the electorate. The primary control of policy decisions was regarded to be in the hands of elected representatives, that is, parliamentarians and political parties. Randall Stewart (1999, p. 134) described this approach in the following way:

> (It) puts the executive at the heart of the policy process. The best way to get a policy developed, it seemed to say, was to get the Minister to think of it and formulate it, then get the Cabinet to sign off on it and get it through Parliament, and then wait until the Minister has another bright policy idea. Public servants were thought to be administrators, not policy-makers.

The executive is the branch of a government charged with executing the law and managing the affairs of the government or state. In parliamentary systems, the executive consists of the prime minister or executive president, the cabinet and the executive departments or ministries of the government. In the executive model of policy-making, the key actors are the government ministers and senior public servants who work in the departments and statutory authorities over which the ministers preside. One of the main objectives of these public servants was to provide 'impartial expertise' to assist politicians in their decision-making (Bridgman and Davis, 1998, p. 8). In this model, policy-making is an elite activity undertaken by a combination of elected and non-elected expert officials. The Westminster model assumed that policy decisions were then administered by an obedient, neutral career public service and implemented by an obedient and well-controlled public service (Gardner and Barraclough, 2007). Another way of describing this model is through the metaphor of 'command and control'.

According to Anna Yeatman (1998), the executive model of policy treats the service delivery level of the policy process as a variable to be manipulated and controlled. It does not consist of people who should be invited to become involved in the making of policy. While service deliverers can make more or less creative adjustments regarding the policy created from on high, it does not acknowledge that *how* they interpret and implement policy contributes to the *making* of policy (Yeatman, 1998, p. 28). The executive model of policy-making does not allow for describing the way new policy issues often arise out of program delivery, setting off a need for new policy developments and responses. Furthermore, the model clearly overlooks the significance of non-elected agents—administrators, professionals, 'experts', pressure groups, the media, front-line workers—in the processes of policy formulation. It also obscures the broad range of both formal and informal extra-parliamentary mechanisms that exist and facilitate input into policy processes. Some of these mechanisms are quite recent developments; others have a longer history. In the following section, we describe some of the historical shifts in modes of governance that have produced the range of formal mechanisms now available to contemporary human service workers. These include advisory and consultative mechanisms, policy units and agencies, social planning processes, mechanisms for consumer and service user participation, policy research and development channels, service agreements and formal partnership agreements (often called 'compacts') that have a policy development dimension.

During the 1970s and 1980s, the 'new public administration movement' was centrally concerned with challenging the executive (or Westminster) model of policy-making whereby public officials were conceptualised as the tools of government ministers. The movement argued that policy and the administration of policy could not be separated in practice or in theory. It highlighted the way in which public servants are active in their own right and insisted that public servants should be positively situated as active agents (Yeatman, 1998). This critique resulted in important reforms of public administration, including: the promotion of 'representative bureaucracy' in which decision-makers in the bureaucracy more comprehensively reflected the diversity of the community (to include women, people from diverse ethnic groups and people with disabilities); the de-centralisation of decision-making within government agencies; and increased opportunities for professional, community group and consumer participation in bureaucratic policy processes. The most tangible evidence of a shift in public administration in this direction is perhaps the development of 'policy units' in many government social service and social policy departments. While policy units and policy positions are now an essential part of social service departments, they need to be seen as a relatively new development.

Various interest groups and pressure groups have always been incorporated into government policy-making processes. Parliamentary systems in the UK, Europe and Australia have long had institutional mechanisms in place for interacting with pressure and interest groups, particularly those concerned with economic and industrial issues (Marsh, 1994; Goodwin, 2006). These mechanisms include advisory committees or arrangements such as summits and royal commissions, which provide opportunities for 'representatives' of particular professional or producer groups to participate in policy-making. According to American political scientist Samuel Beers (1969), new levels of interdependence between government and pressure groups occurred in the 1950s and 1960s in the US and the UK. They were a product of the new roles governments had taken on in relation to the management of the economy and the provision of welfare. He argued that the motives for both pressure group formation and government incorporation of pressure groups originated in the 'egalitarian aspirations' of the welfare-state-managed economy. Ian Marsh (1994) suggests this account broadly fits with the Australian experience, and explains how the development of the welfare state empowered pressure groups, such as business associations and trade unions, in new ways and provided the impetus for the development of new organisations (Marsh, 1994, pp. 262–263). The establishment of mechanisms for interest group participation, such as government advisory committees, has thus been associated with the development of the post-war welfare states.

From other perspectives, such as the corporatist, these mechanisms are a way of privileging the participation of particular interests and enabling them to have more influence in policy-making than other groups or citizens have. This is seen to be the case particularly where governments allow for the participation of businesses, producer groups, unions and elite professional bodies like medical or legal associations. From both perspectives, mechanisms for interest group representation are considered to have both inclusionary and exclusionary tendencies.

For example, the United Associations of Women in Australia was an early pressure group that raised the issue of the exclusion of women from some earlier government advisory committees. In the 1930s and 1940s, the group wrote to government ministers urging them to consider appointing women to advisory bodies in policy areas such as health, housing, rationing and citizenship. The pressure group drew on two important rationales to support their claims, both of which remain relevant in pressure and interest group politics today. First, they argued that they had knowledge and expertise in these areas, and so their input would contribute to the development of 'sensible' (today we would say 'informed') policies. Second, they argued that as *citizens* they had a right to participate in decisions that would affect them (Radi, 1990). A range of groups in the community has made claims for participation in similar ways: as citizens, they have the right to be the creators, not simply the *objects* of policy.

By the end of the twentieth century, most government agencies concerned with social policy had established bodies to institutionalise links between government, the public service and pressure groups. Dean Jaensch (1992) argued that institutionalising relationships between the executive and pressure groups was based on the recognition that governments need advice, specialised information and co-operation from pressure groups. They established these mechanisms in order to maintain the flow of information needed to frame viable policies and ensure that policies would be acceptable to the community. As stated earlier, these mechanisms were often established in the areas of economic and industry policy, but from the 1980s they spread across all areas of social policy. It is now commonplace for housing, health, education and social service ministers to establish and develop advisory councils or committees.

In turn, groups of human service agencies, consumers and community groups often organise themselves into associations, federations and peak bodies specifically for the purpose of participation in social policy processes. Jeff Cheverton (2005) makes the point that Australia is unique among English-speaking countries in the use of the term 'peak body' to describe these types of organisations. He argues that the privileged status they have held within public policy processes is not replicated elsewhere. Indeed, some Australian governments, recognising the social and bureaucratic benefits of institutionalising avenues for advice from the human service sector, have provided significant resources to subsidise the operation of peak bodies or councils (Hogan, 1996). That said, Rose Melville's more recent review of Australian peak bodies demonstrates that many of them lost funding and the favour of government during the Howard Liberal-National Coalition Government (1996–2007) (Melville, 2003).

Government advisory mechanisms have been important channels for human service providers to participate in social policy processes. They provide opportunities for the interests of social service sectors to be represented directly to the executive arm of government. The representative nature of these mechanisms is, however, important to keep in mind. Where unions, peak bodies, associations or federations are charged with providing advice to government *on behalf of* member organisations and agencies, and with representing members' views to government, members need to be actively involved in policy development processes within their organisations.

Broadening participation in social policy processes has also been associated with the demands for greater participation in public decisions made by new social movements (Byrne and Davis, 1998; Painter, 1992; Burgmann, 2003). These movements include the second wave women's movement, civil rights movements, the gay rights movement, environmentalist movements, student movements and various consumer rights movements. These movements have articulated demands for participation in policy processes in terms of 'citizen' or 'community' participation, representing a shift away from interest group or pressure group politics.

Social movement efforts to change social practice and public opinion have affected social policy processes in various ways. For example, they often result in public pressure to address new problems or issues. They also demand new procedures or the inclusion of new groups. One of the first areas in which social movement action opened up conventional government decision-making processes was urban planning. The formation of resident action groups in response to urban development proposals resulted in alliances between local communities and unions. Consequently, governments began to create new structures for participation in urban planning decisions; there is now an expectation in most rich democracies that local communities will be 'consulted' on any major developments. Indeed, 'community consultation' has become a field of practice in its own right. Human service professionals and human service users not only expect to participate in consultations; they will also be involved in developing community consultation guidelines and protocols and evaluating the efficacy of consultative processes.

In the sphere of social planning, grassroots action around welfare issues has led (in some jurisdictions, at some points in history) to the devolution of authority to local groups for making decisions about social welfare priorities. It has also encouraged the formation of local groups to provide community services. In addition, social movements have formed organisations specifically for engagement in policy processes. They have thus transformed institutional arrangements for policy-making by championing the legitimacy of participation—by community, service provider and service user groups—and by creating new mechanisms for dialogue and collaboration between government and political organisations.

In the health arena, the 'new public health movement' underlined the importance of wide participation in policy processes, particularly the significance of service user participation in social policy-making. The central premise of the Ottawa Charter for Health Promotion, established by the World Health Organization—that people should have control over their own health—has supported the development of a range of institutions and mechanisms for consumer and health provider participation in health policy processes (Raeburn et al., 2006).

Advocates of user participation in policy-making argue that it has tended to fall into two main approaches, the democratic and the consumerist. In the democratic approach, involving people in policy-making can be seen as evidence of shifts to empower groups of outsiders who were traditionally excluded from the policy-making process. Service user movements such as those developed by disabled people, mental health survivors and older people have called for more participation; they wish to move beyond being 'users and choosers' and have framed their claims in terms of civil and political rights.

The consumerist approach to user participation in policy processes is initiated by government rather than by users themselves. This push by government to involve service users has been related to the pursuit of market approaches in the provision of welfare, whereby the role of government is seen as responding to the market (Bochel et al., 2007). Mechanisms for user participation in policy processes include consumer representation on advisory boards and participation in consultative processes, as well as the development of user councils to provide expert advice to government. In addition, consumers are 'involved' in policy processes through a whole range of consumer feedback mechanisms, such as consumer surveys. Indeed, in some areas of social policy, consumer participation in policy development is embedded in legislation. Mechanisms for consumer participation in policy-making, however, can be used to legitimise pre-determined agendas or act as token gestures towards participation.

Closing governance? Emergence of New Public Management

The opening up of policy processes came under attack when 'New Public Management' ideas began to dominate. (NPM is discussed further in subsequent chapters.) Alongside the push to rationalise administration of social services and install a performance management culture across all levels of publicly funded organisations, a belief that participatory modes of policy-making were, in essence, 'undemocratic' was promulgated. Here, a theory called 'public choice theory' emphasised that many groups that were actively involved in participatory policy processes not only failed to reflect the public good, but also seriously distorted public policy. For instance, the social services involved with issues of gender, race, public health and even local communities were regarded as having captured the policy agenda, promoting 'special interests' over the interests of the general community. It was suggested that in some cases, they had built 'service empires' for themselves. For human service workers, this critique limited their capacity for advocacy in real ways. The de-funding of peak bodies representing women's, migrant and environmental issues emanates from public choice discourse; workers in a range of areas have found their input into policy processes curtailed.

New Public Management can also be seen in new approaches to policy-making developed for the public services. An excellent example of this is Australian public policy analyst Randall Stewart's 'strategic framework approach', which has been extensively drawn upon by public administrators in Australia. Stewart applies the aspirations and tools of the business sector to the Australian public policy process. Just as business is in the 'business' of producing 'private value' through 'commoditisation', so too, he says, is the public sector engaged in creating 'public value' (Stewart 1999, pp. 27–28). So, for Stewart, the role of public administrators in policy-making is like the work of business executives, analysts, managers and planners whose major responsibilities are to know and understand their 'markets', 'products' and 'customers'. The policy process was thus conceived as one largely conducted by experts whose success depended on their mastery of the tasks involved in each of the four main 'steps and stages' (Stewart 1999, p. 68). In sequential order, these are, according to Stewart, strategic planning, formulation and resource allocation, strategy implementation and evaluation. Stewart's strategic framework approach captures what we know of recent developments in public administrators' roles in Australia and comparable countries such as Canada and the UK.

Interestingly, the strategic or 'technocratic' approach to policy-making has resulted in making the role of health, welfare and social service *research* and *researchers* more significant. The strategic approach to policy development relies on 'evidence', a concept which is explored further in chapter 8. It is therefore not surprising that the research capacity of non-government and government social service agencies has been expanding and that research units within these organisations, as well as standalone social policy 'think tanks', have proliferated (Egan, 2008). It is also important to emphasise that governments often 'buy in' expertise and it is here we have seen the rise in numbers of social policy 'consultants'. These are often human service professionals with management, research or program development expertise who have set up agencies to provide advice to governments. Thus, the strategic approach to policy-making has resulted in new organisational locations and positions from which human service professionals participate in policy processes. We have also seen a significant shift in the way social needs are championed in the policy process.

A critical interpretation of New Public Management suggests that it re-centralised policy-making, particularly through centralising control over finances and the articulation of policy priorities. Dalton and colleagues (1996, p. 95), for example, argued that managerialism deals with the politics of administration by removing politics to the executive level and conceiving of the administration as a 'machine designed to achieve political objectives'. New Public Management also positions service delivery as an *output* of policy, rather than social policy in action. In some sectors, this division has led human service providers to be excluded from formal policy development activities. Rather like in the Westminster model, social policy is regarded as being made at executive and management levels, rather than at the service delivery and implementation levels.

Reopening governance? Networks, compacts and a new role for communities

There has recently been a resurgence of pressure on governments to involve citizens and local service providers more directly in policy-making decisions. This pressure has come from within national communities, but also from trans-national organisations such as the United Nations, the World Bank and, in Europe, the European Union. References to social capital, communitarianism, partnerships and community have been used to frame these new relationships between citizens and the state. This approach to opening up participation in policy-making has been referred to as a 'community governance' model and is discussed in more detail in chapter 11. This model emphasises the heterogeneity of interests in society and the importance of representing those interests in policy processes. Because governance is seen in terms of 'networks of intersecting interests' and the role of government is conceptualised within this, the approach is also referred to as 'network governance'. Melville and colleagues (2008) argue that in various countries, one tangible outcome of this rhetoric is the increase in written protocols governing relationships between governments and community service organisations. These involve the development of compacts between community service organisations and governments. Such compacts recognise the legitimacy of human service providers in NGOs engaging in political advocacy and policy-making processes, but they also structure the terms of this engagement.

While new approaches such as community and network governance appear to open up the policy process to human service professionals, these developments must be viewed in relation to some of the new ways in which policy-making can be closed or centralised (see Melville, Casey and Onyx, 2008; Barnes et al., 2003; Brown and Keast, 2005; Archon, 2006). Kerry Brown and Robyn Keast (2005), for example, suggest that new ways of funding and providing social services, such as the 'purchaser-provider split' and the introduction of contractualism, may have strengthened government control of policy-making through the introduction of coercive regulatory arrangements. It has been suggested that where human service organisations primarily become service providers, their capacity to engage in advocacy, lobbying, research and advisory or consultative activities can be significantly diminished (Dalton et al., 1996; Barnes et al., 2003; Casey and Dalton, 2006). Others argue that in the new modes of governance, decision-making rests too heavily on appointed technocrats and experts in closed policy communities, in essence 'privatising governance' (Rhodes, 1997). In addition, it has been suggested that the growing emphasis on evidence-based policy (discussed in more detail in chapter 8) is closely tied to the politics of a strong central state and centralisation of policy-making to command and control processes (see Wells, 2007). In a more optimistic vein, it has been suggested that the changes constitute 'post-bureaucratic' forms of organisation, which may well open up policy processes to include new players and new interests, and encourage more democratic interaction within policy communities.

Conclusion

This historical account of the opening and closing of social policy processes referred to a range of *institutional mechanisms* available to human service providers in different policy contexts within different modes of governance. These include but are not limited to government policy units, government advisory mechanisms, government consultative mechanisms, devolved social planning, consumer councils and consumer surveys, public sector management structures, think tanks, research bodies, partnership agreements and compacts. The historical account suggests a range of policy-making activities that human service providers may be involved in. These include (but again, are not limited to): lobbying politicians; interpreting policy at the service delivery level; participating as members of peak bodies, federations, unions or professional associations; representing services or issue areas on advisory committees, summits or royal commissions; writing submissions; participating in community consultations or undertaking consultations with consumers; working in policy units or managing programs; undertaking and communicating research; participating in policy networks; and participating in partnerships.

On the surface, it appears that human service workers have abundant opportunities to participate in the making of social policy. Yet an enormous body of research demonstrates that service deliverers and service users feel marginalised in policy processes. Very few people involved in human services regard themselves as the producers or even co-producers of social policy. On the one hand, this may be a result of inaccurate representations of what social policy-making is, such as maps of the policy process that obscure certain types of activity and input. On the other hand, it may flow out of the rules of engagement in contemporary modes of governance. As such, important questions of how power, authority and influence are distributed in the policy process arise. These are questions about the political nature of social policy. Social policy is political because it arises out of the conflict over the nature of problems confronting society and what, if anything, should be done about them. These conflicts, particularly those over ideologies and values, are addressed in the following chapters.

CHAPTER 3

Politics: conflicts over ideas and resources

Introduction

This chapter aims to communicate the essentially political nature of social policy, and to explain why human service professionals need to understand this. Throughout the chapter, we analyse major issues and interests involved in the conflicts over social policy and the struggles for resources. Following on from the focus on the social policy *process* in chapter 2, we also explore the range of players in policy processes and the interactions between them. This includes those directly involved in social policy-making and delivery (politicians, bureaucrats, activists and human service providers) and organised bodies that advocate on behalf of different interests in the policy process (advocacy NGOs, peak bodies, advisory and consultative bodies, business groups and social movements). The political nature of social policy is most apparent in the interactions between key players and policy-makers. It is also where the struggle for influence in the production and implementation of social policy takes place.

Power, ideology and politics

Key conflicts in the social policy field often occur because of differences in ideology. Stakeholders have different ideas about how the world *should* be, and therefore about how social policy should change or not change it. Although the struggle over ideas is important in defining social policy problems and their solutions, it is also a struggle to assert and use *power* to gain resources for certain interest groups or causes. 'Power' in this context is not understood in the sense used in classical political theory, where it is thought of as wielded by the state as sovereignty to maintain order and control. Rather, in much the same way that Michel Foucault understood power, we understand it as 'productive'—as producing effects, often fluid, reversible and invisible (Nash, 2000, p. 20). As Kate Nash points out, Foucault saw power as plural, exercised from a range of points of inception, not from a single political centre 'as the possession of an elite or the logic of bureaucratic institutions'. He did not see it as governed by a single overarching structure such as government (2000, p. 20).

This view of power helps to explain why certain interest groups recognised as 'powerful', such as corporate or religious groups, manage to get what they need or want from policy decisions. It also explains why other players, such as NGOs, social movements and 'the media' can succeed in effecting change or affecting social policy. Of course, this concept of power as flexible and un-centred is not a naïve view. It does not mean that productive power equals 'good' power. Indeed, much social policy analysis concludes that power is often abused and there are winners and losers from the exercise of it. It is therefore useful to engage with how we can understand social policy as inherently political by analysing how power is applied in different instances (or cases) and in different contexts for social change.

One of the most obvious examples of where conflicts over ideology and struggles for power occur is between political parties. Although their most important goals are gaining political office and the pursuit of specific policies that suit their ideological goals (Schmidt, 1996, p. 156), the need to appease or support other social policy actors means they are also involved in constant, multiple struggles over policy. These political struggles may take place between political parties within formal government processes but also within the parties themselves. Indeed, political parties such as the Australian Labor Party (ALP) have a range of policy committees that allows for grassroots input into policy positions, thus creating a policy constituency within the party on a range of issues. Many grassroots members of political parties are also members of other interest groups and have opportunities to contribute to policy change and development from within.

Political parties also deliberately create opportunities for external influence or input into policies. The ALP has continuing links with the union movement, which has structured representation at party conferences where policy issues are discussed. On the conservative side of Australian politics, external input seems less public and less structured. In 2001, for example, the Australian Liberal Party sent letters to selected executives in the information technology and communications industry inviting them to join a new party forum to 'facilitate regular communications between the Minister, industry peers and Federal Secretariat to make a direct input into the Party's policy formulation' (ABC Radio, 2001). This forum required a substantial joining fee and it was clearly aimed at providing exclusive access for stakeholders with shared political goals.

Students of social policy are often introduced to the concept of the welfare state through comparison of how various models of the welfare state work. They are also often introduced to ideological debates about what the welfare state *should* do in any given society. Models of the welfare state have been described in chapter 1, where they serve as a framework for understanding competing interests and structures to influence and change social policy. Ideological views are often aligned with traditional distinctions in political thought: Marxist, social democratic, liberal, neo-liberal, conservative and so on. Different ideologies are embedded in different models of the welfare state, and the range of positions in any particular model of the welfare state will influence how social policy is developed, reformed and implemented. This is important in a discussion about social policy for social change, because the ideological positions of policy-makers can promote, limit or even prevent social change. It is also important in the contemporary context as global strategies, such as international agreements on trade, investment, climate change or world poverty, and the extent to which governments agree with such strategies, can have a dramatic impact on the delivery of human services within individual countries. This is becoming evident in health and education services, where corporate involvement in investment and service provision is increasing (Jordan, 2006, pp. 89–118).

Social policy is unique among the various fields of public policy because so much of how we measure the quality of life in a community depends on what social policies underpin its members' day-to-day experiences. Because social policy affects so many people and touches on so many issues of daily life, it attracts diverse players, therefore the stakeholders are often in conflict. However, there is also a great deal of collaboration among stakeholders as many shared agendas emerge from shared goals for social change. For example, the role of NGOs in human services has grown over recent decades, as the diversity of society has demanded more flexibility in the delivery of human services (Lyons and Passey, 2006, p. 90). With greater participation in the delivery of human services, NGOs have also moved into the struggle over ideas, power and resources in shaping social policy. This will be explored not only in this chapter, but also across a range of topics in this book.

As discussed in chapter 2, making social policy is part of what contemporary governments do. Indeed, the daily lives of many citizens are more affected by social policies than anything else their government does. Most citizens really only get to know the wide range of social policies their government has when political parties are campaigning for elections, when a crisis or problem precipitates media coverage of a particular issue or when government decisions have an impact on a particular human service or resource that they use. Therefore, in a very general sense, the public often sees social policy as part of the political nature of government through government decisions about the distribution of resources. As noted by many social policy scholars (Dalton et al., 1996; Williams, 1989; Drake, 2001), the failure to respond to a particular social issue or problem—or, indeed, the broader idea of the need for human welfare or services—also indicates a certain view or political position. It is not surprising, then, that one of the key points we are making in this book is that social policy is inherently political and that understanding this is important for effective engagement in social change. The remainder of this chapter uses a range of contemporary and historical examples to demonstrate this point.

Politics and healthcare policy: the key role of private interests

Healthcare is a core social policy field, and the effectiveness and equity of the healthcare system is often seen as a key measure of the quality of a welfare state. This view is highlighted in international surveys in rich democracies, which find that a large majority of people think the government *should* have responsibility for providing healthcare (Howard, C. 2007, p. 113). However, regardless of the views people hold, the politics of health policy is very much contingent on the wider political, economic and social context. In some countries, the government's involvement in ensuring adequate hospitals, community healthcare, access to a physician, preventative care and access to medical services is seen as a fundamental part of what governments do for their citizens. This is the case in the UK,

Australia, New Zealand and Sweden, for example, where, in a universal model of national healthcare provision, most people receive healthcare funded primarily through public resources. In other countries, such as Germany and Japan, the government also provides most health infrastructure and services but healthcare is funded through government-managed self-contributory and employer funded insurance schemes (Busse and Riesberg, 2004; NIPSSR, 2000).

In other countries, such as the US, health insurance is seen as the responsibility of the individual but is provided mainly via employers as part of employment conditions. Provision of healthcare is largely private. This results in a healthcare system that is very much embedded in the market. There are some public insurance programs to pay for care. For example, all Americans over 65 have access to a public health insurance program called Medicare. Poor Americans of working age, people with a severe disability, pregnant women and parents and their children also have some access to a scheme called Medicaid. However, Medicaid is administered by the states, which have significant discretion to define the rules of access and they have tightened them considerably in recent years to contain enrolments. Overall, then, the system works well for people with formal, ongoing employment or wealth, but it is highly rationed for people without money (Blau and Abramovitz, 2007, p. 385). The key flaw in this system is that a large proportion of people are uninsured. If a person does not fit into one of the extremely vulnerable categories, they fall outside the system and are eligible only for emergency treatment in some hospitals (OECD 2008a, p. 124). In the US in 2007, the number of people without health insurance rose to 46 million, or 16 per cent of the population. People without insurance are concentrated among low-income households, 80 per cent of which are working families, most with members employed by firms that do not offer health benefits or who are not eligible for their employers' scheme (Kaiser Commission, n.d., p. 2; OECD 2008a, p. 126).

Although total health spending in the US is considerably higher than in other rich countries, outcomes on average are considerably worse (OECD 2008a, chapter 3). For example, life expectancy rates are lower and infant mortality rates higher than in many comparable countries, and there is a strong relationship between economic resources, access to healthcare and health outcomes (OECD 2008a, p. 109). People without insurance receive much less healthcare than those with insurance, and when they do receive care, it is of inferior quality (OECD 2008a, p. 124). One measure reveals the human cost of the lack of a universal insurance system: a recent study found that the number of avoidable deaths if timely and effective healthcare had been available was significantly higher in the US than in comparable countries, and that American 'underperformance on this measure had coincided with an increase in the uninsured population' (OECD 2008a, p. 114). Media reports sometimes provide stark indications of the problems of the system. In 2008, within a short time frame, security cameras in two hospitals in different parts of the US caught the deaths, in public hospital waiting rooms, of two people neglected while waiting for many hours to be treated (CBS News, 2008).

Reviewing the history of how the American healthcare system came to be in this position reveals that the decisions, which brought the current model into being, were clearly political and very much rooted in the power of private sector providers. But the struggles over health policy and their outcomes also reflect conflicts in the wider political economy (Gottschalk, 2000, p. 160). For example, there have been many attempts to achieve a universal health insurance system in the US. Mass mobilisations of the union movement, coalitions of Democrats in government and the unions under Clinton and social movement organisations have variously worked towards this change over many decades. However, each time they have been defeated by a more powerful interest group, namely, private healthcare providers and the private health insurers (Gottschalk, 2000, p. 160). On one side was the call for an allocation of resources via the state in a universal system, and on the other were the private sector organisations that fought, resisted and won their struggle to continue to be the providers. This type of conflict was also evident during the last Democratic administration (1993–2001), when there was a strong ideological commitment to state-funded universal health insurance. It did not succeed in transforming healthcare policy because private interests had a stronger hold over resources and a clear economic interest in the existing arrangements (Gottschalk, 2000; Howard, C. 2007). This highly abbreviated example demonstrates that, despite majority public political support for public provision of healthcare, once private for-profit interests are established, they will strive to maintain their interests, especially in a political model dominated by neo-liberal market values (discussed in chapter 4 in this book).

Some countries, such as South Korea, have hybrid health systems, where the state imposes a mandatory system of self-insurance, manages health insurance funds and regulates fees and charges. Nevertheless, individuals remain responsible for maintaining their contributions and there is a high user-pays component in the delivery of services (Hwang, 2006)—approximately 37 per cent of all healthcare expenditure in Korea is in the form of 'out of pocket' expenses for consumers, compared to 18 per cent in Australia and 13 per cent in the US (OECD 2008a, p. 128). This model faces two areas of risk. One is the growing burden on the state due to changes in demographic demands, such as the ageing population (Kang, 2007, p. 202). The second is that, because it is based on a model for the employed, like the American system discussed above, the Korean model has a tendency to exclude economically marginalised people (including people who work in casualised and low paid jobs) from insurance and, consequently, from access to adequate healthcare.

Key differences between healthcare models arise from social policy decisions about who or what should be responsible for healthcare. This highly political issue will affect almost everyone working in health-related human services. Under each model, human service providers in health will be educated, trained and organised towards practice in ways that align with the model's broad approach to service delivery. Under a universalistic welfare state model, the notion of equal access and equal quality of service will predominate, whereas in a predominantly self-funded model, the more a person pays for healthcare the better the service they receive. In a mixed model, a two-tier or dual system of care is likely to emerge, offering prompt preferential treatment for the privately insured, and less client-orientated responses for those covered by government managed or funded health insurance (Busse and Riesberg, 2004).

The politics of health policy also happen at the sub-national level, as the Australian case powerfully illustrates. One of the defining features of the Australian Government is its federal structure, which divides power and policy responsibilities through the constitution between the national government on one hand and the six states and two territories on the other. Australian social policy is dominated by the Australian (federal) Government, but with a significant state government and inter-governmental dimension. One reason that the Australian Government dominates is that the bulk of social policy *funding* comes from the federal level, while state governments provide most *services*. Therefore, in all areas in Australian social policy, except income support payments, social policy involves negotiation between the two levels of government and it is framed by political struggles, both for ideological dominance over what social policy *should* do and by the struggle for resources to provide services.

For example, private medical practitioners in Australia have fought hard to maintain their interests and private status as the primary providers of medical services (Gray, 2004, pp. 42–51). Despite this attachment to a private model of service provision, medical practitioners enjoy significant subsidies from the Australian Government, which funds 80 per cent of the cost of their services, primarily through Medicare (calculated from table S43 in AIHW, 2008, p. 288), or in the case of children, 100 per cent of their costs. Meanwhile, public hospitals are run by the states but are also funded significantly by the Australian Government. Between 2004 and 2005, it provided 47.2 per cent of public funding to public hospitals, with states providing the remainder. Significantly for our analysis here, the Australian Government had reduced its share of funding to public hospitals over the preceding decade: between 1995 and 1996, it had contributed 50.7 per cent of all public funding (calculated from table S43 in AIHW, 2008 and table S44 in AIHW, 1998). Across roughly the same period, the share of hospital beds in private hospitals grew from 28.5 per cent in 1996 to 33.3 per cent in 2006 (AIHW, 2008, p. 347). Services in private hospitals are also publicly subsidised by the Australian Government's Private Health Insurance Rebate, introduced in 1999. This subsidy has involved a significant reorientation of Australian Government hospital spending away from public to private hospitals: between the periods 1995 to 1996 and 2004 to 2005, the share of total Australian Government spending on hospitals going to *private* hospitals increased from 5.4 to 19.3 per cent (calculated from table S43 in AIHW, 2008 and table S44 in AIHW, 1998).

So why and how has this happened? Across the decade between 1996 and 2007, there was a strong partisan divide between the federal and state levels of government, with a conservative Coalition Government at the federal level, and mostly Labor governments in the states. The Coalition Government had a strong ideological commitment to enhancing private health services, drawing on the arguments of enhancing patient choice and relieving pressure on the public system (Gray, 2004, pp. 89–97). Also, the Australian Government had little political incentive to support the state governments, which run public hospitals, to increase the quality and quantity of public hospital services. The Coalition was able to use its hold over the purse strings to engineer a shift of beds from public to private hospitals. As their share of relative funding fell, the public hospitals run by Labor state governments seemed to groan under long surgery waiting lists and bed closures. This example demonstrates the importance of the broad political and social context, especially in rich democracies where people can choose to change governments at different levels. They may end up with a system that is not ideologically uniform, or with different levels of government at odds with one another. This can create a state of ongoing struggle for power over the social policy that should be pursued and for priorities in the allocation of resources for services.

A further demonstration of the political nature of health policy is when a government changes or transforms its broad economic or political agenda. For example, a post-Mao economic growth-orientated Chinese Government reduced its commitment to state-funded healthcare during the late 1970s and early 1990s. The government reduced its health spending from 0.11 per cent of GDP in 1978 to 0.04 per cent in 1993, and thereby shifted the burden of the cost of healthcare back onto the consumer (Zhu 2000, p. 45, cited in Jordan, 2006, p. 95). Jordan sees this as a deliberate strategy by the Chinese Government to maintain a 'largely state-socialist rural sector' while relying on economic growth from an emerging 'capitalist, industrialised urban fringe'. It resulted in a divided health system, as support for rural health services, previously established under the support-led infrastructure of the Maoist period, was withdrawn and most doctors ended up residing in cities (2006, pp. 95–96). This shift in economic and political priorities meant that a privatised system of healthcare emerged in rural areas to fill the gaps of the previously state-funded services, with nearly 90 per cent of rural people having to pay for healthcare from their own pockets (Jordan, 2006, p. 96). The overall impact of this social policy decision meant that people in rural areas, where poverty is predominant, have the least amount of healthcare and the poorest states of health (Reuters, 2007).

According to a World Health Organization (WHO) report, the Chinese Government has recently made a commitment to addressing this inequality and has announced that it will support universal access to basic healthcare by 2020. However, it faces major challenges because previous economic development policies have limited the capacity to breach the inequities between rural and urban areas of China (WHO, 2008). This change of direction demonstrates how international institutions and interests can also exert influence over what was previously a governmental system closed off from the rest of the world. By exercising political engagement, the World Health Organization has had an effect on social policy direction in China, as this nation works towards integration in global markets and seeks legitimacy in global politics.

Women and the politics of welfare: from the outside in?

As discussed in chapter 1, the welfare state is the structural manifestation or main producer of social policy in most rich countries. Since its inception in the late nineteenth century, the welfare state has been a key site of political contestation and debate at all levels of society. The welfare state is the primary vehicle for social policy processes, notably the distribution and redistribution of resources that are hotly debated in wider society, as we have seen in relation to healthcare. Welfare states are run by governments where a political party is in charge. Thus, politicians tend to deliver policies 'in exchange for specific or generalised political demand and support' (Schmidt, 1996, p. 155), which politicises the policy process. However, as Manfred Schmidt points out, it is also important to recognise the influence of institutional and cultural circumstances on the process and outcomes of political influences on social policy (1996, p. 155). These circumstances can be expanded to include universal social distinctions that have emerged across all societies, such as ethnicity, class or gender.

In this section, *gender* will be highlighted as a key factor that affects the way social policy and/or the welfare state developed from a political point of view, with the aim of placing the position of women at the centre of social policy analysis. Women as an interest group in the politics of social policy have clearly been instrumental in one of the most dramatic and significant periods of social change for rich democracies. The feminist revolution turned many social relations upside down, and issued a challenge to society to rethink some powerful taken-for-granted relations of power. Thus, the ongoing struggle to pursue social change that is good for women exemplifies the kinds of broad conflicts over resources and power that occur in the social policy process.

Understanding the history of how politics shape social policy is important, because events distant in time often provide foundational politics for the type of welfare state that develops in a country. This is clearly demonstrated in Theda Skocpol's (1992) research on the political origins of social policy in the United States. Skocpol demonstrates that a quirk of progressive politics in the post-Civil War period saw the crushing of a move for a universal state-funded old age pension based on a fledgling system of pensions developed for Civil War veterans. She also reveals a general trend in the early makings of the US welfare state model in describing the emergence of a *maternal* welfare state at a time that many other western democracies (including Australia) were developing *paternal* welfare states, based on the male breadwinner or wage earner model.

Skocpol describes how women took 'the lead in US social welfare politics' in the maternalistic model of the late nineteenth and early twentieth century United States. She also shows how maternalistic policies such as mother's pensions, minimum wage regulations for women and the creation of the federal Children's Bureau were achieved, due to the efforts of 'nation-spanning' women's civil society organisations (1992, pp. 2–3). Skocpol attributes the development of the US public school system to women's civil society action, as they were able to utilise the 'domestic morality' of the nineteenth century's 'separate sphere' as leverage for public school provision (1992, p. 3). Thus, the prevailing social view of women as belonging to a separate, unworldly, domestic sphere rather than to the masculinised public sphere gave women's voice a moral leverage, such that the need for universal education came to be equated with higher morality and personal betterment. Skocpol (1992) argues that because women were relatively late to gain the vote in the US compared to other western democracies, and because they were excluded from the mainstream of party politics, they gained impetus to create policy demands from the relatively non-partisan political arena of civil society organisations.

Although Australian women achieved the vote in 1901, they were largely outside the formal political system until the 1970s. Nevertheless, in the more direct interplay of gender politics in contemporary Australia, it can be seen how women have been instrumental in placing key social policy issues on the governmental agenda. Without the agitation of women's groups born from a strong women's movement and the voicing of the politics of 'making the personal political', key social policy concerns such as domestic violence, childcare, sex discrimination and child sexual abuse may have taken many more decades to become part of the mandate of state responsibility (Chappell, 2001; Phillips, 2006a; Summers, 2003; Thorpe and Irwin, 1996).

Relatively sympathetic Labor governments in the early 1970s and again between the mid 1980s and mid 1990s, meant that the politics of feminism had a direct and long-lasting impact on social policy in Australia, as policies that recognised women's specific disadvantages and needs were introduced and implemented (Summers, 2003; Phillips, 2006a; Lake, 1999). These included initiatives such as the establishment of national funding programs for refuges catering to women escaping domestic violence and the instigation of government support for formal systems of childcare via subsidised community-based centres, in response to women's workforce participation needs. Other initiatives were the introduction of anti-sex discrimination laws and equal opportunity programs, programs to enhance girls' equal educational outcomes, specific policies on women's health, income support for sole parents and direct funding of women's advocacy organisations, to name a few.

The political forces that combined to ensure a more women-focused social policy agenda were multiple and diverse. They included a broad-based international women's movement, radical activist groups, formal women's groups (such as the Women's Electoral Lobby), active participation in the institutional political process via participation in political parties and gaining places in parliaments, identified places for women in governmental bureaucracy, formal political and governmental advisory groups on women's policy, and effective use of the media in gaining attention for women's demands for change. As in the case of healthcare in Australia described above, many of the initiatives that came about through the emergence of women's policy were split between the federal government that made legislation and provided funding, and state governments that took on much of the service delivery. This was an important configuration in the case of women's policy, because it ensured that many women's services, such as domestic violence support and sexual assault services, could continue to be offered, even though the broader support by the federal government for women's policy was curtailed by the election of the Howard Liberal–National Coalition Government (1996–2007) in 1996 (Summers, 2003).

The ideology of the Howard Government included a strong anti-feminist sentiment. Many of the gains made for women's policy were adversely affected by its policies, which included the dismantling of women-specific policy infrastructure (Summers, 2003; Chappell, 2002). The Howard Government's hostility towards feminism was successfully pursued at that time because reactionary minority groups appeared to be able to assert greater influence on social policy. This was evident, for example, in the reintroduction of debates around abortion (not debated in the federal parliament since 1979), given public voice by senior members of the government and via access to policy influence from conservative churches (Maddox, 2005, p. 103). These debates gained purchase through the issue of Medicare-funded late-term abortions. They gave an opportunity for the polarised views of the conservative, anti-feminist 'right to life' and pro-choice feminist positions to re-enter the public sphere. One benefit of the state/federal government divide was that a direct negative impact on abortion services was largely curtailed by the ongoing support of access to abortion by the state Labor governments that were responsible for providing such services. However, a lasting manifestation of the abortion debates under the Howard Government related to international aid. The Howard Government introduced a ban on foreign aid being used to give women in poor countries advice and access to safer abortion services (Schubert, 2008; Lane, 2008). Reflecting a significant shift in politics on this issue and feminist politics more broadly, the Rudd Labor Government, elected in November 2007, publicly stated its intent to reverse that decision (Schubert, 2008; Lane, 2008).

Women's or gender politics have played a significant political role in the development of social policy. This is not a recent phenomenon, as the early development of a 'maternal' welfare state in the US shows; it has spanned more than a century. In some ways, core values of feminist politics, such as equality, have become basic political expectations of what welfare states in rich democracies will do. That includes equal access to education for girls and women, equal employment opportunities, reproductive rights and appropriate women's healthcare. However, as the history of women's policy shows, these demands can be denied resources or be de-prioritised by governments that do not support a feminist or pro-women's political agenda. Thus, it is important to understand how conflicts of ideology are played out in conflicts over resources within institutional contexts (such as federal systems of government, which fragment power) that also shape social policy decisions.

The percentage of women in government has increased dramatically in the past 50 years across the world (Paxton et al., 2007, p. 266). It is likely, then, that efforts to shape social policy agendas in ways that meet women's needs are going to have a continued presence, providing ongoing opportunities for human services for women to be developed. The most 'women friendly' policies exist in Nordic states where women's representation in government, education and paid work has been high since the 1970s and where an ongoing emphasis on gender equality in public debates and policy-making has emerged as a strong characteristic (Marques-Pereira and Siim, 2002). This arose from exhaustive efforts towards gender equality; women across these societies were mobilised and had support from the various governments. 'Nordic state feminism' was coined by feminist academics to describe how much feminist ideology has been taken on by the Nordic states and become integral to social policy (Bergman, 2008). However, as Solveig Bergman (2008) points out, even in these high performing states inequalities remain. The labour force is highly gendered, with women more likely to be employed by the state and men more likely to be employed in the private sector. Further, more women than men are primary carers, and men dominate in core leadership positions (Bergman, 2008).

However, a high proportion of women in politics is not always a necessary, nor a sufficient, condition for policy outcomes that work for women. For example, in the US, where the achievement of programs for women may be surprising, this has occurred because women in political power have been shown to prioritise policies relating to women and children, and introduce bills on women's rights, sometimes overriding formal political party affiliation in support of such issues (Paxton et al., 2007, p. 273). However, in other countries and in differing political contexts, such as where women are elected under very conservative governments, female politicians can adopt an anti-feminist stand and assist in the retrenchment of social policy that supports women. This happened in Canada in 1984, when the Progressive Conservative Party came into power, with a dramatic increase in the number of women members who immediately became vocal critics of feminists and women's interest groups (Chappell, 2002, p. 73). Another example discussed previously was under the Howard Government in Australia. Clearly, being a woman is not the same as being a feminist.

The example of women's policy offers some strong general lessons about the political nature of social policy. It also demonstrates that political engagement in social policy is not confined to party politics or formal political processes. It can emerge from social movements, particularly when it is driven by the desire for significant social change, such as gender equality. It is also a good way of highlighting key points of application or pressure that can be placed across the social policy process. However, more than anything, the struggle for women's policy highlights the need for multiple players in the process of achieving significant social change. The women's movement was so successful in the Nordic states because a feminist agenda was incorporated into the policy of a strong welfare state. The important gains in Australia were achieved through a combination of an active women's movement, increased women's participation in formal political institutions and the development of women's services and formalised lobby groups working to develop social policy responses that achieved key women-friendly policies and increased resource allocation to women's services.

Politics, NGOs and social policy

As demonstrated above, making social policy is not the exclusive domain of governments: there are other key actors in the process. For example, NGOs can be a vehicle for citizens to get issues onto the social policy agenda and communicate specific needs in the community they represent. That community may be highly localised or exist across a national or international sphere. NGOs or non-profit organisations can deliver services or function as advocacy groups. In many cases they do both. In the performance of an advocacy function, most human service or social interest NGOs (or non-profits) share the pursuit of a 'collective good framed in the public interest' (Andrews and Edwards, 2004, p. 485). Often, riding on the wave of a timely and influential social movement, such as the women's movement mentioned in the previous section, NGOs will make effective use of the media through protests or public actions.

In the effort to get an issue on the social policy agenda, NGOs (along with other political actors) draw on what Kenneth Andrews and Bob Edwards describe as 'diagnostic' and 'prognostic' frames (2004, p. 493). 'Diagnostic frames' draw on theorised social ideas (such as feminism or racism) to define social problems and assign blame for the cause of those problems. 'Prognostic frames' are used to identify and propose solutions to problems, including making demands for resources to be allocated to programs or services that can solve social problems. Using either frame is integral to the way a political struggle works towards reaching social policy outcomes. In other words, a set of political ideas or theories helps frame the higher goals of a social policy objective and sets a framework for other actors to work collectively towards social change. Often existing within or in alignment with that framework (such as a social inclusion agenda as discussed in chapter 9), human service NGOs diagnose and work on social problems—on how to solve them, or at least how to mitigate their negative impact.

As discussed in chapter 2, NGOs have become central to human service delivery and they are increasingly important players in the development of social policy. The role of NGOs is much debated in international as well as national and local contexts (Ahmed and Potter, 2006, p. 241). NGO performance is more scrutinised than ever before and questions are often raised about their legitimacy, owing to a perception of their greater power and influence (Ahmed and Potter, 2006). A recent report on 'The 21st Century NGO' presented a view of NGOs as moving from being 'outsiders challenging the system' to increasingly being 'part of the system' (SustainAbility et al., 2003). The report refers primarily to the politics of NGO corporate engagement but is equally applicable, at a global level, to the increased legitimacy of the influence of NGOs on global social policy, as developed by international institutions such as the United Nations. One example of NGO legitimacy in social policy development on a global scale was their important role in the development of the Millennium Development Goals, a core set of internationally supported objectives for a significant reduction of world poverty between 2000 and 2015 (Brinkerhoff et al., 2007).

NGO peak bodies and larger NGOs have been a key source of knowledge and influence in transformations of social policy in many rich democracies. Of course, there is significant variation within the NGO sector; organisations hold different positions and play different roles in the processes of social policy development and implementation. Further, the influence and role of any particular NGO, or of the NGO sector as a whole, varies under different governmental regimes, depending on the ideology or political goals of the government and the level of development of public social provision. Indeed, the role of NGOs in social policy development can evoke a negative political response, because NGOs pose a challenge to the power of the state in controlling the social policy agenda. In Australia, for example, politically conservative commentators have made a concerted attack on the legitimacy of NGOs in social policy agenda setting (Hywood, 2004; Johns and Roskam, 2004; Maddison et al., 2004).

It is widely acknowledged that NGOs and social movements act as alternative democratic vehicles for social change and, with a growth in capacity for influence via contemporary communication technologies such as the internet, are able to wield social policy influence at many institutional levels (Phillips, 2006b). Reorientations of some welfare states have resulted in a new set of relationships between NGOs and governments in the delivery of a range of human services and the development of the entire breadth of human service policies. For example, governments in Australia have expanded services by contracting out new initiatives, leading to a greater proportion of services being provided by NGOs and businesses.

In rich countries, NGOs often provide services on behalf of or alongside government, and are heavily subsidised by public funding. In contrast, in poor countries, where the welfare state is underdeveloped, NGOs are often central to the provision of human services for the majority of people. In the Philippines, for example, a vibrant NGO sector actively seeks to influence social policy. With poverty as the most pressing and widespread social policy issue, the key objectives of many NGOs are aligned with multiple forms of poverty alleviation. However, due to poor state infrastructure, many NGOs are doing the work that people in rich democracies expect of state-funded human services. One example is the Kapwa ko Mahal ko Foundation, which funds essential medical services and medical training for preventative health and public health education. The foundation began with a regular television program on health education that has continued for 25 years. In addition to its educational goals, the program provides a means of connecting poor people with medical needs that they could not otherwise afford and voluntary donors who assist with medical costs via the television program (Alampay and Ong, 2007, p. 151). The foundation had to employ medical staff to assess patients due to an overwhelming demand and later began providing primary healthcare and community-based health programs across the Philippines (Alampay and Ong, 2007, pp. 151–165).

As stated in chapter 1, in Australia, most non-institutional human services are delivered by the NGO sector (although funded by the state). This places them in a unique sphere of political policy influence, especially given their capacity to conduct grassroots research and use it in a 'prognostic' way for social policy development or change. However, another characteristic of the human services NGO sector is that it is often poorly resourced; many service organisations do not have the capacity to take on multiple roles within their sector. Accordingly, many human service NGOs rely on peak bodies that form to represent the political interests as advocates for the sector. In this way, the NGO sector is often well organised to mobilise public interest and support for particular issues. Large peak bodies, which represent various areas of human services, can be very influential in developing social policy through direct lobbying of ministers or other politicians, producing submissions to government budgets or analysing election promises.

This means that the capacity of NGOs to exert political influence varies from government to government and between nations. For example, in the US, there is a strong culture and significant financial investment in political lobbying by advocates for 'public interest claims promoting or resisting social change' (Minkoff et al., 2008, p. 526). NGOs are often in a struggle not to be hijacked by powerful business, moral or religious lobbyists or think tanks that represent certain views on the state's role in the affairs of families or in human relations. In Australia, under the Howard Government, certain NGOs were favoured and others excluded from access to policy influence. Whether an NGO found favour was often determined by its ideology, and some key peak bodies, such as the Australian Council of Social Service (ACOSS), found themselves outside the political process. ACOSS had enjoyed a high level of legitimacy with previous governments in its role as a representative of human service and welfare advocacy organisations across the country (Mendes, 2005; Mendes, 2006; Phillips, 2007).

Think tanks as players in the social policy process

Think tanks are another source of evidence and argument in social policy debate, and they often play a role in raising the profile of social policy issues in the public domain. Opinion is nevertheless divided on just how much they influence governmental policy development (t'Hart and Vromen, 2008, p. 138). A range of types of institutions or bodies do this kind of research and policy advocacy work, including research centres within universities, research centres established and funded by governments but operating independently of government, centres or research businesses set up to contract out their services and 'policy advocacy' organisations that seek to influence specific sectors or policies. Of all of these types of knowledge producers, think tanks are of great interest in a discussion about the political nature of social policy because they tend to have overtly political alliances or agendas and, unconstrained by government or electoral politics, they can campaign for or against specific social policy agendas.

Because think tanks tend to have a clear political identity, they are often referred to as 'left wing' or 'right wing'. This political labelling usually occurs because there is some kind of financial or executive connection to a political party or movement. For example, policy think tanks in Australia include some clearly identifiable right-wing organisations, such as the Centre for Independent Studies, which has a strong negative position on welfare and income support, the Institute for Public Affairs, which pursues free market policy objectives, and the Menzies Research Centre, which is funded by the Liberal Party (t'Hart and Vromen, 2008, p. 140). Conversely, there are also clearly identified and influential left-wing think tanks in Australia, such as the Australia Institute, which focuses its research on social policy and environmental issues, and the Chifley Research Centre, which is linked to the Labor Party but is funded by the Australian Government and private corporations.

Because they tend to have an ideological base, think tanks take a 'prognostic' approach on many social policy issues. In doing so, they often issue strong attacks against other actors in the struggle over resources and ideas. In order that their research is considered authoritative and to ensure that they are called upon to comment on governmental policy decisions or other research, they claim expertise in their field. It is evident that right-wing think tanks have been most successful and have long histories, often because they have support from wealthy corporate and business interest groups (Cahill, 2002, p. 21). In Australia, the Centre for Independent Studies has grown from strength to strength over 30 years and claims that it is a 'rare day that CIS research or researchers fail to appear somewhere in the media' (Norton, 2006, p. 44). Despite its claims of independence (Norton, 2006, p. 45), the CIS gained significant favour under the Howard Government and a number of its staff contributed to bolstering anti-welfare state debates and policies (Mendes, 2003; Cahill, 2002). It has also been combative against other NGOs and academic research on issues of measuring poverty, income support and sole parent families (Saunders and Tsumori, 2002). Left-wing think tanks appear to have had much less public exposure and success at influencing thinking. Philip Mendes points to the success of the Australia Institute in promoting progressive alternatives to the neo-liberal ideas put forward by right-wing think tanks but indicates that they tend to have more limited resources (2003, p. 49).

Some think tanks manage to preserve a sense of independence from insti-tutional politics although, according to t'Hart and Vromen (2008, p. 144), this is increasingly difficult in Australia. Indeed, the very nature of projects that think tanks tender for, and the expertise they hold, means that political identity (as left or right in their thinking) is often assumed. Committed to researching key issues of concern to governments, scientists, academics or the public, they play an increasing role in influencing social policy directions. This is achieved primarily by funding research that 'proves' a certain position or provides evidence that calls for specific or general social policy responses.

T'Hart and Vromen (2008) emphasise the political nature of think tanks and point to the wide variety of political positions that they reflect—despite the clear need, in a market-driven and competitive context, that they present a 'balanced' research brief and report. Think tanks also depend heavily on the media for influence. The media plays a key role in determining how influential or controversial think tank research and position papers will be, thereby affecting how much public pressure may be generated about a particular social policy issue. If the media fails to take up findings from these organisations, no matter how true their findings are, their work may have no impact or only a 'slow trickle' impact on public policy (t'Hart and Vromen, 2008).

Being aware of the existence and influence of think tanks is important in social policy. The source of ideas promoted from think tank research should be carefully scrutinised and, if necessary, countered by alternative, sometimes more rigorous, research. Human service professionals are often well placed to present evidence to counter some of the ideologically driven research put forward by anti-welfare think tanks. They should therefore take opportunities to engage and utilise the media when social policy issues are publicly aired.

The power of the media in social policy

Alongside the various political actors we have discussed in this chapter, the media (print, television, radio and increasingly internet based) is also a key agent or direct political player in social policy. From a broad perspective, the media is central to the public sphere, which is, as Iris Marion Young points out, the 'primary connector' between people and power (2000, p. 173). The public sphere is the stage on which all the actors in social policy play out their influence by raising issues, formulating problems, publishing or broadcasting information, putting forward opinions, criticisms and artistic expressions and proposing new policies and solutions to social problems. If widely disseminated, reported and debated through the media, these problem formulations, criticisms and policy proposals can sometimes provoke political and social change (Young, 2000, p. 174).

The media has a high profile in the public sphere and is both a device for and a reflection of a well functioning democracy. In most rich democracies, it is important to have an unrestrained and active critical media, reflecting the principle of freedom of expression and speech. Media can operate to control or moderate power through exposing corruption, exploitation and false information. However, it can also be used to manipulate thinking or values in certain circumstances or within certain communities. Media ownership is a big issue in debates about the quality of interaction in the public sphere, because concentrated ownership is often cited as a cause of media manipulation on specific issues or in meeting particular political ends. In Australia in 2006, for example, changes to media ownership policy made it easier for media companies to own more kinds of media outlets (television, newspapers, etc.) than they previously had been able to. This development prompted senators from the National Party to submit a dissenting report to a senate committee looking into the implications of the change in policy. In that report, they quoted a small media owner, who responded to a question about whether increased concentration of ownership could affect the democratic process as follows:

> Absolutely. We have no doubt about that … We are not trying to demonise the owners of the media. That is their role. But if you look at the track record of media owners in this country [Australia] in terms of directing the information traffic, when they want to, on issues that they are interested in—on big political issues, on societal issues—they have done that (Joyre and Nash, 2006, p. 1).

Fear that media corporations will exploit their power is widespread in Australia. A survey of social attitudes in 2003 found that around 80 per cent of people agreed there was too great a concentration of power in media ownership (Denemark, 2005, pp. 232–233).

The media influences social policy in many ways. In some cases, news and current affairs programs will act as a provocateur for social policy change, as an informational or educational tool or as an advocate for causes, individuals, groups or communities. A positive outcome can arise when the media effect-ively influences political decisions or policy responses by shifting the focus on a specific social policy problem to the 'consumer' end where, for example, parents, young people and carers engage with social policy when it directly affects their lives. This often allows specific social policy decisions to influence the way they vote at elections. This was exemplified in recent calls in Australia from people affected by alcohol-related violence to extend the level of health education and regulation against smoking in public places to excessive drinking in public places (ABC News, 2008). Such a call for social policy intervention is often driven by individual citizens' preparedness to speak publicly in the media about the catastrophic effects of social problems on their own lives. In this case, the family of a young man who received head injuries as a victim of alcohol-fuelled random violence has stepped to the forefront of media calls for greater restrictions on alcohol consumption (ABC News, 2008). Hence, we see the role of media as an advocate representing people affected by a social policy problem brought about by the failure of government to act and address the problem. The extent to which a government responds to such a call for policy action will affect how people can relate to, or are associated with, the key stakeholders in a debate. On occasion, this type of pressure can escalate into a national campaign that has a timely impact leading up to an election. This type of policy influence for social change can be described as grassroots campaigning that draws on informal political power.

By contrast, child protection is a prominent example of an area of social policy that has a long history of being affected negatively by media reporting, often leading to moral panic. The neglect and abuse of children is a highly sensitive social problem, and when a child dies at the hands of a carer, or is found to be living with extreme violence or neglect, it is always a 'big' news story. There are many interest groups or players in child protection in rich democracies and they all expect that the state will take ultimate responsibility to protect children from harm. The media usually takes up a 'prognostic' role in child protection cases, sheeting blame to either the social workers or the agency that failed to remove children known to be at risk (Goddard and Liddell, 1995; Ayre, 2001).

Patrick Ayre has assessed media influence in serious cases of child protection over three decades in England and Wales. He observes that each scandal was followed by three responses (2001, p. 888). First was a media attack and blame on agencies deemed responsible. Second were announcements of recommendations for welfare agencies by public inquiries convened to analyse the tragedies. Third, revised, detailed practice policies were propagated to prevent the same thing happening again (Ayre, 2001, p. 888). Ayre described how the media contributes to creating a climate of fear, mistrust and blame, which invariably forces the government's hand to make promises to protect children (Ayre, 2001, pp. 889–891)—promises that governments cannot keep. The same patterns can be observed in most rich democracies, highlighting the powerful role the media plays in instigating debate or division on sensitive social policy issues.

Human service workers in child protection are from many disciplinary fields and have to think strategically about using the media and strategically responding to the media. Ayre emphasised a need for political awareness among professionals in this field, suggesting that appropriate public knowledge and understanding about child protection interventions could only become part of media representations when they become 'aligned with wider, stronger and more influential political and social currents within the body politic' (2001, pp. 899–900).

Conclusion

Most struggles over ensuring the best social policy are motivated by a desire for the best outcomes for the people affected by the policies. Yet people disagree about what the 'best' is, and how it can be achieved. These disagreements are legitimate, and politics is the realm of society in which these differences are played out in the struggle over ideas and for resources and power. Many areas of social policy prompt keen interest from a range of players with different interests. The political nature of social policy means that there is ample opportunity for different kinds of actors to take up a range of roles in the process of social policy development and implementation. This diversity of interests and actors highlights the multiple opportunities for human service practitioners, as citizens and as participants in the social policy domain, to participate in the social policy process. There are opportunities to influence how social policy is framed and developed, and how it is channelled through the allocation of resources. There are also opportunities to participate in the competition for ideas that create a wider social and political environment and where new social policy direction is accepted.

In the next chapter, we turn our focus to the wider community and specific professional communities in an examination of the role that values, ethics and rights play in the social policy process.

CHAPTER 4

Values: social policy and contested domains

Introduction

The provision of human services is inextricably linked to values that operate at a range of levels, spanning the macro to the micro. Within this range, values shift and change and are influenced by ideology, orientation and context. Human service professionals have to operate in this complex arena and contend with political, organisational and individual value systems. In this chapter, we explore the relationship between values and policy processes. We begin by examining the connection between ethics, morality and values before reviewing the ways in which the addition of rights influences the discussion. We then consider the associations between different political approaches, which comprise social democratic, neo-liberal and 'third way' orientations, and their underpinning value systems. Throughout, we appraise the implications for human service professionals.

The relationship between ethics, morality, values and rights

Any discussion of values requires a review of the terminology and an appraisal of the ways in which associated concepts relating to ethics, morality and rights can be understood. All may have different meanings, which evolve and change over time and differ according to context. With regard to contemporary definitions as well as the connections that can be made between these concepts, Banks

(2006) distinguishes between ethics, which she sees as synonymous with moral philosophy, and ethical behaviour, which she relates to norms or standards. She acknowledges that there are, of course, many variations between these two areas, but in relation to moral philosophy, she differentiates between three main types. First is 'meta-ethics', a set of ethics associated with critical and analytical thinking about the meaning and use of moral terms such as 'right', 'good' and 'duty' and issues related to the nature of morality. Second is 'normative ethics', used to try and provide answers to moral questions such as what is the morally right course of action in a particular case, and how a morally good person can be defined. Third is 'descriptive ethics', a way of looking at the moral opinions and beliefs that people hold and how they act in relation to them. It is at this level that social policy is most obviously affected by ethical understandings, as these drive broad political as well as personal agendas.

In relation to ethical behaviour, there is usually a connection between ethical understandings drawn from moral philosophy and the standards of behaviour viewed as acceptable by the prevailing consensus opinion. In turn, there is much debate about whether understandings of ethics and standards of behaviour are internally developed by a moral agent, externally imposed by external authorities, such as governments, or acquired through a combination of internal and external factors. Although Banks (2006) suggests that a combination of morality and ethics can be used to formulate a code of ethics or a system of moral norms or standards, others disagree and see ethics and morals as distinct entities. Ife (2008), for example, makes a clear distinction between the two and views ethics as a yardstick to measure and evaluate society's underpinning morality. A different understanding is drawn from Greek and Roman interpretations, where morality is viewed as being nestled within the wider parameters of ethics, rather like a yolk within an egg (Bowles et al., 2006). From a sociological perspective, Bauman (1993) sees 'ethics' as an externally imposed code for universally prescribing correct behaviour and views morality as a set of personal perspectives that are both internal and autonomous. In contrast, Foucault (1984), another prominent social theorist, sees morality and ethics as forming distinct parts of discourses that dominate general or normative thinking in a society. He regards these as being based on the links between power and knowledge frameworks and the popularising of certain sets of ethics, which are then used to promote particular social policy directions and justify specific forms of social change.

This overview of the associations that can be made between ethical under-standings, standards of behaviour and morality further emphasises that meanings are not fixed in stone and can be endlessly debated. It also draws attention to how ethics, standards and morality inform values and the ways in which values shift and change according to context, culture and prevailing dominant perspectives. Although all concepts have to be viewed as fluid, O'Connor and colleagues (2008) offer a useful organising perspective with their suggestion that values are simultaneously held by organisations, groups and individuals at abstract as well as at specific levels. This combination can be seen to produce legitimising frameworks for action at macro and micro levels, influenced by key players such as governments, the media and, drawing from Foucault (1981), the interplay of dominant discourses.

At the micro level, Ife (2008) makes a useful contribution when he explores professional codes of ethics and how human service professionals, such as social workers, critically reflect on the ethical issues they deal with in practice. He highlights that codes of ethics encourage ethical behaviour and control unethical behaviour by applying sanctions. Further, he argues that rights and ethics can be seen as two sides of the same coin, with the principles and practices involved in statements of ethics implying a set of rights. However, he does note two main differences between a code of ethics and a set of rights. The first is that rights do not contain professional sanctions as control functions. The second is that rights imply a set of truths or convictions of certainty that rarely accord with the messy and contradictory world of practice. Looking at human services in terms of social work, he states:

> A social work dilemma, framed in 'ethical' terms, sees the social worker as the actor with decision-making discretion; there is no clear role for the client in the social worker's ethical decision. On the other hand, a human rights perspective … allows the possibility for the client to be an active participant in the decision-making process (Ife, 2008, p. 122).

The point that Ife makes here is that an emphasis on ethics and codes of ethics can subtly reinforce conservative and disempowering guidelines or rules for social work practice. However, Ife (2008) takes on board a key point made by Bauman (1993) and accepts that, although professional ethical codes can support 'top down' imperatives or directives on how to practise, they can also operate as constraints on those with power, creating some balance in influence by those with less power.

An example of the operation of a legitimising framework at a macro level can be seen in the way the Howard Liberal–National Coalition Government (1996–2007) dramatically adjusted Australian social policy on the immigration of refugees. This was in response both to racially motivated policies promoted by the far right and to the 'war on terror' campaign enacted in the aftermath of '9/11'. Here, policy can be seen to have influenced values, with values influencing policy in a circular manner. The result was a shift in values, which made it acceptable to the majority for an uncompromising stance to be taken against asylum seekers (Mares, 2001, p. 3; McAllister, 2003, p. 448).

However, to take this example further, it is notable that even though the Howard Government actively discouraged any debate on the moral issues generated by its immigration and asylum seeker policies, critical analysis of the changes to refugee policy by churches, NGOs, some parts of the media, academia, legal experts and human service professionals eventually brought a moral dimension to the questioning of such policies (Jupp, 2005, p. 186). Revelations that the government had lied about asylum seekers on a sinking boat throwing their children overboard, and the sinking of a further boat carrying asylum seekers, brought the moral integrity and ethical behaviour of the government into question (Jupp, 2005, p. 187). Values were influenced to the extent that there was a shift away from such unbending policy responses. This serves as a demonstration of how human service professionals can engage in debating core values in the public domain and how particular social policy platforms can be undermined.

Value systems, policy analysis and social policy orientations

A key concern explored in this book is how value systems can affect the type of social policy developed for the wide range of human service contexts. One means of investigating this is to think about how it applies to three different political frameworks discussed in chapter 3: social democratic, neo-liberal and third way approaches. Our emphasis here is on the ways that particular social policy 'platforms', or sets of promises, appear to be underpinned by inherent values operating within these political perspectives.

Social democratic politics and policies can be seen to draw from a strong set of egalitarian values derived from a tradition that recognises equality as something everyone shares from birth. This encompasses equal rights that extend to political, civic and social dimensions. Equality is regarded as a key means of achieving individual freedom and this is applied through a range of policies that aim to bring about equal opportunity so that everyone can develop their full potential (McClelland, 2006, p. 22). There is also emphasis placed on the 'decommodification' of individuals, with understandings of citizenship and participation defined by solidarity rather than by participation in the market (Stephens, 1996, p. 36).

The underpinning value base of social democratic politics and policies incorporates a strong pluralistic element that can lead to social policies being developed from compromises between different competing groups. In this, as Henderson and Thomas (1987) point out, competing interest groups are seen as vital to democracy and stability because they divide power and prevent one group exerting exclusive influence or power over decisions that affect everyone. Where pluralism is present, the state or government has an important role in balancing different competing interests and ensuring that political decision-making takes account of a range of views.

In general, social democratic social policies promote values that are in contrast to neo-liberalism, for example, as they begin on a premise of collective 'good' rather than individual interests. Burdens are spread across society, and wealth and benefits are redistributed via a heavily redistributive tax and social spending regime, as a means of addressing social problems or needs. Where social democratic governments exist, such as in the Nordic states, defining characteristics of a strong welfare state can be found. These include non-gender-specific benefits and services based on a notion of equal responsibility between men and women for such things as parenting, and an aim to shift the burden of responsibility from the family unit to the state and the wider community. One example is in the positive support given to publicly financed childcare in Sweden. Values emanating from an acceptance of gender equality—the right of all adults, including mothers, to support themselves by undertaking paid work—together with a strong represent-ation of women politicians, has led to pre-school, publicly funded childcare being regarded as a universal right. This has been sustained through challenging economic circumstances and has in turn reflected a changing value base with the increasing prioritisation of equality in opportunity for children.

Neo-liberalism or economic rationalism is often used to describe the dominant set of political values that currently prevail in liberal welfare states, although this varies from country to country depending on the wider social and political context. In the US, for example, the 'liberty' of 'free economic action' and a neo-conservative discourse of 'individual solutions to myriad social problems' tends to be given particular attention (Ong, 2006, p. 2). In Australia, neo-liberalism is informed by a social liberal tradition that places high value on individual freedom in both a positive and a negative sense, but with the ultimate goal that social (and economic) policy is made within the ideal of achieving the greatest good for the greatest number (McClelland, 2006, p. 22). That means that freedom from coercion is just as important as freedom to achieve economic well-being and that state intervention in the market is justified in the pursuit of 'social goods' (McClelland, 2006, p. 22). The values underpinning neo-liberalism also shape how people are defined and how they act as citizens. For example, it promotes the freedom and 'natural' rule of markets as a primary goal and in doing so reflects a key characteristic in the transition from production to consumption and ultimately to 'commodification' (Baudrillard, 1998). 'Commodification' also applies to citizenship, as it suggests that 'good' citizenship is based on economic participation, therefore the value of having a job is strongly emphasised in neo-liberal welfare policy. This explains, to some extent, the constant reference to *work* as the best form of welfare for all, as discussed in chapter 9.

The economic downturn, experienced by all industrially developed countries in 2008, allowed these differences in values within neo-liberalism to be played out on the global stage. In the context of the collapse of core free-market economic institutions such as the stock market, investment markets and mortgage lenders, and the impact of this financial crisis on large business sectors such as housing, motor vehicle manufacturing and retail industries, some argue that the individualistic, non-interventionist neo-liberalism of the US has failed. This failure is part of the explanation for the Democratic Party's win in the 2008 presidential election (Komblut, 2008; Rudd, 2009). Strategies put forward to address the collapse of the free-market system have relied on social liberal values that support heavy investment and intervention (via market regulation) by the state to protect individuals from poverty and long-term unemployment. A turn to social liberal values is a driver for governments in other rich democracies such as Australia, Germany and the UK, which have made massive investments in the market to protect their citizens from social problems that arise from a widespread economic downturn.

Overall, the values that underlie the 'commodification' of human services have influenced most liberal welfare states by extending market principles through privatisation and reducing the role of the state in health and welfare services (discussed further in chapter 6). Examples include legitimising the view that profits can be made out of caring, and the ways in which individual responsibility for family support, characterised by the 'user pays' principle, have been emphasised (Mendes, 2008a; Western et al., 2007). This points to the core value of the importance of the individual over community or society as a lens for citizenship in a neo-liberal world. The dominance of the neo-liberal values found in the effects of 'New Public Management' and the prioritisation of economy, efficiency and effectiveness can also be seen to have fragmented the skills of those working in the human services, which has led to the increased casualisation of jobs. It is also evident in many human services that professional judgment has been devalued, an issue we take up again in chapter 7. The imposition of managerial cost and efficiency objectives has led to the breaking down of jobs into segmented roles that have specific skill levels attached (Clarke and Newman, 1997; Thornley, 2008). Dustin (2007), in *The McDonaldization of Social Work*, for example, points to the intensification of 'Fordist' (work efficiency) management techniques, originally used to produce tangible goods, being applied to the intangible arena of 'care'. This brings about an emphasis on dividing work roles into unpaid, paid but unskilled, skilled and managerial aspects. It also results in the tendency to avoid costs by maintaining a highly casualised workforce undertaking less skilled roles.

Although dominant or prevailing value systems can be linked to particular social policy orientations, it is also important to recognise that within these there can be variations. This is particularly apparent in the Australian context where the social and economic policy agenda of the Howard Government found its roots in the values of economic rationalism rolled out by the Hawke-Keating Labor governments (1983-1996). Their commitment to free market economic policies was clearly demonstrated in the sale of government assets, the deregulation of the financial market, the maintenance of social security as a targeted 'safety net' and the establishment of the reintroduction of fees in tertiary education through the introduction of the Higher Education Contribution (Mendes, 2008b, pp. 158–159; Ziguras, 2006, pp. 161–170).

Looking further back into Australia's welfare history, values supporting the free market and the rights of the individual can be seen to have influenced pre-Federation welfare arrangements in Australia. They have also been continually reflected in the emphasis placed on participation in the economy and the labour market as the most effective means of promoting people's welfare (O'Connor et al., 2008; Carney and Hanks, 1994, p. 49), albeit tempered by the settler society values of social equality (Smyth, 2006, p. 102). Indeed, the Australian welfare state that emerged after Federation earned the title 'wage-earners' welfare state', given that it was based on the costs of the basic needs of a 'working man (sic) and his family' (Castles, 1985, p. 103).

The dominance of free market values, so central to neo-liberalism, has been interspersed with a conservative emphasis on 'family values' under different governments and in different periods of history. It is a basic tenet of social conservatism that the family should be the primary site of welfare, particularly in regard to the care of dependent groups such as children and older people. Recognising how this set of values can be utilised in differing formations of social policy, Fiona Williams points out how the place of the family in social policy fluctuated, based on the values or ideology of various governments in the UK at different points in political history (1989, p. 176). She observed that in the post-World War II period, the ideology of the traditional family (married to notions of national unity and British culture) was used to *justify* state intervention in the market in efforts to rebuild the economy (1989, p. 176). However, during the later dominance of neo-liberalism in the 1980s, the same ideas of traditional family were used to justify *less* state intervention in welfare by elevating the family to a level of high responsibility for the welfare of its members, the types of school and health systems (based on choices made by families), upholding public notions of morality and promoting British cultural values (1989, p. 176). The 'neo-conservatives' who have risen to prominence in the US since the 1980s have also focused attention on the value of the family in this way (Isgro, 2005, p. 48).

The principles behind 'third way' political frameworks clearly link responsibilities of rights and citizenship to responsible participation in community affairs. As part of this process, emphasis has been placed on making labour markets more flexible, investing in human capital rather than in social protection, reforming public services to guarantee value for money and reducing the size of government bureaucracy (Hudson et al., 2009; Mendes, 2008a).

When considering the associations that can be made between 'third way' approaches and particular value orientations, chapter 9 provides insights into how 'third way' perspectives are translated into policies. However, at this juncture, a useful example relates to the promotion of the social inclusion agenda in the UK following the election of the New Labour Government in 1997. The values of social inclusion are influenced by the view that disadvantage is cyclical and it is repeated through the generational consolidation of living in 'poor' neighbourhoods, as discussed in more detail in chapter 9. This has resulted in a significant social policy emphasis on community regeneration with Labour's 'New Deal for Communities' and then, a decade later, the 'Communities and Local Government' framework, as an important part of this agenda.

As Andrew Wallace (2007) points out, the 'New Deal For Communities' incorporated a recognition that top-down decision-making and bureaucratic service delivery could be disempowering and could exacerbate social exclusion. This was based on a view that people in local poor communities did not have the necessary networks of support and trust that provide protection against dislocation and fragmentation. Strategies for promoting local community opportunity placed emphasis on the value of *active citizenship*. This meant working towards increasing security for government investment by dynamic community activists participating in and being committed to building community capacity and achieving sustainability.

The underpinning values of community regeneration initiatives clearly link responsibilities to rights. As Allan Cochrane (2000) highlights, this marks a shift away from community regeneration being driven by purely commercial or market concerns towards communities being promoted as moral frameworks which can change the behaviour of residents and regenerate impoverished community environments. Wallace (2007), however, argues that this value base fails to take account of conflicting needs and values within communities. He maintains that, rather than being characterised by co-operation and working towards agreed goals, communities can be patterned by conflict and contestation over physical spaces, facilities or different needs. This can result in the needs and values of senior citizens, for example, directly conflicting with the needs and values of teenagers, or division continually being recreated and reinforced by the ongoing 'othering' (or exclusion) of devalued groups. This analysis clearly illustrates how the heterogeneous values produced and sustained by a range of interactive processes within excluded communities can run counter to the overarching value platform that informs a particular policy initiative.

Values and human services

Values can be regarded as universal, context specific or occupying different spaces where the tensions between the general and the particular are continually played out. These considerations can quickly lead to significant philosophical debates about the nature of certainty and whether, in an era often referred to as post modern, late modern or post-post modern (Smart, 1993; Bauman, 1992; Lyotard, 1994), it is ever possible or even appropriate to refer to the existence of *certainty* with any degree of confidence. It is argued, for example, that the 'large certainties' of modernism (such as ideas of economic or social class, truth in science and the binaries between genders) often used to underpin values in a particular context, have been translated into 'small certainties' and that these are played out in the management and assessment tools that characterise 'New Public Management' (Fawcett and Featherstone, 1998).

From a post-modern perspective, it is possible that in the context of professional practice, an emphasis on making early and certain judgments leads to the acknowledgment of values and evidence that supports the decision and ignores a greater critical interrogation (Taylor and White, 2006). Carolyn Taylor and Sue White promote the idea that professionals should adopt a stance of 'respectful uncertainty' (2006, p. 944) that takes on board the possibility of other interpretations and courses of action. They also highlight the ways in which value judgments about the worthiness of service users continue to inform decision-making processes. They call for critical reflection by professionals on their value judgments and on how they apply personal values or professional codes of practice. This approach suggests that a lack of reflection can result in individuals or groups being rendered legitimate or illegitimate, with resulting consequences for the action taken. As an approach for human service professionals, it rejects the uncritical use of rigid technical or rational approaches to assessment and decision-making and the unquestioning application of a fixed set of values, and argues for reflective processes, critical thinking and the use of context-specific material.

From an alternative perspective, Ife (2008) maintains that neither a straight-forward modernist construction of ethics nor a post-modern emphasis on relativity is useful for human service professionals. He advocates the importance of placing emphasis on 'practising ethically', which can be understood as practising morally. An understanding of human rights is used as a reference point for what that morality might be. This perspective incorporates respecting the human rights of the client or group, but also maximising human rights, in that the role of human service workers goes beyond simply providing the best service available within the social worker's agency. According to Ife (2008), it also necessitates looking at all of the person's human rights and ensuring they are realised and protected. As a result, in a hospital setting, for example, a human service professional has a responsibility to work not only for a patient's human right to health, but also for their right to adequate housing, employment and social security. Additionally, it includes incorporating a set of human rights that spans civil, political, collective and environmental rights within ethical social work practice.

The approach advocated by Ife (2008) places expectations on human service professionals that could be difficult to meet in institutional contexts. However, he highlights that there are no quick and easy prescriptions or 'how to do it' procedures. Instead, he argues that the key question for practitioners is not 'what should I do?' but rather 'who should I talk to?' and 'what should we do?'

Human service professionals operate in a terrain that is often complex, where a range of values can have diverse effects on practice as well as on social policy, and where macro and micro frameworks both intersect and interact. However, this is not to say that social change cannot be achieved at a variety of levels. From the events surrounding a shift in ethics in Australian refugee and asylum seeker policy discussed earlier in this chapter, it is clear that the actions of advocacy groups operating at a micro level appealed to macro level human rights frameworks as a means of assembling a greater moral and ethical position. This not only served to obtain funds for the advocacy and support of refugees and asylum seekers, but also effectively brought together a diverse coalition of actors sharing a set of values different from those promoted in the government's policy responses. This network was able to form a co-operative association to draw attention to what they considered unethical and immoral responses and practices and to campaign for policy change.

The above example demonstrates how individual action can lead to a range of diverse groups placing pressure on government for significant policy change to occur. Within organisations, practitioner action evaluations, such as that described in chapter 8, can generate pressure for policy change, as can the marshalling of various interconnected arguments all making pertinent points as to why a particular practice ought to be abandoned or a policy and practice initiative undertaken.

Conclusion

The key aim of this chapter has been to appraise how values contribute to and often underpin social policy. Human service professionals are under increasing pressure to apply prescriptive universal solutions to complex problem areas. They are also expected to subscribe to value systems and practice requirements that are adopted or developed in the agency within which they work. Although, as highlighted, professional codes of ethics can bring their own set of strengths and weaknesses and possibly provide alternative sets of values to draw from, they also direct attention to the tensions that can exist between value systems. Understanding different political frameworks and recognising competing value systems not only highlights the necessity of taking account of the operation of various interlocking and interrelated layers of values, but also emphasises the utility of applying values and evaluating criteria in context-specific ways. In our next chapter, we go on to explore social policy in relation to economic considerations. Specifically, we pose the questions who pays, who benefits and by how much?

CHAPTER 5

Economics: who pays, who benefits and how much?

Introduction

In chapter 1, we defined social policy, among other things, as what governments do to affect the quality of life of the people. In this chapter, we examine the economics of social policy: how and how much governments tax and spend, how they organise spending and the impact of the pattern of government taxing and spending on citizens' lives, as measured by changes in income difference and access to services. Taxing and spending patterns are underpinned by different entitlements and responsibilities for citizens, and these patterns are one key to understanding how social policy works. They determine the distribution of benefits of social policy between various groups of citizens, include different points for contestation and intervention and define the differences between kinds of welfare states.

Human service professionals can benefit significantly from understanding the economics of social policy, for several reasons. First, many social problems have their roots in economic problems, such as poverty and inequality, and so at least part of the solution to these problems lies in the redistribution of economic resources. Human service professionals will better understand both problems and their solutions if they can grasp their 'money and measurement' as well as their 'people and practice' dimensions. Second, economic discourse dominates public policy debates and has had a profound impact on social policy. In a direct and concrete way, economics affects social policy because money talks—and powerfully. We see this in the way that social programs are increasingly expected to contribute to economic goals of increased productivity and competitiveness (see also chapter 9), and to demonstrate that their benefits meet or exceed their costs. Less concrete is the effect of economic ways of thinking on social policy and practice. For example, under the influence of economic ideas, policy frameworks have come increasingly to model social policy and practice as production processes, with 'inputs' and 'outputs' to be counted, measured and costed (Meagher, 2002, p. 2). Another example of the power of economic ideas in social policy is the increased use of market mechanisms to organise service provision, which we discuss in this chapter and chapter 6.

Human service practitioners tend to think of themselves as people and values-orientated, rather than numbers and money-orientated. Yet those who are able to understand and engage the economic dimensions of policy formation, change and debate are better placed to participate in social policy development and resist the inappropriate application of economic ideas. Much economic information is presented in numbers, thus 'critical social numeracy' (Lake, 2002) or 'quantitative literacy' (Wiest et al., 2007) is also a crucial skill for human service practitioners who seek social change through social policy. Critical social numeracy enables practitioners to read, interpret and, where necessary, challenge the proliferation of quantitative data produced for and in social policy processes, and increasingly in social policy implementation and human services practice. This chapter aims to set out some key economic dimensions of social policy, to demonstrate how and why understanding quantitative and monetary dimensions of social policy matters. In the next chapter, we discuss some of the economic concepts and arguments associated with the growing role of the market in social services. Our hope is that by presenting some quantitative data and economic concepts within the context of social policy analysis, our readers will become more proficient in, and more confident about, using and criticising them.

Our framework for thinking about the economics of social policy focuses closely on the instruments governments use, on expenditure and on the consequences of these instruments and expenditure for the distribution of resources within societies. These are very important dimensions of the economics of social policy, but not the whole picture. Other dimensions include the use and impact of cost-benefit analysis in social policy-making (Beresford,

2005; Burch, 1998; Nathan, 2000, pp. 73–79) and the macroeconomics of social policy. This latter is a 'big picture' approach to framing the economics of social policy that we outline briefly and set aside. From a macroeconomic perspective, which looks at the economy as a whole and conceptualises government taxing and spending as 'fiscal policy', social expenditure is an instrument governments can use to *manage the economy* as well as assist individual citizens (Atkinson, 1999; Barr, 1992). A concrete example helps here. As experience of recessions shows, unemployment can be made worse if people who lose their jobs also lose all their income and can no longer buy the things they need. When people stop buying, those who produce the goods and services that the unemployed people would have bought can also lose their jobs, in a vicious cycle. By guaranteeing a minimum level of income to unemployed people, and thereby smoothing some of the risks of the business cycle, government can help maintain purchasing power. Because government payments to the unemployed go down when economic times are good, and up when times are bad, this kind of spending acts as an 'automatic stabiliser' on the economy. Another way of thinking about this is that the welfare state helps governments pool risk and smooth consumption over the life cycle and between good and bad times, and these activities enable and sustain economic growth (Quiggin, 2007). This 'demand management' role of social policy, many economists argue, is crucial to the successful functioning of market economies. However, it is not simply a technical matter of governments 'pulling levers' to increase or decrease demand in the economy. There are strong political constraints, which differ between countries, on how much revenue governments can raise through taxes and other means. The politics of raising revenue ultimately determines the size and form of the welfare budget.

Social spending: structure and instruments

The OECD defines social expenditure as '[t]he provision by public and private institutions of benefits to, and financial contributions targeted at, households and individuals in order to provide support during circumstances which adversely affect their welfare ...' (cited in Adema and Ladaique, 2005, p. 7). As a first cut, expenditure on social policy measures can be divided into *income support* and *social services*, as we saw in chapter 1. Governments pay income support to replace labour market income for specific groups of citizens, typically those who are either *unable* to work because no work is available, or because they are sick or disabled (unemployment benefits, disability pensions), or *not expected* to work because they have reached retirement age or have caring responsibilities (age pensions, maternity payments). As well as replacing income for those not in the labour market, many governments also offer support to parents in the form of income *supplements* to assist with the costs of raising children. Often, these payments go to families with working parents. Overall, then, income support payments are tied to *socio-economic* (unemployment, disability) or *life cycle* (parenthood, retirement) risks. Governments also provide (or fund) social services, including care for the elderly and people with disabilities, healthcare, housing, childcare and social welfare services such as child protection, family support and drug and alcohol rehabilitation.

How governments come to fund income support and social services distinguishes different kinds of welfare states. Income support can be funded from general revenue, that is, straight out of the public purse, using money collected in taxes. This is how most income support payments are financed in Australia. Income support can also be funded by social insurance schemes, with contributions from some or all of the government, employers and employees. Various insurance schemes operate in most other countries, especially in continental Europe.

When it comes to human services, our focus in this book, governments may provide them directly or fund other organisations (either wholly or partially) to do so. When governments provide services directly, public sector organisations employ human service workers—nurses, teachers, social workers, home care aides—and these workers provide services to citizens directly. When governments fund private (for-profit and non-profit) organisations to provide services, they use one or more of a range of instruments (Davidson, 2009; Gilbert, 2005). Often, governments privatise service provision by *contracting out* to private sector organisations, either for-profit or non-profit, effectively paying these organisations to deliver services on the government's behalf. Under this 'purchaser-provider split' model, contracts often specify the kind of services to be offered, service performance standards and the criteria determining who is eligible to receive them. This model of service provision draws on faith in the efficiency of private provision and the virtues of 'competitive neutrality' (sometimes called 'quasi-markets') in the selection of organisations and the allocation of public funds to provide these services (see chapter 6).

Human service provision can also be publicly funded through subsidies paid directly to citizens, who purchase services for themselves using a rebate or voucher of some kind. Under these kinds of arrangements, governments may, but do not always, regulate which organisations service users can purchase services from. In Australia, childcare subsidies to parents are paid only for care purchased from accredited childcare providers, and rebates for healthcare services are paid only for approved services from approved providers under the national health insurance scheme, Medicare. In both service domains, for-profit and non-profit providers can be accredited or approved.

Because access to significant public subsidies can be a good 'business model' for private sector providers, the kinds of providers and services that governments approve can become the focus of intense lobbying action by interested parties. In other fields of human services in recent years, some governments (for example, in the UK, the Netherlands, Italy and Australia) have also begun to grant funds directly to the elderly or people with disabilities so they can buy personal care services from providers of their choice; this is one model of 'consumer-directed care'. In some countries, policy allows recipients to spend money granted to purchase services on hiring a family member to provide care. This can result in a kind of hybrid of income support and social service provision, when the 'cash-for-care' payment enables a family member who might otherwise have been in paid work to receive an income to provide what is effectively a form of publicly subsidised care.

Whether public funding meets the full cost of providing social services is another matter. Sometimes, policies are designed only to provide a partial subsidy for service provision. Partial funding can occur through the mechanism of a planned service user co-payment or by rationing services. These mechanisms can operate to distribute services unevenly, creating groups with access and those without. Services can be rationed by creating 'places', which may be notionally fully funded but not provided in numbers that serve all the need in the community. Services may also be funded by allocating service users fewer hours (or instances) of service than they need, even though, again, the services allocated may in principle be fully funded.

The implications of partial funding can vary according to the broader policy context, and for different social groups. When services are only partially funded, there is an implicit or explicit expectation that the family sphere (service users and their families) or the community sphere (primarily NGOs) will make up the gap. The family sphere can provide services itself. In Australia, for example, much care for elderly people at home and for children and adults with disabilities is provided by family members alongside or instead of services provided by other agencies (AIHW, 2007, pp. 308–310). Families and individuals may also buy unsubsidised services in the open market, if social provision falls short of need. Obviously, this has implications for the distribution of access to services; those with fewer resources are more likely to find themselves with fewer or even no services. Where the community sphere, primarily NGOs, is only partially funded to provide government services under contract, agencies charge service fees and/or draw on donations of money or voluntary labour to make up the shortfall. Sometimes, community agencies are ostensibly fully funded to provide services but believe that additional expenditure will result in a higher quality standard of service. Community sector agencies can also provide services the government does not fund to meet needs that would otherwise go unmet. In both these cases, unless the agency has some independent means (as some foundation-funded or religious organisations do), it will need to rely on service user payments or donations of money or labour.

Partial funding can provide extra incentives for market sector organisations to become involved in human services. In Australia, for example, parents paying for childcare or elderly people paying for residential care can 'top up' subsidies to purchase higher quality services than public funding provides. These services may be offered by for-profit enterprises, which can derive income from a combination of public subsidies and user fees. When 'topping up' is permitted, it can encourage the development of a tiered system of provision, in which people with more money can purchase higher quality services than those with less. But consumer co-payments do not necessarily lead to topping up and a tiered service system. For example, although consumer co-payments are part of childcare provision in Sweden, since 2002 the national government has imposed a cap on the fees parents can be charged (Nyberg, 2007, p. 49). This means that incentives for developing a system with different quality 'tiers' are weak.

So far, we have focused on more or less direct public funding of public or private provision. But governments can also subsidise social service provision by giving families and individuals financial incentives to buy services wholly in the private market. One frequently used instrument to promote the purchase of services on the private market is 'tax expenditure', which operates by giving tax concessions to the income that people spend on private social services. In Australia, private health insurance and superannuation are heavily subsidised this way.

As we discussed in chapter 1, a complex 'mixed economy' of human service provision arises when governments use a variety of these instruments to organise and fund services. And it should be obvious from the preceding paragraphs that the way services are funded has a crucial role in shaping the sectoral mix of social services (see also Healy, 1998, chapter 1; chapter 6, this volume). If governments provide services directly, services are 'public'. If governments contract out to non-profit or for-profit providers or offer tax concessions to households making provision for their own needs, the private sector becomes involved. The kind and mix of private sector participants (for-profit, non-profit) depends on the funding rules and the structure of incentives those rules establish. Meanwhile, some kinds of cash-for-care payments bring the family directly into provision of publicly funded social services. We have also begun to point out how different approaches to organising social spending have consequences for the distribution of the costs and benefits of that spending, something we return to later in this chapter.

Underlying all this is the overall level of government funding: the less support that government provides to households and individuals (or mandates that private institutions, such as employers, should do so), the more households and individuals must rely on informal supports within the family and community or on wholly private provision through the market—or go without assistance altogether. Thus, the level of resources governments devote to social expenditure, and the instruments they use to deliver income support and social services, are of critical interest to citizens. But public social supports cost money, much of it provided by households through the tax system. Hence, voters' interests in social provision can conflict with other interests, such as low taxes. As we discuss in chapter 6, the institutional mix of providers has implications for the quality of services and jobs for human service workers. Further, the instruments governments use to deliver social policy shape the points of intervention in the policy process and the extent of democratic control.

Social spending: how much and on what?

So what do governments in rich democracies spend on social policy measures and how do they spend it? Answering this question is becoming less straightforward, primarily because of the complex mixed economies described above. What we might call 'headline' figures of public social expenditure as a proportion of a nation's total resources (or Gross Domestic Product—GDP) are typically used to measure governments' social policy efforts and compare welfare states. Table 5.1 presents public social spending as a percentage of GDP, with expenditure divided between cash benefits and services. Cash benefits are further divided into spending on pensions for the elderly and 'survivors' (which include widows and orphans), and on income support to the working age population (such as disability and unemployment benefits and payments to families, including child benefits or family allowances and sole parent income support). Public expenditure on services is also divided into two categories: spending on health and spending on all other social services.

A careful look at table 5.1 reveals several interesting and important patterns in public social expenditure. The first is perhaps the most obvious, which is just how much *variation* there is in the proportion of national spending devoted to social purposes in rich democracies in 2003: from more than 30 per cent of GDP in Sweden to around 16 per cent in the US and Ireland, and less than 6 per cent in Korea. This variation arises because of differences in the social policy instruments used by governments of different nations and 'families of nations' (Castles, 1993) or welfare regimes, instruments determined by each nation's distinctive political, ideological and institutional structures and priorities.

Thus, we come to a second pattern in the data, providing some concrete evidence of a point we raised in chapter 1: Nordic welfare states devote considerably more resources to social services other than health in their social policy budgets. The table shows that governments in Norway, Denmark and Sweden spend between 4.9 and 7.4 per cent of national resources, compared to 3.2 per cent in the next highest spender, the United Kingdom. This has led Jorma Sipïla and colleagues (1997) to call social care services 'the key to the Scandinavian welfare model'. Put in simple terms, the British spend about 1 dollar in 30 on services while the Swedish spend about 1 in 14. If we were to rank the nations in the table by the proportion each spends on social services, the UK, at 3.2 per cent of GDP, would come in fourth after the three Nordic

Table 5.1   Public social expenditure in selected OECD countries, per cent of GDP, 2003.

	Cash benefits		Services (a)		
	Income support to working age population	Pensions (old age and survivors)	Health	All other social services	Total public social spending (b)
Sweden	7.4	8.0	7.1	7.4	31.3
France	5.4	12.0	7.6	2.7	28.7
Denmark	8.8	5.3	5.6	6.3	27.6
Germany	4.8	11.5	8.0	1.9	27.3
Austria	6.0	12.8	5.1	1.6	26.1
Norway	7.6	5.4	6.5	4.9	25.1
Italy	2.7	13.8	6.2	0.8	24.2
Spain	4.9	8.2	5.2	1.3	20.3
United Kingdom	4.2	5.6	6.7	3.2	20.1
New Zealand	5.7	4.5	6.3	1.1	18.0
Australia	5.3	3.4	6.2	2.5	17.9
Japan	1.5	8.2	6.1	1.6	17.7
Canada	3.0	4.4	6.8	2.7	17.3
US	2.2	6.2	6.7	0.9	16.2
Ireland	5.1	3.3	5.6	1.2	15.9
Korea	0.9	1.3	2.9	0.4	5.7

Source: OECD (2007, p. 20)
(a) There may be some double counting of services provided to elderly and/or disabled people in institutions other than hospitals for some countries, where these services are included in calculations of both health and social service expenditure. Adema and Ladaique (2005, p. 10) estimate that the value may exceed 1 per cent of GDP.
(b) Total spending includes the cost of active labour market programs, for which a breakdown between cash and services is not available.

countries, while the five countries at the bottom of that ranking spend less than 1 per cent (Ireland, New Zealand, Italy, the US and Korea).

Third, and in contrast to the wide variation in total public social spending and spending on social services, public spending on health is far more similar between the countries we are considering (see figure 5.1). With the exception

Figure 5.1   Public social spending on health and all other social services, selected OECD countries, per cent of GDP, 2003 (ranked from highest to lowest total public expenditure on total social services).

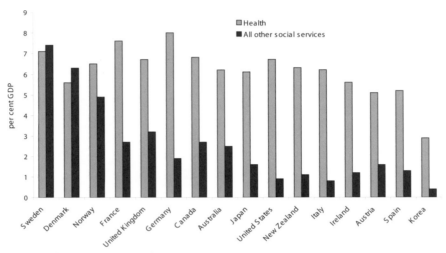

Source: OECD (2007, p 20; see table 5.1)

of Korea, governments of all countries for which we present data spend between 5.1 per cent (Austria) and 8.0 per cent (Germany) on health services, compared with variation between 7.4 (Sweden) and 0.8 (Italy) on spending for other social services. The fourth pattern we note is that *pensions* form a particularly high proportion of total public spending in key European welfare states (Italy, Austria, France, Germany and Spain) and in Japan. Unsurprisingly, these states fall into the 'conservative' group identified by Gøsta Esping-Andersen (1990).

This data is informative, particularly about the role that spending on services plays in distinguishing the social democratic (or 'Nordic') welfare states, and the important role of social insurance-funded pensions in conservative welfare states. However, as the OECD researchers responsible for collating this data argue, the figures do 'not give a full picture of collective social effort across countries' (Adema and Ladaique, 2005, p. 6). Their study points to two reasons. First, gross spending data does not deduct the cost to recipients of *taxation* on social benefits, especially income support payments, which 'claws back' some portion of social spending in every country, via direct or indirect means. Second, not all benefits are fully publicly funded, as we have seen. In many countries there is also significant *private* expenditure for social purposes, either mandated by government policy (such as compulsory superannuation levies in Australia), or encouraged by government policy (such as the health insurance rebate in Australia). Accordingly, the OECD argues, measures of 'net social expenditure' are required to measure 'what governments "really" devote to social spending' (Adema and Ladaique, 2005, p. 6). Significantly, measures of net social expenditure also aim to capture expenditure by 'private agents', such as businesses and NGOs, because, as we have already suggested, these institutions are involved in delivering social policy in the broadest sense. Table 5.2 presents some more detail on the composition of total social expenditure in different countries, ranked this time in order of net social expenditure.

Table 5.2 Gross and net public and private social expenditure in selected OECD countries, per cent of GDP, 2003, ranked by net social expenditure.

	Gross public social exp.	Net public exp.	Gross mandatory private exp.	Gross voluntary private exp.	Net private exp.	Net social exp.	Rank in Table 5.1
France	28.7	25.5	0.4	2.3	2.5	28.0	2
Germany	27.3	25.8	1.2	1.8	2.2	27.6	4
Sweden	31.3	24.3	0.6	2.4	1.8	26.1	1
US	16.2	17.3	0.4	9.7	9.2	25.2	14
UK	20.6	19.3	0.8	6.0	5.4	24.6	8
Italy	24.2	20.6	1.8	0.5	1.9	22.3	7
Austria	26.1	20.6	0.9	1.2	1.5	22.2	5
Norway	25.1	20.2	1.6	1.0	1.5	21.7	6
Denmark	27.6	20.3	0.2	2.3	1.2	21.6	3
Canada	17.3	17.2	0.0	5.4	4.3	21.2	13
Australia	17.9	17.2	1.2	3.2	3.7	20.6	11
Japan	17.7	17.6	0.7	2.6	3.0	20.6	12
Spain	20.3	17.6	0.0	0.3	0.3	17.7	9
NZ	18.0	15.1	0.0	0.5	0.5	15.5	10
Ireland	15.9	14.0	0.0	0.5	0.5	14.3	15
Korea	5.7	5.9	2.2	0.2	2.1	8.0	16

Source: OECD (2007, p. 82)

Column 1 in table 5.2 is simply the last column of table 5.1, and shows total public social spending before the impact of taxes on benefits. The second column shows the impact of the tax system on benefits. By comparing these two columns it is clear that in some countries, such as Denmark, Sweden, Austria and Norway, the impact of taxes on total spending is significant— these governments are clawing back between 7.3 and 4.9 per cent of GDP from their public social spending, mainly through income taxes on income support payments. In liberal welfare states—Australia, the UK, Canada and the US—clawback of public social spending tends to be much lower, mainly because low benefit rates incur low taxes, and because indirect tax rates (like goods and services taxes) tend to be lower, so the difference between columns 1 and 2 is smaller. Indeed, in the US, the impact of the tax system is to *increase* slightly public social spending, because tax *breaks* rather than *payments* are used to deliver certain social benefits. (These 'tax expenditures' are a commonly used instrument in liberal welfare states.)

When we move to private social expenditure (columns 3, 4 and 5), we see, first, that liberal welfare states, notably the US, the UK and Canada, stand out, with net contributions from private agents (companies, individuals) ranging from 4.3 per cent of GDP in Canada to 9.2 in the US (column 5). Indeed, private social spending is more than one third of all social spending in the US, and around a fifth in the UK, Canada and Australia. Given the lower level of public spending, and a tendency to favour individualistic or market approaches to social provision, this is not surprising. Second, about a third of all private social spending is mandatory (column 3). In Australia, for example, employers are obliged to pay for employees' sick leave, to insure against occupational accidents and diseases and to pay into private superannuation funds on behalf of employees (OECD, 2007, p. 24). The majority of private social spending, then, is voluntary and mainly funds pension benefits in countries where public pension benefits are low—such as Australia, Canada, Japan, the UK and the US (Adema and Ladaique, 2005, p. 13). In the US, employer-provided health insurance is an exception to this generalisation; in the absence of public provision for most of the working age population, significant private expenditure fills the gap (OECD, 2007, p. 25), at least for those who receive this benefit. Indeed, private social spending is typically tied either to employment, such that employers pay for employees, or to individual or family capacity to 'top up' public schemes.

Thus, we would expect the *redistributive* impact of private social spending to be weak (Castles and Obinger, 2007, offer a cogent critique of the OECD's work on net social expenditure).

Including private spending and the impact of taxes gives a more comprehensive picture of the resources devoted to social policy objectives in different countries. However, even then, it is not the whole picture. As discussed above, many non-government agencies raise funds from sources other than governments, and individuals and families spend for 'social purposes' in ways that are not accounted for in these measures. Australian non-profit organisations that provide social services, for example, obtain on average 9 per cent of their funds from the sale of goods, 22 per cent from service fees and a further 4 per cent from donations and other fundraising (ABS, 2008). All these are funds not accounted for in official social policy statistics. Depending on the role and extent of charitable provision and user co-payments in different countries (higher in liberal countries, lower in social democratic ones), the 'undercounting' of private resources devoted to social purposes will be higher or lower.

Social spending: on whom and for what purposes?

What or *how much* governments spend for social purposes is clearly important for understanding the impact of social policies on the living standards of different groups of citizens. *Who* governments spend on, for what *purposes*, is just as important, and the redistributive impact of social expenditure is not always neatly aligned with the size of the 'welfare effort' as measured by spending. Two of the key goals of social policy are to reduce inequality and poverty (Goodin et al., 1999, pp. 26–27; Korpi and Palme, 1998, p. 661). In this section, we explore how well different approaches to social spending work to reduce inequality and poverty in several of the countries discussed in the previous section, using data that have only recently become available.

In the previous section, we saw that understanding an apparently basic concept like 'social spending' requires careful definition and measurement. The same is true for measuring inequality, poverty and the impact of social spending on these social problems, not least because these are highly charged political issues. This is not the place to engage deeply with debates about the meaning and measurement of these key concepts (Goodin et al., 1999, chapter 1;

Saunders, 2004; 2005; Saunders and Bradbury, 2006). Rather, the aim here is to set out some key findings on inequality, poverty and their redress, or otherwise, by different approaches to social policy.

Inequality

Research has firmly established that income inequality has increased in most rich countries in recent decades (Mahler and Jesuit, 2006; 2008; OECD, 2008b). Using data compiled and standardised within the Luxembourg Income Study since the late 1970s, Vincent Mahler and David Jesuit calculate that in Australia, for example, the Gini coefficient increased from 0.396 to 0.460 between 1981 and 2003 (2008, table A.1).

The Gini coefficient summarises the distribution of income across the whole population into a single statistic, which varies between zero (complete equality between units measured, in this case households) and one (when one unit receives all the income) (ABS 2007a, pp. 42–43). The measure used here is *private* income, which is income received from wages and other market sources, excluding government benefits and taxes. We might say that this is a measure 'before' social policy has done its work. Income is measured at the *household* rather than the individual level, because economists and social researchers recognise that when household members pool resources, individuals within them are likely to have a higher standard of living than they would if they relied simply on their own capacity to generate income. The household income measure is also *equivalised*, or adjusted to take into account the fact that households of different sizes have different needs. (Mahler and Jesuit, 2006, offer more information on data sources and measures.)

So what the Gini coefficient for Australia tells us is that household incomes from private sources, adjusted for household composition, have become more unequal over approximately the two decades up to 2003. Similar trends are evident in other countries. In the US, the Gini coefficient increased from 0.402 to 0.481 between 1979 and 2004, and from 0.396 to 0.498 in the UK between 1979 and 1999. Thus, this data shows that inequality was worse in the US than in Australia and the UK at the beginning of the period, and worst in the UK at the end. Interestingly, in 1981, inequality of private household income in Sweden was higher than in all three 'liberal' countries we have just mentioned; the Gini coefficient was then 0.411, rising to 0.447 in 2000, the latest year for which data is available (Mahler and Jesuit, 2008, table A.1). Thus, although inequality of private income was already high at the beginning of the period, it has not risen as much as in Australia, the US and the United Kingdom.

However, these statistics tell us only the first part of the story. The policies that affect the distribution of private income are primarily those governing the labour market. But our focus in this chapter is on social policy—what governments do, after the labour market has established the primary income distribution, to reallocate resources between households by levying taxes and distributing benefits. Once these instruments of social policy have done their work in the process of 'fiscal redistribution' (Mahler and Jesuit, 2006), we use the concept of 'disposable income' to measure household resources. We can use the same summary statistic, the Gini coefficient to measure fiscal redistribution within and between countries. In Australia in 2003, the Gini coefficient for household disposable income was 0.312, a decline of 0.148 from the coefficient for private income. In the US in 2004, the Gini coefficient for household disposable income was 0.372, a drop of 0.109 from the coefficient for private income. In the UK, the Gini coefficient for disposable income fell to 0.343, a decline of 0.155. Meanwhile, in Sweden in 2000, the Gini coefficient for disposable income was 0.252, a huge decline of 0.195 from the coefficient for private income in the same year. What are these changes in inequality—after social policy has done its job—telling us? They show that the US redistributes least, and Sweden most. Australia and the UK fall somewhere in between. (Mahler and Jesuit (2008) present data on several other countries, including Canada, Norway, Finland, France, Switzerland, the Netherlands and Germany.)

These findings are not surprising: we saw in the previous section that the governments of the US, the UK and Australia spend considerably less than the Swedish Government on income transfers, so social policy in these liberal countries does less to reduce inequality. But there is an interesting complication to this story, one that Walter Korpi and Joakim Palme call 'the paradox of redistribution' (1998). A well-known characteristic of liberal welfare states, especially Australia's and New Zealand's, is that publicly funded income support is highly targeted, that is, focused on benefits for the poor. In social democratic countries, a more universal approach to social policy means that income benefits are more widely distributed across the population. We might expect, then, that because benefits are directed to the needy in liberal countries, there is *more* redistribution than in social democratic states. Yet this is precisely what we do *not* find. The measured 'target efficiency' of benefit spending is higher in the UK, Australia and Canada than it is in Sweden, Norway and Denmark (Mahler and Jesuit, 2006, pp. 492–493; 2008 table A.3). In other words, these welfare states tend to target poor people progressively. But here is the catch—even though these governments focus spending on the poor, they spend much less on welfare, limiting their overall redistributive impact when compared to universal welfare states that spend more on a wider group of citizens.

Often overlooked, social *service* provision also has a role in reducing inequality. A recent assessment of how publicly funded services, such as health, education and social care services change the distribution of income finds that '[p]ublic expenditure for the provision of social services to households significantly narrows inequality' (OECD, 2008b, p. 245). The impact is not as great as that of taxes and transfers; however, it is significant. Such studies show the important and under-recognised role that publicly funded human services, and hence human service workers, play in equalising living standards.

It is important to reinforce, though, that not all social spending reduces inequality. Two kinds of policy instruments are particularly relevant here. First, employment related benefits are mainly distributed to the formerly employed, in the case of pensions, or the currently employed and their families, in the case of health insurance in the United States. Second, tax concessions for private pensions and health insurance, such as are available in Australia, tend to benefit those on higher incomes rather than being redistributed to the poor (Adema and Ladaique, 2005, p. 10).

Poverty

Poverty can have serious consequences for those who experience it. According to a recent review of evidence on its impact, poverty can interfere with the development of cognitive, language and socio-emotional skills in children and adolescents. These developmental problems in early life affect the chances of poor children, who are more likely, as adults, to have reduced earnings, involvement in crime and mental illness (Dearing, 2008, p. 324). We have seen that inequality of private income is widespread, even in countries with an egalitarian reputation, like Sweden. So is poverty also a widespread problem? Are members of some social groups more likely to live in poverty? And what of the role of social policy in poverty reduction?

We noted earlier that the measurement of poverty is complex and contentious. However poverty is measured, though, Peter Saunders points out that the key idea underpinning the concept is that poverty *'prevents people from consuming, owning or doing things that are an essential part of belonging to the societies in which they live'* (2005, p. 59, emphasis in original). Two common measures are some form of *absolute* 'poverty line' or threshold, defined as the monetary value of a 'basket of socially perceived necessities' (Saunders, 2005, p. 60), and a *relative* measure, typically defined as a percentage of median household income (OECD, 2008b, p. 126). Using these measures, researchers arrive at the poverty rate by calculating the proportion of households whose income falls below the poverty line, or below 40, 50 or 60 per cent of the national median income.

Social scientists use these measures or variations on them to compare the poverty rate between social groups in a country, to compare countries and to compare social groups or countries before and after the impact of redistributive policies. The Luxembourg Income Study has provided researchers with unique opportunities to measure poverty and the impact of social policy on reducing it, both within and across countries. Using this data and a modified measure of the poverty rate designed to take into account how *many* poor households there are and by how *much* these households' incomes fall below the median, Mahler and Jesuit (2006) report poverty ratios for a range of welfare states before and after taxes and transfers. Table 5.3 shows their findings for nine of the countries we have focused on in previous sections. Their results show that among these countries, what we might call the 'raw' poverty ratio, which measures the extent and depth of poverty in private income before the impact of social policy, is highest in Sweden and the UK and lowest in Norway and Canada. Thus, we have what seems like an unusual mix of liberal and social democratic societies among those with relatively high and relatively low poverty ratios.

However, a more familiar picture emerges when we look at poverty ratios for disposable income, which is a measure of income that takes into account the impact of redistributive taxing and spending policies. Among the chosen countries, poverty reduction is highest in Sweden and Denmark and lowest in Australia, Canada and the United States. These three liberal countries also have the highest poverty ratios for disposable income—as high as 11.6 in the United States. Again, we see the paradox of redistribution at work: in countries where public income support programs are designed to reduce poverty and are targeted at the poor, the poverty reduction is smallest (see also OECD,

Table 5.3 Poverty ratios for private and disposable income, selected countries, ranked by poverty reduction.

	Private income	Disposable income	Poverty reduction
Sweden	25.7	4.4	21.3
Denmark	24.1	5.6	18.5
United Kingdom	25.4	7.3	18.0
France	22.7	5.3	17.4
Germany	21.5	4.4	17.1
Norway	19.3	4.4	15.3
Australia	21.3	8.0	13.3
Canada	19.1	7.6	11.5
US	20.1	11.6	8.5

Source: Mahler and Jesuit (2006, table 2).

2008b, pp. 139–44). This is because the good intention of focusing welfare on the poor is not accompanied by a sufficiently large welfare budget to make a significant difference.

The measures we have been looking at measure poverty at a point in time. Perhaps higher poverty rates in some countries are not too much of a problem, because people who fall into poverty in those countries do not stay there for long. Unfortunately, available evidence suggests the reverse: countries with a higher average poverty rate for disposable income are significantly more likely to have higher rates of persistent and recurrent poverty (OECD, 2008b, p. 158).

Who is poor?

We have surveyed evidence about poverty at the national population level. However, the risk of being poor is different for members of different social groups and it changes over time. Over recent decades, for example, poverty among older people, although still significant, has tended to decline, while poverty among children and young adults has grown. There are also significant gender differences in the risk of poverty (OECD, 2008b, pp. 130–39). Indeed, social researchers have called the phenomenon of the over-representation of women among the poor in rich societies 'the feminisation of poverty'. The feminisation of poverty has been described as a 'nearly universal' problem, evident in 'almost all affluent Western democracies', and among both women of working age and older women (Brady and Kall, 2008, p. 986). Further, the risk of *persistent* or chronic poverty was always higher for women than men, a recent study of 17 rich countries found, mainly reflecting the situation of single women, whether or not they have children (OECD, 2008b, p. 161).

An Australian study has examined the composition of households with low incomes and low wealth, defined as those falling within the lowest three deciles (bottom 30 per cent) of the income and net worth distributions, adjusted for household size, for the financial year 2003 to 2004 (ABS, 2007b). The study found that 14 per cent of households overall had low incomes and low wealth, while among one-parent family households, 44 per cent fell into this group, as did 18 per cent of single people under 35 years of age. Poverty remains a problem among the elderly in Australia, especially those living alone: 21 per cent of people over 65 living alone had low incomes and low wealth. Couple households, with or without children, were much less likely to be poor. For example, among couple families with dependent children, approximately 10 per cent had low incomes and low wealth, while among couples without children or with non-dependent children, only 4 to 5 per cent were poor (ABS, 2007b, p. 166).

The feminisation of poverty is also evident in Australia. In 2006, a large majority of one-parent families was headed by women (87 per cent), and these mothers had lower incomes and wealth than single fathers or couples with families (ABS, 2007c, pp. 49, 51). Among older Australians, women are more likely to rely solely on the age pension and are over-represented among age pensioners who are single (FACSIA, 2006, p. 8). Policies on private retirement incomes in Australia, which are tied to labour market earnings and give substantial tax benefits to high income earners, are also 'stacked against' women, because they are over-represented among low-income earners (Sharp and Austen, 2007).

Although the feminisation of poverty appears to be, as David Brady and Denise Kall put it, 'nearly universal', differences in the instruments governments use to accomplish social policy goals, and, perhaps, differences in those goals themselves, can make a profound difference to the level of gender inequality within a country. Priscilla Lambert (2008) has developed an index of maternal employment policy (MEP) to analyse international variation in policies that support working women and mothers. The social policy instruments she includes are maternity and parental leave provisions and publicly funded childcare. Thus, the MEP includes both income support or replacement (leave) and social services (childcare). The insight underlying the index is that these '"women-friendly policies" promote gender equality, remove family care burdens, and increase the range of choices available to women' (2008, p. 316). She finds that the countries that do most to encourage the employment of women using these policies also have high rates of participation by women in the workforce and more equal contributions by women and men to household income (2008, p. 316). Interestingly, Lambert also finds that the percentage of women in parliament is one key variable in explaining international differences in women-friendly social policies.

From poverty to social exclusion; from expertise to experience

An important debate among social scientists and policy-makers is whether poverty measures should focus on material resources only, or broaden out to capture a range of dimensions of social disadvantage. Over the last two decades, many development economists, social policy researchers and policy-makers have come to understand that lack of income is a rather narrow concept for measuring disadvantage, and have sought to develop multi-dimensional poverty measures. New concepts have emerged, such as 'deprivation', 'capability' and 'exclusion' (Saunders, 2005, chapter 3). There has also been a move away from expertise and towards experience as the foundation for understanding poverty. Accordingly, social policy researchers have made increasing efforts to understand poverty from the perspective of those who experience it (Peel, 2003; Saunders et al., 2007). This kind of research provides new perspectives to inform the development of social policy. In chapter 9, we return to examine the impact of the idea of social exclusion on social policy in liberal welfare states.

Social spending: economic drain or gain?

We have seen that governments in many rich countries spend a great deal on social policy measures—close to a third of the total value of all national production in Sweden, and more than a quarter in France, Germany, Austria, Denmark and Norway (see column 1 of table 5.2). However, economists, social policy analysts and policy-makers have argued long and heatedly about the economic implications of devoting so many of a nation's resources to social purposes. On one side are those who argue that redistributive social spending is a drain on the economy—a 'leaky bucket' as Arthur Okun (1975) famously called it. On the other side are those who argue that social spending might actually support economic growth, or operate as an 'irrigation system' for the economy, as Walter Korpi (1985) put it.

Korpi explains that arguments against redistributive spending have tended to be *theoretical*. They have relied on economic theory to make claims that, in various ways, the welfare state inhibits the growth that genuinely increases welfare by interfering in the market mechanism. Yet, as he points out, it is ultimately an empirical question whether the welfare state, the organisation and impact of which is highly varied, is 'negative, neutral or positive for economic efficiency' (1985, p. 115). Since Korpi issued this challenge more than two decades ago, much evidence has been amassed to explore the question. So what does the evidence show? It does not confirm the fears of conservative economists and social philosophers: economic growth is not harmed by social spending and under certain circumstances, it may be enhanced by it (Lindert, 2004; Mares, 2007). Evidence on the relationship between employment and the size of the public sector is mixed; it seems that how wage bargaining is organised is a much more important variable than the size of social spending.

Theories about the deleterious effect of social spending on economic growth and employment have roots in long-standing fears among policy-makers, social philosophers and other political actors, such as business lobbies, about the effect of welfare measures on work incentives. In the context of the economic crisis of the 1970s, these ideas and the theories associated with them achieved great currency, and many books and articles proclaimed a 'crisis of the welfare state'. The welfare state survived the 1980s, only to be threatened again in the 1990s and the 2000s. This time, globalisation is thought to be impelling a 'race to the bottom' among welfare states forced to cut taxes to maintain their position in the global competition for investment and jobs—if population ageing and fertility decline don't get them first. Francis Castles calls these 'crisis myths' and, like Korpi, emphasises the value of evidence in assessing what is really going on. Confirming the findings of previous research (including Bernard and Boucher, 2007; Korpi, 1985; Lindert, 2004; Mares, 2007), Castles finds that, on the evidence, 'neither the "race to the bottom" predicted by the globophobes nor the expenditure blowout predicted by the gerontophobes [is] taking place on anything like the scale assumed by the crisis scenarios' (2004, p. 7).

One consequence of the 'drain or gain' debate has been the emergence of the idea of the welfare state as a vehicle for 'social investment' rather than 'social protection'. By reframing and reorientating social policy towards *investment*, proponents hope that a new 'productive' direction for the welfare state will enable it to *contribute* to rather than inhibit economic growth. In chapter 9, we explore these ideas further in a discussion of the reorientation towards 'workfare', among other developments, in liberal welfare states.

Conclusion

Clearly, social policy settings, including the level and reach of income support payments and the extent and kind of public provision of human services, profoundly affect the living standards of national populations and groups within nations. That there is significant policy variation between countries with broadly similar levels of wealth shows that there is more than one way to 'do' social policy, which remains under some degree of social and political control. Writing about poverty in the US, Brady and colleagues (2008, p. 27) make this point very sharply:

> … working-aged adults with the same disadvantaged work, education and family characteristics in other affluent democracies are far less likely to be poor simply because they reside outside of the U.S. political context.

Within nations, too, partisan changes of government or changes in economic circumstances are often linked to changes in social policy. Eligibility for certain benefits might be widened or narrowed, benefit rates might be increased or allowed to languish and new programs might be introduced or existing programs retrenched. Any such changes will produce sets of winners and, often enough, losers. We discussed some of the political dynamics of social policy in the previous chapter and will return to discuss policy shifts, both progressive and less so, in the final three chapters of the book.

CHAPTER 6

Organisations: which should provide human services?

Introduction

Governments develop, legislate and fund social policy, but as we have seen in the preceding chapters, many other actors are involved in the policy development process. Many actors are also involved in the *implementation* of social policy, particularly in human service provision. Human service practitioners are crucial players, as are service users and, in many countries and fields of human service, volunteers are important participants. Yet all these people operate in different kinds of relationships with *organisations*, which enable and constrain their actions in various ways. Because service encounters always take place in an organisational context, the interaction between personnel and organisations is also critical. Accordingly, to understand how and why social policy does or does not enable change in the lives of service users and in society more broadly, we need to understand how people and organisations interact in the process of social policy implementation.

Our focus in this chapter is on the different types of organisations involved in social provision. Throughout this book, we have referred to the significance of the mixed economy of welfare or the mix of public, for-profit and NGOs involved in provision. Here we suggest that understanding the 'welfare mix' has become a crucial element of contemporary social policy analysis: human service professionals located in different kinds of organisations need to be cognisant of the theories and debates about the welfare mix, and how and why this mix is developing and changing.

We begin our analysis by exploring systematically some of the theoretical arguments for and against involvement of different kinds of organisations in human service provision. We then consider some of the consequences of the changing organisational structure of the human services field in rich democracies. This analysis complements our examination of quantitative and monetary dimensions of social policy in chapter 5, by extending the economic analysis of social policy to include theoretical arguments and empirical evidence drawn from economics, public administration and social policy research. The theoretical arguments we discuss here underpin contemporary social policy debates around the world. A grasp of this theory, and of the evidence that enables us to evaluate its claims, enables critically engaged participation in social policy development and change.

Public, for-profit or NGO: which type of organisation and why?

In liberal welfare states, which operate with a highly developed mixed economy of social provision, a diverse range of organisations implements social policy: public sector, non-profit and for-profit; large and small. In the social democratic regimes of northern Europe, mixed economies are emerging and consolidating from a domain previously dominated by the public sector. In conservative regimes, such as Germany and Austria, voluntary or non-government organisations have always been important and are now being joined by for-profit organisations in some key fields of service. We describe and evaluate these developments in more detail in the next section. The point here is that, as discussed in some detail in chapter 5, governmental choice of social policy instruments will determine what types of organisations are involved in policy implementation.

The very use of the term social *policy* implicates government in social provision. As we noted in chapter 1, however, the state is actually a relative latecomer to its role in maintaining the welfare of citizens. What is now called the 'third sector' or the 'NGO sector' has a much longer history of social provision, going back centuries, with the work of religious organisations and mutual aid societies, including both charitable and self-help models of support. There is a sense in which, in the twentieth century, public provision took over and universalised the somewhat haphazard coverage of voluntary organisations. Yet despite this history, the increasingly prominent role of NGOs, and the emergence and growth of for-profit organisations in human service provision in recent years, is often justified in terms of 'government failure'. This is a clear reversal of the theory of 'market failure', which offered justification for government engagement in the social field in the first place. Because many of the arguments for and against public (government) and for-profit (market) provision are framed as almost mirror images of each other, we discuss them together here.

Arguments in favour of for-profit and market provision

Arguments in favour of for-profit organisations providing human services have become prominent in recent decades, with the rise of New Public Management in the context of a resurgence of market-orientated ideologies in economic and public policy circles during the 1980s and 1990s. These arguments are based on ideas about competitive markets developed within neo-classical economic theory. In theory, at least, markets work to match supply and demand for goods and services through the price mechanism. In markets, people purchase, as individuals, what they decide they need at a price they are prepared to pay. If the price of goods or a service offered by one provider is too high or the quality too low, individual consumers will shop around to find a provider offering a lower price and/or better quality. Because consumers *can* shop around, providers have an incentive to compete with each other to attract them. This means that for-profit providers try to meet consumer demand at as low a price as they can. Consumer choice and competition, then, drive prices and costs down and quality up. Arguments for for-profit provision assume these processes work well, or well enough, while arguments for public provision point to 'market failure'. (For a more detailed discussion of arguments for and against for-profit human services, see Meagher and Cortis (2009).)

Of course, theorists and some proponents of the use of market mechanisms (choice, competition) in human service provision recognise that privatisation creates '*quasi*-markets' or 'managed markets', which do differ in critical ways from markets for other goods and services (Le Grand and Bartlett, 1993; Davidson, 2009). Julian Le Grand and Will Bartlett (1993, p. 10) explain that, on the supply side, not all non-public providers will be for-profit organisations, and so maximising profit may not be their organisational goal. On the demand side, they note that consumers do not express their 'purchasing power' through money. Indeed, consumers may not pay for or even choose the provider or the service. Nevertheless, the core ideas about the positive role that competition between providers and consumer choice can play in social policy draw on the economic theory of competitive markets and on assumptions about the way self-interested actors (consumers, profit-seeking enterprises) behave.

Ideas about market competition have been used to develop a theory of 'government failure' (Le Grand, 1991), which furnishes the key arguments against public provision of human services. As noted above, these arguments are framed in terms of how the public sector *lacks* key features of markets: efficiency in the use of resources and in getting what is provided to the right people.

First, public providers are not subject to the discipline of competition in the market, which, in theory at least, drives prices down as far as technically feasible. This means that resource use may not be 'optimised' in the public sector. In other words, time, money and other resources may not be used as efficiently as possible in the public sector, so that taxpayers' funds do not buy as much as they potentially could (Le Grand, 1991, p. 432). The implication is that *privately* organised provision through competitive markets will be more efficient and cost-effective.

Second, when publicly provided goods and services have no price (that is, are free) to consumers, or have a lower price than the market would set (that is, are subsidised), public provision is likely to be either wasteful or misdirected. When the price of public goods or services is set lower than the market price, more people will take or purchase the service than really want or need it (as measured by their willingness to pay), and so there will be oversupply and therefore waste. If the government knows what quantity of goods or services is the right amount to produce, but distributes it using a non-market means, those goods or services might not get to the right people. Non-market means of distribution include queues or allowing bureaucrats or professionals to decide who receives goods or services. The problem with a queuing system is that there is no guarantee that those most in need will come to the head of the queue. The problem with allowing professionals and bureaucrats to decide who gets services is that they may use their discretion to shore up their own interests, rather than the taxpayers' or service users' interests. They might *over-service* to increase their income, in the case of private professional practitioners, or *under-service* to decrease their workload, in the case of public employees (Le Grand, 1991, p. 435). Over-servicing is wasteful, while under-servicing leads to unmet needs.

These are some of the arguments against government provision. While they have been strongly contested, they have been and remain powerful, as the rise of the New Public Management and the dominance of pro-market arguments show. Significantly, these arguments attribute rather base motives to human service practitioners. Because neo-classical economic theories assume that individuals are self-interested, criticisms of public provision that build on these theories assume that human service practitioners will primarily focus on meeting their own needs at the expense of other stakeholders. We discuss these ideas in more detail in the next chapter.

Arguments for public provision

As noted above, and indicated in chapter 1, arguments *for* government provision arise from criticisms of markets, but also from criticisms of community and family provision. Because consumers in markets must have resources to participate, markets cannot meet the needs of people with no or too few resources. Organisations in the community sphere can choose those to whom they provide services or benefits. In a similar vein, families may care for their vulnerable members, but not every person in need has a family, nor does everyone in need have a family that can or will assist them. Further, it is not clear that care and assistance from family is always best, even when it is available. Family care and assistance arises from or creates bonds of obligation that may not be sought or valued by the family members involved. Familial bonds of obligation can also impinge on the freedoms of both the family members providing care and support and those receiving it. Thus, one argument for public provision is that governments can meet the needs of people who are too poor to buy what they need, or who are without community and family supports. Public provision can also relieve family members, particularly women, of some of the pressures of caring responsibilities, and can relieve people who need assistance with activities of daily life, or high levels of specialised support, from unwanted dependency on other family members. In this way, government can be the great equaliser—citizens' rights give them a claim over income or essential services that other social spheres are not obliged to recognise. Further, because of their potentially universal reach, public services may be uniquely able to ensure universal and uniform minimum standards. Because of its democratic accountability, there are also good reasons for public provision in areas that involve control over citizens' lives, such as citizens in need of protection (for example, children, people with mental illnesses), punishment (such as prisoners) or opportunities (for example, educational opportunities).

Another argument for public provision of human services is based on the intuition that human services give benefit to society as a whole as well as to the individuals who receive them. From this perspective, services like health, education and social care are what economists call 'merit goods' or 'public goods'. The two terms have slightly different meanings but they point to the same basic idea: human services have spillover benefits for society or, as economists put it, 'positive externalities'. In this case, relying on the market mechanism or private provision for profit would lead to under-supply of the goods and services in question, at a cost both to individuals who might personally invest too little in health and education and suffer the consequences, and to society overall (Stiglitz, 1993, pp. 180–82, 597–98).

The arguments for and against public and for-profit provision are linked to a debate we discussed in chapter 5 about whether social spending is a drain on the economy or a support for economic growth and development. And as with that debate, there is a clear empirical question about the relative efficiency and efficacy of public and market organisations (Le Grand, 1991). A values component also resonates with ideas discussed in chapter 4. Neo-liberal ideologies that favour market or for-profit provision over public provision value individual freedom very highly, and hold that government intervention through taxes and public programs should be kept to a minimum. Social democratic ideologies value freedom too, but place a premium on equality, which only public provision is able to guarantee.

Arguments for NGO provision

Values are also a significant feature in arguments about the advantages of NGOs in human service provision and, perhaps unsurprisingly, arguments for NGO provision point to both government failures *and* market failures (Wallis and Dollery, 2006). Yet the relatively neat symmetry of advantages and disadvantages that we see when we compare public and for-profit provision is not easily replicated in analysis of NGOs, which 'present a far more complex challenge for analysis' (Billis and Glennerster, 1998, p. 86).

Notwithstanding this complexity, arguments for and against NGOs in social provision include the following. First, we consider the advantages that NGOs have over for-profit organisations, which are suggested by a specific theory of market failure called 'contract failure' (Davidson, 2009). In markets for many goods and services, the quality is easily assessed by the consumer, who is also generally able to choose and change their provider at will. A consumer does not find it difficult to judge the quality of a restaurant meal, a box of cereal or a haircut. If they are not satisfied with the offerings of one provider, they can find another easily enough. Not so in human services, where market mechanisms for monitoring the behaviour of providers, and the quality and outcomes of services, do not operate well. When it is hard for consumers to monitor the quality of goods and services, for-profit sellers can make extra money by skimping on quality: if consumers are not able to tell the difference between good and bad products easily, they are unlikely to become dissatisfied and change suppliers. In this context, NGOs have an advantage over for-profit firms in human services, because they do not face the 'redistribution constraint' that for-profit businesses do. In other words, unlike private businesses, NGOs do not need to make a profit for shareholders, and so are not 'in it for the money' (Davidson, 2009 p. 65). This enhances trust in NGOs, because they do not have an incentive 'to take advantage of customer ignorance' about their services (Wallis and Dollery, 2006, p. 494). Because they do not need to make a profit, NGOs might also be able to provide higher quality services than for-profit organisations, as NGOs can devote relatively more resources to delivering service (Salamon et al., 2000, p. 5).

Second, NGOs have some advantages when compared to public providers. As noted above, one argument for government provision is that standards can be uniform and universalised, although this can also work as an argument *against* government provision. A commonly cited advantage of NGOs is that, freed from bureaucratic procedures and the requirement to provide uniform service to all, they are better able to cater to the specific needs of particular service user groups (Wallis and Dollery, 2006, p. 493). Indeed, David Billis and Howard Glennerster argue that NGOs have a 'comparative advantage' in meeting certain kinds of specialised and complex needs because their roots are in the associational world (that is, the community sphere discussed in chapter 1). This means that the clear-cut differentiation of roles (between employer and employee or between service provider and service recipient) that operates in both public bureaucracies and private for-profit firms does not operate within NGOs (1998, p. 91). Thus, 'stakeholder ambiguity' prevails in NGOs, in which service users can be on the board of the organisation providing services, or become human service practitioners themselves. Consequently, 'the gap between users and those in authority can be less, given the potential for greater motivation, sensitivity to and knowledge about client need' (1998, p. 91).

Third, it has been suggested that NGOs have heightened capacity to innovate and respond more nimbly to emerging needs, when compared to government (Wallis and Dollery, 2006, p. 493).

Fourth, Josie Kelly points out how the associational roots of NGOs could heighten their capacity to contribute to forming social capital in communities. Their stakeholder ambiguity and greater sensitivity make NGOs, in theory, more inclusive of a range of actors from service users to interest groups and local communities. Thus, they build social capital and community cohesion, considered goods in themselves, above and beyond the 'good' delivered through providing the particular service an agency might offer (Kelly, 2007, pp. 1010–11). Further, the capacity of NGOs to draw in volunteers can have both economic (cost reduction) and social (community development) benefits.

Fifth, as Lester Salamon and colleagues argue, NGOs can also play a critical advocacy role, pushing for policy change or social change more broadly because they are free from market disciplines and separate from the state. This advocacy role is also tied to the strong values orientation thought to underpin NGOs in human service provision, and can be enabled by the community-building dimensions of their work (Salamon et al., 2000, p. 6). Indeed, as we discussed in chapter 3, NGOs can provide an organised institutional means through which social movements can engage with the social policy process.

Some of the arguments against NGO provision have already been suggested, such as, citizens' rights do not give them a claim over services from NGOs, which may be free to serve only groups they choose to serve. This may lead to duplication of services to popular or deserving groups, and service gaps for unpopular or undeserving groups. This problem is more likely if services are funded and provided by discretionary (charitable) giving (Wallis and Dollery,

2006, p. 498). Another argument is that expertise may be underdeveloped in organisations that use volunteers as practitioners (Salamon et al., 2000, p. 8). If so, the quality of services could be lower in these NGOs than in public or market organisations that use only qualified employees. (We discuss this issue further in chapter 7.) In addition, the more the NGO sector relies on private philanthropy, the more likely it is that NGOs will not have sufficient resources to meet overall demand for services. This is because of what economists call the 'free rider' problem. As Salamon and colleagues put it, 'Since everybody benefits from a society in which those in need are cared for, whether or not they have contributed to the cost of the care, there is an incentive for each person to let his neighbor bear most of the cost' (2000, p. 8). According to this proposition, then, the total amount of charitable giving will be lower than the total social demand for services.

Yet another argument against NGO provision is that accountability mechanisms may be underdeveloped in these organisations. For-profit businesses must answer to a board of directors and to customers. Public agencies are responsible to elected representatives and voters. NGOs are not subject to these kinds of accountability mechanisms, and so may rely largely on the trustworthiness of managers (Salamon et al., 2000, p. 9). Indeed, it has been argued that the pivotal role of values in NGOs can actually *undermine* sound organisational governance. Catherine McDonald (1999) argues that the pivotal role of values in non-profit organisations makes it very difficult to establish the internal accountability and control mechanisms needed for effective evaluation of their performance. Reporting on fieldwork she conducted in non-profit organisations in Queensland, Australia, McDonald found that formal program evaluations 'had a ceremonial quality, validating performance *by reference to values or beliefs*, not performance' (1999, p. 18, emphasis added). Within the organisations she studied, managers, boards and workers thought all was going well, as long as they believed themselves to be '"doing good", committed to a set of legitimate beliefs, and therefore beyond reproach' (1999, pp. 18–19).

These arguments about the relative strengths and weaknesses of different kinds of organisations are largely built around ideal types, which are in turn based around a set of defining characteristics of each organisational type. Further, ideal types of organisations assume ideally typical institutional frameworks for action. In theory, for-profit organisations are assumed to interact with one another and consumers in competitive markets, public organisations are assumed to operate within an overarching hierarchical command structure, and NGOs are assumed to operate in the associational world of civil society, separate from both market and state.

Ideal types can be analytically useful but ultimately they are theoretical constructs or distilled generalisations. In reality, organisations of the same type operate in different contexts. The regulatory environment may differ—in Australia, state governments make policies in many human service areas, for example, so that the same type of service is organised differently in each state—as may policies in other relevant areas such as industrial relations, education and training and human rights. The characteristics of service users and available human service workers can also vary between contexts. At another level, for-profit organisations are not 'cordoned off' in markets, nor are NGOs restricted to the associational sphere. Institutional frameworks such as 'competitive markets' and 'the associational world' are not entirely separate spheres—they shape each other, and ideas and practices are shared and transferred between them. This means that although the theoretical arguments we have considered in this section are powerful, we cannot assume that organisations of a particular type will always show the strengths or weaknesses that theory predicts. In the next section, the focus is on the 'real world' of the mixed economy of human services.

From public to market and third-sector provision: evaluating the consequences

Exploration of the advantages and disadvantages of human service provision by different kinds of organisations has, inevitably, political and historical dimensions, in addition to the primarily theoretical dimensions discussed in the previous section. The evolution of a country's 'economy of social provision' is shaped by political conflicts, which themselves involve conflicts over ideas and interests, as we saw in chapter 3. An understanding of these conflicts is crucial for understanding how organisational change happens in the human services field. As discussed in previous chapters, governments in many countries have been expanding social service provision in recent decades by directly and indirectly funding private sector organisations to provide social services. In this section, we explore the emergence and consequences of this privatisation.

In chapter 2, we introduced New Public Management (NPM) ideas, which have emphasised corporate-like management practices within government organisations and justified attempts to reduce, or at least contain, the size of government overall (Bredgaard and Larsen, 2007). Proponents of NPM argue that private providers, both for-profit and non-profit (NGOs), are motivated to deliver services more efficiently and effectively than public services, in ways discussed in the previous section. From this perspective, privatisation should reduce costs and increase the quality of human services. While the governments of different countries have adopted these ideas to different extents, NPM has had a strong impact on social policy in the US, Sweden, Australia and the United Kingdom. In these countries, NPM ideas have taken deep root, in the context of rising demand for services and associated rising pressure on government budgets. In all, there has been an increasing use of the private sector (non-profit and for-profit) to deliver mandated services (Gilbert, 2005). Indeed, one of the most striking developments in social policy in many countries in recent decades has been the emergence of for-profit providers of human services. We begin by setting out three examples of the growth of for-profit provision, by way of illustration: care for older people and people with disabilities in Germany, childcare in Australia, and childcare, elder care and residential care for children in Sweden.

Human services as a business: the rise of for-profit providers

Before introducing the Long-Term Care Insurance (LTCI) scheme in 1994, Germany provided no public support for long-term care of frail older people or people with disabilities, apart from means-tested income support for people with little or no private income (Rothgang, 2003, p. 25). Heinz Rothgang (2003) explains the operation and uptake of various forms of assistance under the LTCI scheme in detail. The key points for us from his account are as follows. Those receiving formal home care can choose between in-kind provision or cash benefits, and the rates of benefit are legally set at different levels according to the need for services, not financial need. Benefits for in-kind care are offered at about twice the rate of cash benefits: that is, a person assessed as requiring moderate (Level 1) support, for example, is eligible for *either* €205 per month in cash *or* in-kind benefits to the value of €384 (Rothgang and Igl, 2007, p. 79). Recipients of cash benefits can use them to pay a family carer, but are not required to. In-kind benefits are provided by both for-profit and non-profit organisations, and fees for services are covered by the insurance fund, up to a ceiling.

Before LTCI was introduced, government policy prescribed that only non-profit organisations could provide formal (paid, non-family) care, even though service users paid for services entirely from their own pockets. Critically, when the German government introduced the LTCI scheme in 1994, it removed the restriction on the kinds of organisations that could provide care, to promote competition. In other words, NGOs were no longer privileged, and the field of care provision was opened up to for-profit providers, which could also draw on the newly available insurance subsidies. Five years later, for-profit providers of care comprised 47 per cent of the approximately 11,000 organisations operating in the field, and served fully 62 per cent of service users (Rothgang, 2003, p. 34). In 2001, approximately 30 per cent of people receiving benefits under the LTCI scheme received some formal care, nursing home or home-based. By 2005, this had increased to 54 per cent (Rothgang and Igl, 2007, p. 87). Clearly, formalisation, privatisation and defamilialisation in long-term care are not complete in Germany. However, the rapid rise to dominance of private, for-profit involvement is particularly noteworthy.

In Australia, long day care for children shows a similar pattern: once restrictions on subsidies to for-profit providers are lifted, for-profit provision mushrooms. Public funding to childcare has increased significantly in the last decade and a half, and two specific changes to funding policy have dramatically altered the mix of organisations providing subsidised services. In 1991, in order to expand service provision rapidly during a recession, a Labor government removed the prohibition on public subsidies going to for-profit childcare providers. It did so by extending fee relief, which was one key subsidy mechanism, to parents using for-profit services (Brennan, 1998, p. 203). Fee relief was paid directly to centres, which charged eligible parents a lower fee. In 1996, the newly elected Coalition government removed the other key subsidy mechanism: operational subsidies to community-based childcare centres (Brennan, 1998, p. 222). Instead of offering operational subsidies to some centres and fee relief to eligible parents, the government now directed all federal subsidies to childcare through funding to *parents* with quasi-vouchers rather than directing funding to *providers*. These two measures promoted the disproportionate growth of 'for-profit' childcare provision, and the movement into the sector of corporate players. Some figures demonstrate the rapid change in the mixed economy of the childcare sector. In 1991, when subsidies were extended to for-profit providers, for-profit centres accounted for 48 per cent of all centre-based long day care places receiving federal government funding. By 2004, 70 per cent of all such places were in for-profit centres, according to the most recent data that links childcare places to ownership of centres (calculated from table A3.3 in AIHW, 2005). Between 1991 and 2008, the number of places in subsidised long day care had nearly quadrupled, from 76 267 to 285 989 (AIHW, 2005 and Review of Government Services, 2009, table 3A.9). Overall, 83 per cent of all new subsidised places in long day care centres between 1991 and 2004 were in for-profit centres (calculated from table A3.3 in AIHW, 2005; no new data linking places to ownership of centres has been published since then).

A further, significant development is that for-profit ownership became increasingly concentrated over time in Australia, as corporations entered the childcare field. One company, ABC Learning Centres, was the first childcare company ever to be listed on the Australian Stock Exchange. The company pursued an aggressive global acquisition strategy, and at its height was the largest childcare corporation in the world (Fraser, 2008). In 2008, having bought out many competing corporate providers, ABC Learning owned 1042 centres in Australia and cared for more than 100 000 Australian children ('ABC Learning', 2008). (As we shall see, the unregulated growth of a single corporate player had significant consequences for the whole childcare field in Australia.)

The examples of elder care and childcare just considered are in what we might call 'mainstream' human service domains—significant proportions of older people and children, respectively, use these services as part of the normal unfolding of the life course. As defamilialisation occurs, albeit at a different pace in different countries, the demand for these services grows. Rich democracies have market economies based on for-profit enterprises, so the fact that 'ordinary businesses' might offer these mainstream services is not entirely surprising, especially where governments seek to contain the size of the public sector.

The next example takes a more specialised social service: residential care for children who have been removed from their families. This kind of service often involves more intrusive intervention into family situations that are, by definition, unusual. Further, residential care is offered—for some, it is mandated—to a very small proportion of the relevant population. Thus, the establishment of for-profit providers is less expected. Nevertheless, this is precisely what has happened in Sweden, a country more typically associated with public provision of human services.

Research by Marie Sallnäs (2009) explains how for-profit organisations came to be so prominent in Swedish residential care for children. In 1982, the Swedish Government introduced the Social Services Act, a piece of legislation usually understood to be a cornerstone of universalistic, rights-based human service provision to Swedish citizens. However, the Social Services Act also enabled the entry of private individuals to establish residential care homes for children. Before 1982, 90 per cent of homes were publicly run, with the remainder run by non-profit organisations. Now, only around 10 per cent of homes are publicly owned, and the vast majority of the remainder is owned by for-profit companies (SCB, 2006, p. 25).

However, the case of residential care for children is, at this stage, a relative outlier in the Swedish case. Overall, the scale of for-profit provision of social services in Sweden is not vast, although it is growing. In 1993, less than one per cent of people employed to care for older people and people with disabilities combined, worked in for-profit organisations (Trydegård, 2001, p. 116), with most of the remainder working in the public sector. By 2005, the proportion working for for-profit companies had increased to 11.2 per cent (Szebehely and Trydegård, 2007, p. 206). However, the growth in for-profit provision has been very uneven between municipalities, which have considerable control over how service provision is organised. In some, more than half of all elder care is privately run, while in about one third, private provision is negligible (Gustafsson and Szebehely, 2009, p. 85). The share of non-profit organisations has also grown, as part of an overall trend to privatisation. However, non-profit growth has been much more restrained: from 1.8 per cent in 1993 to 3.5 per cent in 2005 (Trydegård, 2001, p. 116; Szebehely and Trydegård, 2007, p. 206).

For-profit provision of centre-based childcare (called *förskolor* or preschools) is also growing in Sweden. In 1990, before the decision by a conservative government to extend public subsidies to private operators, about 5 per cent of children were in privately run preschools (both non-profit and for-profit) (Nyberg, 2007, p. 42). By 2006, 16.9 per cent of all Swedish children in preschool attended private centres (including 6.2 in for-profit centres, and 7.2 per cent in preschools run by parent or staff co-operatives). Almost all of the remaining children (more than 80 per cent) had places in preschools run by the municipalities (Swedish National Agency for Education, 2007, p. 39).

These case studies confirm something we discussed in chapter 5: that the kind and mix of private sector participants (for-profit, non-profit) depends on funding rules and on the structure of incentives that those rules establish. Where subsidies are available to all providers, who are also able to set their own fees and work under relatively light regulation, for-profit provision grows rapidly. Long-term care in Germany, childcare in Australia and residential care for children in Sweden are all examples here. Where opportunities to charge higher fees are constrained, as they are in preschools in Sweden, the development of for-profit provision is slower, presumably because the opportunities to make significant profits are also somewhat constrained. Models and regulation matter, and these are decided *politically*. This is also why the development of for-profit provision of aged care is so patchy in Sweden; municipalities decide themselves, and make very different decisions.

So what has been the impact of these developments? In Sweden, privatisation has involved replacement of public with private organisations, while in Germany and Australia, privatisation has often been a means of expanding service provision. Despite differences in the organisational configurations of care sectors before and after privatisation in all three countries and elsewhere, researchers have raised concerns about the emergence, and in some cases the rise to dominance, of for-profit provision (Blomqvist, 2004; Bode, 2007; Meagher and Cortis, 2009). There are also the questions of whether privatisation has reduced costs and increased quality, as theory predicts it will, or whether the project of turning human services into businesses is simply too high risk.

The case studies set out briefly above allow us to explore some of the problems that research has identified with the privatised provision of publicly funded human services. A critical challenge is the regulation of quality, when services are provided at 'arm's-length' from governments that fund them. In Germany, there are 'serious problems of quality assurance' in formal long-term care for older people and people with disabilities (Rothgang and Igl, 2007, p. 102). One reason is that providers developed their own quality assurance procedures, partly to respond to new legal requirements under LTCI arrangements, and partly as a pre-emptive strategy to avoid too much regulation by public authorities (Rothgang and Igl, 2007, p. 102). This does not necessarily mean that quality is poor, just that it is difficult to establish whether or not services are of good quality, both for funders and consumers, because different providers cannot be compared. In itself, this is a problem, since opening provision to a range of actors was intended to promote competition and choice, both of which require good information.

A related problem is that private organisations can gain and exercise significant influence over policy that regulates service quality, particularly if a large proportion of services is privately provided, or concentrated in the hands of one or few providers. In childcare in Australia, for example, Deborah Brennan (2007, p. 220) documents how representatives of for-profit providers have repeatedly and successfully lobbied against attempts to strengthen regulation that would improve the quality of childcare—but that would also make it more expensive to provide, thereby reducing profitability. Several British studies have also found that increasing concentration in residential aged care has shifted political power from regulators to the largest for-profit providers, and have limited the scope for consumer choice between providers (Drakeford, 2006; Holden, 2005; Scourfield, 2007a).

In residential care for children in Sweden, providers have had a great deal of latitude in setting prices, which some have exploited as sometimes desperate municipalities seek to place children, typically troubled adolescents, in care (Sallnäs, 2005). The significant costs of this model are increasingly recognised as a problem by social service managers in municipalities (Meagher et al., 2009). However, once these providers were established in a field where there were few alternatives, it became very difficult for governments to challenge their market power (Marie Sallnäs, personal communication).

Privatisation, then, can be associated with changes to the extent and perceptions of democratic control over the organisation and funding of human services. A study of workers and working conditions in publicly-financed aged care in Sweden, by Rolf Gustafsson and Marta Szebehely (2009), found strong evidence that workers employed by private (mostly for-profit) providers were significantly less likely than those employed by public providers to believe that politicians had control over their working conditions and the resourcing and quality of elder care in the municipality. This is despite the fact that politicians retain primary formal responsibility for the resourcing and quality of elder care in the communities they govern.

Another problem with privatisation that our case studies reveal is instability in marketised care sectors. In Australian childcare, the outcome of the 'vast national experiment' (Brennan, 2007, p. 223) with corporate provision has now been revealed with the collapse of the corporation behind ABC Learning Centres during the closing months of 2008. Some 60 centres have been closed and the Australian Government has been obliged to intervene to prevent the closure of hundreds more ('ABC Learning', 2008; Gillard, 2008a).

A significant body of research has accumulated that seeks to establish whether privatisation has improved quality and reduced costs. Many studies compare the quality of services provided by for-profit and non-profit providers. Meagher and Cortis (2009) reviewed evidence from a large number of such studies in childcare, residential aged care and home care for older people and people with disabilities. They found that research shows that overall, quality is typically lower in for-profit services in childcare and residential aged care than in non-profit or public services. Further, unless regulation is very strict, for-profit childcare centres tend to serve smaller proportions of low-income children and children with special needs (2009, p. 30), raising issues of accessibility and segregation in marketised care. In home care for older people and people with disabilities, results are more mixed, showing that regulation may neutralise differences in quality between for-profit and non-profit providers. Some studies in this sector suggested that the process of privatisation itself (especially managed competition) can operate to bring down the quality of care and jobs in all providers, a process called 'institutional isomorphism' (Meagher and Cortis, 2009, p. 31; see also Baines, 2004; Gustafsson and Szebehely, 2009).

Neither has research established that privatisation is cheaper or less bureaucratic than public services. Thomas Bredgaard and Flemming Larsen (2007; 2008) have analysed the privatisation of employment services in Australia, Denmark and the Netherlands, and concluded that 'the idea that the invisible hand of the market will produce better and cheaper services turns out to be difficult to realise in practice' (2007, p. 290). Without regulation, the social goals of privatised programs would be difficult to meet, and the political accountability of governments as contractors would be impossible to maintain. In the case of employment placement services, Bredgaard and Larsen found that extensive and continuous public regulation of the market for employment services was required to prevent problems such as 'creaming' of the strongest unemployed, 'parking' of the weakest and underinvestment in training. Yet this regulation can undermine another goal of contracting out: that of creating flexible, innovative and responsive services. A range of studies has found that regulated quasi-markets typically become as inflexibly bureaucratised as the public system they extend or replace (Bredgaard and Larsen, 2007; 2008; Schmid, 2003). What contracting out of employment services is well suited to, though, is to 'support a politically intended shift in the content of employment policy' towards a work-first orientation (Bredgaard and Larsen, 2007, p. 296). On the matter of cost, Bredgaard and Larsen find that it is difficult to evaluate the efficiency of private systems because 'there is little valid and systematic knowledge on the outcomes and effects the system is able to deliver' (2008, p. 345). Other research has confirmed the significant difficulty of measuring whether or not privatisation results in cheaper services, and often points to 'weakening the position of employees' as a means to and outcome of cutting costs (Kähkönen, 2005, p. 94).

NGOs in the contracting state

We now turn to exploring the impact on NGOs of participating in privatised human service provision. Some of the problems with private (non-public) provision we have just discussed may apply to provision by non-profit as well as for-profit providers, depending on the way quasi-markets are organised and regulated (Bredgaard and Larsen, 2007; McBeath and Meazan, 2008; Morris and Helburn, 2000), although that is not our primary concern here. Earlier in the chapter, we saw that the advantages of NGO provision of human services are, in theory derived from the relative *independence* of these organisations from market and bureaucratic imperatives. The question, then, is how do NGOs fare when they are drawn into provision of mandated services through government contracts, often in quasi-markets?

Government funding provides a significant proportion of the income of social service organisations in many countries: 58 per cent, in Australia, according to the most up-to-date data (calculated from ABS, 2001, p. 29). Thus, many NGOs rely greatly, some completely, on government funding. When governments pay organisations to deliver specific programs, and regulate and monitor delivery of those programs, there is a risk that the space for NGOs to define their own approach to service delivery can be considerably constrained (Rawsthorne, 2005; Kelly, 2007; Rogers, 2007). By working on behalf of government, NGOs risk becoming 'positioned merely as "service providers" rather than partners with government in solving social problems' (Rawsthorne, 2005, p. 228). If so, NGOs may lose their reputation for independence, as they become 'perceived as an agent of government' (Kelly, 2007, p. 1015). Indeed, NGOs may actually lose their autonomy, as they become aligned with the purposes of the government programs they deliver and drift away from their original mission and purposes (Rawsthorne, 2005, p. 228). The responsiveness and innovation that governments ostensibly seek in engaging the NGO sector in service provision can also be eroded (Smith, 2005, p. 602) and the scope of services narrowed to those that governments will pay for (Rawsthorne, 2005, p. 228). There is also the risk of curtailed advocacy activity by NGOs, particularly against government policy or for more resources. NGOs may censor themselves, or be censored by contracting conditions, under the potential or actual threat of having their funding withdrawn (Kelly, 2007, pp. 1016–17). The contracting environment may engender competition rather than collaboration between NGOs, undermining some of the means of social capital development they would otherwise engage in (Rawsthorne, 2005, p. 229). Finally, the organisational demands of contracting with government funders, including service design, monitoring and accountability frameworks may reorientate the internal operations and cultures of NGOs towards more corporate and/or bureaucratic models. If this happens, the way NGOs design and deliver services and their relationships with their service users and the human service workers they employ can also change.

Although the nature of the relationship between governments and NGOs varies from place to place and service type to service type, there is evidence that some of these problems have arisen in Australia. Margot Rawsthorne and Sheila Shaver (2008) conducted a study of more than 600 organisations providing a range of social services under contract to the federal government in 2002. Their questionnaire sought service providers' perspectives on the impact of changes to funding arrangements, such as the introduction of contracting, on their agencies and the sector in general. On issues of responsiveness and innovation, 42 per cent reported that they were less likely under the new funding models to receive funds for innovative prevention and development work (2008, p. 80), and 61 per cent believed that the changed funding arrangements had led to a lack of response to emerging needs (2008, p. 88). On issues of autonomy and community orientation, 47 per cent of respondents agreed that contracting arrangements had made their organisation more cautious in advocacy (2008, p. 88), 18 per cent reported that their agency had been diverted from its vision and purpose (2008, p. 82), and 48 per cent agreed that their agency was 'now more accountable to the Department than the community' (2008, p. 84). On issues of the impact of changes on internal operations and on relationships within the sector, 39 per cent believed that their agency had to divert resources away from client services to meet reporting requirements (2008, p. 77), 42 per cent agreed that they were 'encouraged to compete rather than collaborate with other agencies' (2008, p. 83), and around 60 per cent agreed that there had been a loss of small services and growth of large organisations (2008, p. 88).

Significantly, Rawsthorne and Shaver's study included only agencies that *had* contracted with the government to offer services—as Rawsthorne notes elsewhere, organisations that were unwilling or unable to contract with the government were excluded. In her survey of the impact of contracting on non-profit providers of employment services, Colette Rogers (2007, p. 402) points out that some agencies did not enter or renew contracts with the Australian Government to provide 'Job Network' services because the program conflicted too deeply with their organisational values. For the same reason, most Christian charities declined to participate in the then government's financial case management program in 2006 (Rogers, 2007, p. 401). It therefore seems that NGOs can face a serious dilemma, especially if they do not have substantial alternative sources of funding. They can participate in programs that the government chooses to fund, and face the various risks outlined above, or withdraw from the provision of services they find too compromising and be unable to offer services.

Conclusion

In this chapter, we have examined theoretical arguments for and against different kinds of organisations in human service provision, and some evidence about the impacts of diversifying the kinds of organisations involved in human services. From a policy perspective, it is crucial to recognise that the policy *context* in which different kinds of organisations operate is critical to the ability of organisations to pursue their own goals. For non-profits, contracting for government might lead to 'mission drift' and a loss of distinctiveness; for for-profits, the regulatory regime might constrain behaviours that could otherwise undermine the quality of services. Overall, regulation can engender 'institutional isomorphism', such that different kinds of organisations become less distinct from one another and their relative strengths and weaknesses are attenuated. From a service perspective, this may be a positive outcome; regulatory control over the quality and distribution of services is easier to achieve. However, convergence can undermine the very flexibility that diversifying the range of providers was designed to accomplish. Further, there may be significant costs to democratic accountability for the distribution and quality of services when governments put service provision at arm's-length. From a human service practitioner's perspective, the type and regulation of human service organisations operating in the field have a range of implications that we consider in the next chapter.

CHAPTER 7

People: who implements social policy?

Introduction

In chapter 6, we explored how social policies enable or constrain different kinds of organisations in human service delivery, with consequences for the quality and distribution of services in the mixed economy of welfare. In this chapter, we consider how people as implementers of social policy are enabled and constrained by their organisational environments and by broader social structures and discourses. As we pointed out in chapter 2, implementation is not an after-effect or output of the policy process, but rather an inherent part of it. Therefore, to understand how policy is formed and how it works, we need to understand how it is implemented; this is particularly important in policy on human services. Further, because human service provision is a fundamentally interpersonal process, the characteristics and dispositions of the people involved make a critical difference to the outcome of a service encounter. Thus, those who are part of the human services workforce and the ways they are organised are social policy issues in their own right.

Two key groups of personnel who implement human services policy are human service practitioners and volunteers. We examine these two groups and their relationships, and consider some key debates about their identities, roles and motivations. We also include a discussion of the role of the service user in the social policy process, since important developments in both discourse and practice have changed their position in recent decades. Overall, the chapter aims to offer some concepts, arguments and evidence to support practitioners' reflections on their own participation in social policy for social change.

Human service practitioners: motivations, models and contexts

Caring? Controlling? Self-seeking? Autonomous? Bureaucratised? Professional? The capacities, behaviour and motivations of human service practitioners have been characterised in these and other ways, demonstrating the contested nature of human services work. Elements of these debates recur as themes in this section, but we begin with perhaps the most obvious fact about human service practitioners as a *workforce*: they are overwhelmingly women. Some statistics demonstrate the point: in Australia, 90 per cent of registered nurses, 71 per cent of school teachers, 95 per cent of childcare workers, 81 per cent of social workers and 72 per cent of counsellors are female (AIHW, 2007; 2008). In the US, 91 per cent of all registered nurses, 75 per cent of all school teachers and 82 per cent of all social workers are female (US Bureau of Labor Statistics, 2007, table 11). Allied health professions are also strongly feminised, and this overall pattern is evident in most rich countries.

How is the gender of the human service workforce relevant to our theme of social policy for social change? One reason is the complex relationship that exists between gender and human services work in contemporary society, which has implications for the social and economic organisation of this work. Much of the work human service practitioners do can be understood as 'care work'—the work of enabling and nurturance that allows people to achieve their potential and supports humans in times of vulnerability, whether life-course related (childhood and old age), health related (mental and physical) or socially shaped (unemployment, disability and social isolation). (For an overview of definitions of care work, see Meagher and Healy, 2006, p. 12.)

Care and skill in human services work

The concept of care work has become important in the analysis of human services practice and organisations in recent decades. It is associated with a distinctive approach to ethics in human services (Banks, 2006; 2008; Meagher and Parton, 2004). The concept of care has arisen from feminist attempts to think through the nature of and relationships between gender and the care work that is undertaken formally, by paid workers, and informally, by unpaid family members and others. Care has been conceptualised as having both practical/technical dimensions and moral/motivational dimensions because it involves both caring *for* and caring *about* (Meagher, 2006, p. 35). Because care work takes place in both formal and informal settings, and because women bear primary responsibility for unpaid informal care and constitute the vast majority of paid formal care workers, human service work seems inextricably 'feminised' and linked to naturalised activities such as family care (James, 1992). This is not to say, simply, that paid care workers (nurses, social workers, childcare workers) do the same things in formal settings that unpaid carers (mothers, wives, friends) do informally. The point here is that human services work has, as part of its social meaning, a connection with the unpaid work of informal care.

The connection between formal human services and informal family care brings with it some apparent benefits, such as the assumption that human service workers, like family carers, will have altruistic caring motivations. However, it also has costs, some of them in hard cash. Research in the US has found that paid workers in caring occupations receive lower pay compared to workers in other occupations with comparable skill (England et al., 2002). One widespread rationale for this 'care penalty' is that because care workers are altruistically motivated, they are willing to accept a lower rate of pay. On this view, increasing payment for care work would attract the 'wrong kind of people' into human service occupations, that is, people motivated by money (an extrinsic motivator), not by a sense of vocation, altruism or even 'love' (intrinsic motivators). Julie Nelson and Nancy Folbre (2006) strongly rebut this argument. They argue that 'Because skilled, caring, and able people need decent wages, it is quite possible … that higher wages would attract a higher proportion of truly caring, skilled workers' (2006, p. 129). They reject the claim that money will 'crowd out' caring motivations, drawing on Bruno Frey's (1998) theory of motivational crowding. Workers' sense of control and the meaning of payment is crucial here. Where work is regimented, and workers feel controlled by external drivers, caring motivations can be crowded out. One can imagine if nurses' pays were calculated according to the number of injections they gave, dressings they changed and reports they completed, it might be difficult to focus on patients' broader needs. But where payment is understood as recognising and rewarding caring and professionalism, it can 'crowd in' caring motivations and maintain high standards of service (Nelson and Folbre, 2006, p. 129).

The connection between paid care work and informal care work has another cost. The relational values and practices of informal care work seem to belong to the family and community spheres of the social world, rather than to the market and state spheres where money and power reign. Of course, in reality, money and power shape relationships in the family and community spheres, and affective and reciprocal relations exist in the market and state spheres too. But the organisational logics and discourses of the market and the state can make the values and practices of caring harder to see and enact in these spheres. Thus, care workers in all kinds of human service fields and organisations can find it difficult to practise in ways they believe best meet the needs and aspirations of service users. The child welfare social worker who feels she spends more time on paperwork than anything else (McLeod, 2008; Meagher et al., 2009) and the home care worker whose care for her elderly clients is fragmented into discrete tasks to be completed in specified time frames (Eliasson–Lappalainen and Nilsson Motevasel, 1997) are feeling the effects of the undervaluation of care and of New Public Management on the organisation of human services. We return to the implications of NPM on human service workers later in this section.

The gender dimensions of caring work are implicated in a related set of critical social policy questions about human service workers and the human services workforce. How skilled is the work? What kinds of qualifications are required? What sort of workforce is needed? The question of whether or not care work is skilled has been complicated by the association of care work with unpaid family care. Certainly, some tasks in many situations and fields of human services, and even the emotional connections of formal and informal care can be very similar (James, 1992; Himmelweit, 1999). Does this mean that human services work is *not* skilled?

There are three issues here. First, family carers typically have significant but *unrecognised* organisational, practical and psychosocial skills developed in running households and raising families (James, 1992).

Second, there are skills that many family carers do not have or develop in the course of daily life. These may encompass technical skills such as those required to teach mathematical concepts in the primary school classroom, recognise child neglect or abuse, or understand and respond to the psychosocial needs of patients in hospitals or long-term care settings, when the human service worker is not in a long-term intimate relationship with the recipient.

Third, how the work is conceptualised and organised by institutions such as schools, hospitals, child welfare departments and the broader systems in which these operate is in a dynamic relationship with the skills demanded or allowed to be expressed in a job. If, for example, nursing is organised, through task allocations and management oversight, as a job primarily orientated towards physical rather than holistic care that includes psychosocial support, or if nurses are expected to do only tasks assigned to them by doctors, then the range of skills demanded of nurses by the organisation is narrower. Of course, the range of skills called upon by the patient's needs may be much broader, and many researchers have documented how nurses and other care workers work around organisational demands to exercise other skills in meeting service users' needs (James, 1992; Stone, 2000; King, 2007).

How questions about skill and the appropriate mix of workers are answered in a practical sense can have a profound impact on the quality of jobs in human services and of human services themselves. If policy-makers and employers generally agree that human services work is mostly unskilled, with few or even no qualifications required, then the quality of jobs is likely to be poor. If the quality of *jobs* is poor (low pay, poor working conditions, lack of recognition by management of workers' skills and contributions), then there is a higher probability that the quality of *services* provided will be poor (Stone, 2004; Ackerman, 2006; Caspar and O'Rourke, 2008; Healy et al., 2009). If there is not always a straightforward relationship between job quality and service quality in reality, then it is because care workers act on their intrinsic motivations; that is, in response to their emotional and ethical identifications with the service users they work with (Folbre, 2006, p. 18). However, a range of social and economic forces undermines the capacity of organisations to continue to exploit the altruism of care workers (Folbre, 2006, p. 17; Himmelweit, 2007). Recruiting and retaining human service workers has become a significant problem in many rich democracies. As a result, the need to recognise and reward human service workers adequately is increasingly acknowledged by social policy-makers, who are developing explicit workforce strategies.

Professionalism: A contested ideal

One very important, if also somewhat contentious, concept that has been mobilised within human service occupations with the aim of having at least some care work recognised as highly skilled is the idea of the 'professional'. As with the concept of care, the idea of the profession carries traces of a vocation and a strong values orientation, linked to professional ethics (see chapter 4). However, the idea of the profession is also defined by its links to *knowledge*, and the *power* that derives from exclusive exercise of expert knowledge.

As Idit Weiss-Gal and Penelope Welbourne note, there have been numerous attempts 'to develop a theoretical framework to distinguish professions from non-professional occupations and to identify the factors that influence their development' (2008, p. 2). They outline the two dominant approaches to theorising the professions in a review of previous research (see also Macdonald, 1995). One is the 'attributes approach', which attempts to identify the core traits of a profession. Attributes usually include some or all of the following: a systematic body of knowledge; professional authority, autonomy and prestige recognised by clients, the state and the community more broadly; a code of ethics governing practice and linked to a service orientation; and a professional culture sustained by formal professional organisations, which may control access to entry into professional training (Weiss-Gal and Welbourne, 2008, p. 2).

The second is the 'power approach', which focuses on the processes by which occupational groups seek, gain and sustain dominance in areas of practice against threats from other occupations, the state, the bureaucracies that may employ them, or their clients. *Professions* are occupational groups that have successfully achieved control over their work, including its techniques, the selection of members for training and the nature of services and who gets them (Weiss-Gal and Welbourne, 2008, p. 2). Medicine and law are the archetypal professions in both these approaches. Occupational groups that do not have the attributes or, in the power approach, do not achieve autonomy over the relevant activities are, by extension, *not* professions.

One reason why the idea of professionalism has been contentious in human services is because many consider that occupations such as nursing, teaching and social work do *not* have the attributes or the power to achieve professional status. Thus, they have been called 'semi-professions' (Etzioni, 1969) or 'bureau-professions' (Parry and Parry, 1979). A second reason is that many *within* the human service professions, perhaps particularly within social work, have argued *against* professionalism as an ideal. On this view, which takes the power approach, human service professionals should seek to work *with* and *for* service users, not to wield power in the form of expertise *over* service users (Ife, 1997; Healy and Meagher, 2004, pp. 248–249).

How to approach the issue of the 'professional project' is a thorny strategic problem for the female-dominated human service occupations (McDonald, 2003; Healy and Meagher, 2004). On one hand, the pursuit of social and economic recognition seems to cut across the emancipatory, anti-hierarchical, service user-orientated aspirations of human service professions. On the other, the *lack* of social and economic power and recognition in female-dominated human service occupations makes them more susceptible to threats to their capacity to work with and for service users. In other words, appropriately defined and pursued, the power of professionalism can be used productively for social change as well as paternalistically for conservation of existing hierarchies (see chapter 3). Feminist models for professionalisation have been proposed in nursing (Davies, 1995; 1996) and social work (Healy and Meagher, 2004; Meagher, 2006), and these seek explicitly to reconcile criticisms of professional power with the more emancipatory goals of human services. Another alternative is the 'partnership' model of professionalism proposed by Neil Thompson (2002) for social work, but that has broader relevance.

Human service practitioners as 'street-level bureaucrats'

A concept we introduced in chapter 1 has also been significant in theorising human service practitioners as implementers of social policy: the 'street-level bureaucrat'. First proposed by Michael Lipsky (1980), this concept aims to understand the role of front-line workers in public organisations. Lipsky's analysis of street-level bureaucracy is 'complex and multi-faceted' (Evans and Harris, 2004, p. 876), and we cannot consider all its nuances here. The central insight of Lipsky's book is that front-line practitioners *necessarily* make interpretations and decisions in assessing and advising service users and in delivering services, and that these interpretations and decisions make a significant difference as to who gets services and why, and what services they get and how. Thus, he writes, 'the decisions of street-level bureaucrats, the routines they establish, and the devices they invent to cope with uncertainties and work pressures, effectively *become* the public policies they carry out' (Lipsky, 1980, p. xii, emphasis in original). (Significantly, although Lipsky recognises that professionals are already expected to exercise discretion, his theory extends the role and impact of discretion to decisions made by para-professional workers (1980, p. 14).)

A case study from a recent research project illustrates the issues. Michele Foster and colleagues (2006) analyse how human service professionals in English social service departments conduct and document the assessments they undertake with adults with disabilities. A key aspect of the context of the study was the new 'discourse of personalisation of services' in English social services, which aims to give 'individual consumers of public services the opportunity to articulate their preferences and exercise their choices' (Foster et al., 2006, p. 125). We discuss this discourse in more detail later in the chapter. The policy instruments used to deliver personalised services include 'direct payments' (where people with disabilities receive cash to purchase the services they choose from the providers they choose), and 'individual budgets', by which a person has control over how funds allocated for their support are spent, although under this model they do not receive the funds directly (Foster et al., 2006, p. 126). But, as Foster and colleagues point out, to gain access to direct payments or an individual budget, a person must be *assessed* so that their requirements and the areas of support that the allocated resources will cover can be identified (2006, p. 126).

The assessment process is one crucial 'moment' in the social policy system, during which frontline practitioners make interpretations and use their discretion to make decisions in an organisational context. In the case that Foster and colleagues analyse, the context is one where there are pressures to introduce greater choice and personalisation on one hand, and managerialist pressures to apply more explicit eligibility criteria and measure and manage performance on the other (2006, p. 127). In interviews with practitioners, the researchers found that one important area where practitioners used discretion was in choosing topics from the Community Care Assessment form for discussion with service users during the assessment process. Topics that practitioners more commonly considered relevant were physical health, personal assistance, communication and technical aids and equipment, rather than culture, mental health, personal counselling, personality and preferences, employment/education and social/recreational needs. The researchers concluded that it was 'not clear how far these priorities actually reflected those of the people being assessed' (Foster et al., 2006, p. 130).

Practitioners' interpretations and choices during assessment were affected by their professional assumptions (Foster et al., 2006, p. 130), but also by their organisational environment. Working within imposed resource constraints, their perceptions of what could *actually be offered* affected how they conducted assessments and developed Care Plans (2006, pp. 131–132). Practitioners' interpretations and decisions, then, have 'profound implications for the subsequent opportunity to identify personalised service responses' (2006, p. 130). However, Foster and colleagues are not entirely pessimistic. They argue that practitioners' discretion can support rather than compromise choice, depending on how they use it (2006, p. 132). They also recognise the variability between practitioners—another source of difference in service outcomes (2006, p. 130)—which suggests that training and development, as well as improved resourcing and more enabling organisational contexts, could improve the quality of decision-making.

New Public Management: changing human service practitioners and practice?

The impact of the New Public Management on human services has been a recurrent theme in this book. One of the core assumptions underpinning NPM is that professional discretion is 'an obstacle to public service reform—especially if professionals were able to resist change or re-interpret policy at the street level' (Taylor and Kelly, 2006, p. 632). In other words, from the NPM perspective, professionals and other practitioners cannot be trusted to implement policy as policy-makers intend and so require specialised management and oversight. Thus, the way front-line practice is organised has been a primary target of NPM-inspired policies, and practitioners' roles have been increasingly structured and monitored. Further, some human service professions, such as teaching and social work, have come to be more closely regulated *as occupational groups* by governments in Australia and England, in the form of accreditation of training programs, registration of practitioners and other means (Fenech et al., 2006; Cornes et al., 2007). In a burgeoning body of work, researchers have debated whether professions have been de-professionalised, and whether street-level bureaucrats have lost their discretionary powers as NPM policies have taken hold (Exworthy and Halford, 1999; Rummery and Glendinning, 2000; Bradley, 2003; Farrell and Morris, 2003; Evans and Harris, 2004; Healy and Meagher, 2004; Martin et al., 2004; Fenech et al., 2006; Osborn, 2006; Taylor and Kelly, 2006; Ellis, 2007; Burton and van den Broek, 2008; Goldstein, 2008).

As in other situations we have discussed in this book, the impact of NPM on human service workers is ultimately an empirical question. Drawing on a range of studies undertaken over the last decade or so, we can conclude that attempts to control discretion by the proliferation of rules—through detailed procedural guidance on assessment and service delivery, often integrated into information technology systems—and/or by increasing management scrutiny of practitioners' performance, have had mixed results.

Some studies have found that change has undermined the ability of practitioners to undertake their work in ways they think best. In a study of educational reform, for example, Marilyn Osborn found that reforms designed to monitor, measure and change the 'outputs' of school education had led many English teachers to the belief 'that the more affective concerns of teaching—the sense of vocation and investment of self—were being undermined by the pressure for performance, to become "expert technicians" in transmitting externally pre-defined knowledge and skills to their pupils' (2006, p. 243). Judith Burton and Diane van den Broek's study (2008) of child welfare workers using new information technologies in Australia found that many practitioners did not welcome the refocusing of their work away from clients and towards structured information gathering. One group of workers they studied was employed in a call centre established for the centralised reception and initial assessment of child protection reports. These workers were under pressure to meet performance targets for the number of calls they took and processed. Many found this a compromising intrusion on their capacity to assess callers' needs, and believed the system's orientation had shifted from a focus on the quality of work performed to the quantity (2008, p. 11).

However, many other studies have found that the proliferation of rules simply creates new opportunities, or demands, for discretion, since rules must be interpreted (Evans and Harris, 2004; Foster et al., 2006; Ellis, 2007). Also important is the finding that just because NPM ideas are advocated by policy elites does not mean that these ideas are implemented by the managers of service organisations and front-line practitioners in the spirit intended. Indeed, managers may be as resistant to the new discourse of public sector reform as are the professionals (Farrell and Morris, 2003, p. 137). Ultimately, the impact of reform depends on the kind of rules imposed, the technologies (managerial, informational and otherwise) used to impose rules, the sector of practice or occupational group under consideration (for example, doctors retain more power and discretion than nurses, teachers and social workers), and the responses and actions of the specific people and organisations involved.

Discretion, professionalism and service user orientation in implementation

Practitioner discretion is clearly a critical element of social policy implementation, as human service practitioners mediate the generalisations that social policies necessarily make as well as the particular, concrete needs of individuals they work with in the process of providing services (see chapter 1). From the perspective of service quality, practitioners can use discretion to ensure that human service systems better meet the concrete and specific needs of individuals by interpreting, or even working around, policy, rules and organisational structures that make it difficult to do so. From the perspective of human service practitioners working in organisations, discretion can also be used to manage the tensions between practitioners' personal commitments to service, and the reality of service delivery in systems that seem to work as much against as for meeting human needs (Lipsky, 1980, p. xii; Martin et al., 2004). The study of Foster and colleagues (2006) shows how practitioners had to manage the tension between policies imposed from above that promoted an individualised service model yet enforced strict resource constraints. There is also evidence that practitioner discretion can lead to unjust outcomes. This may occur when decisions are not informed by policy requirements on service users' rights, when they are informed by practitioners' personal prejudices, or when they are orientated more towards keeping organisational peace (Rummery and Glendinning, 2000; Bradley, 2003; Foster et al., 2006; Ellis, 2007). Further evidence shows that many practitioners believe new systems of organising and managing human services work make it more difficult for them to act in the interests of service users, particularly in contexts where demand for services is escalating and funding is dwindling (Carey, 2003).

Overall, the impact of discretion on the effectiveness and fairness of social policy systems is highly variable, and social policy systems need to enable the exercise of discretion in meeting needs, and curtail the exercise of discretion that leads to unjust or poor outcomes. One way systems might do this is by developing organisational structures and practices that do not assume human service practitioners have entirely self-interested motivations that need to be reined in by performance monitoring and incentives, or controlled by detailed practice guidelines and IT-bound documentation procedures. Nor should systems assume that practitioners have entirely altruistic motives that must be exploited (and perhaps burned out), or relied on always to provide high quality services (Le Grand, 1997). Systems need to recognise and enable practice that draws on practitioners' intrinsic motivations while also recognising their efforts with appropriate rewards (Frey, 1998; Jones and Cullis, 2003; Nelson and Folbre, 2006).

How might these aspirations be expressed in organisations? The way front-line practice is designed within workplaces (for example, the balance of 'people work' and 'paper work'), and the kind of support that organisations offer to their front-line practitioners (for example, opportunities for professional as well as managerial supervision), are crucial elements. So too are the availability of meaningful career paths and professional learning and development opportunities (Healy et al., 2009). An appropriate model of professionalism can play a role, too, by offering an alternative organisational reference point for human service practitioners, and support for the ongoing development of professional ethics, skills and policy influence (Healy and Meagher, 2004). Unions can also play a role, representing workers' interests in sustainable wages and working conditions that enable them to offer high quality services (Healy and Meagher, 2004; Baines, 2008), especially where professional organisations are not relevant or are weak.

Volunteers: bringing the 'social' back into social policy?

Our focus in this chapter so far has been on paid workers employed by human service organisations. Yet unpaid workers, or volunteers, also play a significant role in social policy implementation. Some figures give a sense of the scale of volunteer participation in organised human services practice. In Australia, in 2006, 1.23 million Australians gave 135 million hours in community or welfare agencies, and a further 309 000 gave 26 million hours in parenting support and child and youth services. Another 120 million hours were given in health and education agencies. Clearly, then, volunteers make a very substantial contribution to human services in Australia.

Of course, 'volunteers' have always been involved in human service delivery, if we conceptualise human services broadly to include the informal support offered within the community sphere. However, in the contemporary context, volunteers are more likely to be associated with non-government organisations. There has been a renewed emphasis on volunteering in recent years, particularly by Australian, North American and British policy-makers on both sides of politics.

Voluntarism: definitions and discourses

Volunteers may be defined as people who perform activities 'which are not socially required as a duty or responsibility' (Hoad, 2002, p. 239). This definition emphasises that what counts as 'volunteering' depends on the social context, and helps distinguish volunteers in the 'care division of labour' from informal carers and paid workers (Hoad, 2002). Another way of putting this is that the 'essence' of volunteering is '*voluntary* rather than *contractual*' (Hoad, 2002, p. 245, emphasis added). This has two implications. First is that volunteers 'cannot be obliged to take on any particular cases or to do specific tasks'—both of which are demanded, in different ways, from informal carers and paid workers. Second is that the ideal of voluntarism has become central in political ideologies, both left and right, that seek to set up the virtues of 'free and spontaneous citizen action' against the destructive force of modernity's 'formal organisations and social institutions', which are thought to undermine social capital and citizen activism (Salamon and Sokolowski, 2001, p. 1). Voluntarism, at the individual (volunteering) and organisational (voluntary organisations, or NGOs) levels, is held up by proponents as 'the needed solution to a vast array of social problems' (Salamon and Sokolowski, 2001, p. 1).

Within these discourses, voluntarism is valued as a representation of the spontaneous self-organisation of individuals in pursuit of collective goals. However, the findings of a study conducted in 24 countries challenge this 'romantic mythology' to show that volunteering is 'augmented rather than inhibited by a formal organisational base, which in turn grows because of state support' (Salamon and Sokolowski, 2001, p. 1). In other words, volunteering is an instrument and an outcome of *social policies*, rather than some kind of independent and self-willed alternative to them (Salamon and Sokolowski,

2001, p. 1). Despite its strong connection to policy, voluntarism remains an ideal imbued with values of individual altruism and community mindedness, manifest as personal willingness to help others. This ideal is opposed, by many proponents, practitioners and recipients of voluntary assistance, to what they see as the impersonal, regimented and often stigmatising services offered by professionals and other employees of human service organisations (Bagilhole, 1996, p. 201; Parrott et al., 2006, p. 153; Ronel, 2006, pp. 1143–46; Cloke et al., 2007, p. 1097).

Volunteers as organisational resources

Bringing these two elements together, we now turn our focus to volunteering as part of the social division of care labour in organisations that implement social policies. From the perspective of service-providing organisations, volunteers are attractive because their labour is relatively cost free compared to that of paid workers, and a supply of people is always available (Handy et al., 2006, p. 28). In addition to the attraction of low cost, there is the ideal of the volunteer as a warm altruist, who has something specific and unique to offer users of human services. This ideal can also have a halo effect for organisations for which volunteers can act as 'goodwill ambassadors' in local communities, providing public relations value that 'cannot be purchased by money donations' (Handy et al., 2006, p. 33). Drawing on volunteers, organisations may be able to offer additional, complementary types of assistance that paid workers normally do not undertake for a variety of reasons. For example, some kinds of services, such as 'befriending', which offers social support to isolated members of the community, seem particularly well suited to volunteer provision. 'Befriending' is a model of semi-structured social support by volunteers who are typically recruited, trained and supported by an NGO. Such programs are offered across the life course to support families (Parrott et al., 2006), children and young people (Wilkes et al., 2006) or older people (Andrews et al., 2003) and evaluation studies find that both volunteers and those they befriend report positive experiences (Andrews et al., 2003; Parrott et al., 2006; Wilkes et al., 2006).

However, volunteers are not entirely cost free to organisations: they may not receive payment for their work, but must be recruited, hired, trained, managed and supervised. Further, volunteers typically work relatively few hours and can stop working for an organisation with no penalty (Handy et al., 2006, p. 31). This means the supply of any particular volunteer's labour is inherently unstable. Further, some services are simply so demanding, in terms of skills required or power wielded, and some clients so vulnerable, that paid workers must assume responsibility in order to ensure the quality and integrity of services and manage liability issues. Thus, the policy of extending the use of volunteers in human service provision needs to be pursued with caution. For organisations that do work with volunteers, the issue of managing boundaries—between volunteers and paid workers, informal carers and service users—is crucial (Hoad, 2002). How organisations manage boundaries, and indeed the kind of boundaries they need to manage, depends on the activities the organisation undertakes and the organisational roles of its volunteers.

We know that policy-makers in some rich democracies have increasingly looked to voluntary organisations and volunteers to deliver human services in recent years, and one vehicle for expanding the use of volunteers has been contracting service provision out to NGOs. Indeed, in Australia for example, some public programs, such as the 'Families First' scheme established in New South Wales in 1998, have been partly built around volunteer service delivery organised by service providers paid under contract. Volunteering within organisations contracting to government to provide services, then, is increasingly common. Peter Hoad points out that contracting out has resulted in a 'bureaucratic rather than a communal/associational way of working', and has increased the likelihood that more explicit boundaries will be set 'around what volunteers are and are not expected to do' (2002, p. 241). Accordingly, there has been a tendency to formalise the roles and work of volunteers, and increase the use of specialised volunteer managers to recruit, train and supervise volunteers and publish advice on volunteer management proliferates (Healy et al., 2008, p. 6). Again, we see the impact of NPM as, on the one hand, contracting out increases the use of voluntary organisations in human services, while on the other, associated issues of contract compliance, risk management and liability affect how direct service providers (in this case, volunteers) engage in the process of human service delivery. Several researchers have argued that organisational change may undermine volunteers' motivations, and that it needs to be carefully managed to preserve their goodwill and commitment (Lie and Baines, 2007; Healy et al., 2008).

Volunteering: motivation, experience and impact

From the perspective of volunteers, research shows that participating in human service provision presents a range of benefits as well as risks. Benefits include the opportunity to participate in the broader community, learning new skills and having a sense of contributing (Lie and Baines, 2007, p. 230). This array of benefits suggests that volunteer motivations are complex, and research has confirmed this. Altruism, derived from a sense of social responsibility, ideological beliefs or values towards assisting others, is typically an important motivation. But it is not the only one. Liat Kulik's review of research on motivations points to several others that are more focused on meeting the volunteer's own needs, including forming relationships, feeling part of a community and gaining recognition from that community, perhaps 'to resolve internal conflicts, or to alleviate anxiety or guilt' (2006, p. 543). In her survey study of volunteers, Kulik also found that conformist motives (where volunteering was a normal behaviour in the respondents' community) and the desire to fill free time were present. Personal and other motivations are not necessarily in tension. Cloke and colleagues (2007, p. 1092) argue that 'the processes of giving and receiving are inseparable for volunteers', and that volunteering offers a 'bridge between ordinary ethics and a more deliberate performance of "ethical citizenship"'.

These motivations and associated benefits stress the ethical and personal dimensions of volunteering. However, studies of volunteering in disadvantaged communities often emphasise its *political* benefits for volunteers and communities. Mary Ohmer (2007), for example, studied neighbourhood organisations seeking to improve the local conditions of four poor neighbourhoods in a large American city in various ways. She found that the more volunteers participated in the everyday activities of and decision-making in an organisation, 'the greater their leadership competence, ability to influence government and neighborhood policy, knowledge and skills in neighborhood development, organisational collective efficacy, and sense of community' (Ohmer, 2007, p. 116). Given that volunteers are working to improve the community they live in, this finding suggests that participation, as a citizen, in determining and delivering services is a very valuable process.

Although their motivations are complex, and not only altruistic, there is evidence that the ideal of the altruistic volunteer is not simply mythological. Natti Ronel (2006) conducted a study of the impact of volunteers on the lives of at-risk youths living on the streets of Israeli cities. She found that, at the very well functioning service sites with stable volunteer bases, the youths' *perceptions* of the volunteers as 'representing pure altruism' (2006, p. 1133) was crucial to the impact on their lives of the services being offered. These young people, whose lives on the street were profoundly difficult, saw the 'possibility of survival without a constant struggle and a growing sense of a meaningful life' in the volunteers' willingness to accept and assist them without payment (2006, p. 1148). This finding does not mean that the volunteers in well functioning services were only motivated by altruism; rather it means that the symbolic value of giving can be powerful to *recipients* of volunteer service.

Volunteers are also exposed to some risks in human services work. Liat Kulik's study (2006, p. 547) divided the difficulties some volunteers experience into two categories: problems in their relations with provider organisations and those with service users. Volunteers' difficulties with provider organisations included ambiguity about the tasks to be performed, their sense that their time was not well used, and their perception that the organisation did not appreciate their work. Difficulties in relation to service users included a sense of frustration at their inability to improve service users' situations substantially, problems coping with service users' suffering, and problems dealing with service users' unrealistic expectations. Some of these issues could be conceptualised as managing boundaries (Bagilhole, 1996; Hoad, 2002) around the role of volunteers, their expectations of what can be achieved, and their relationships with service users.

Relationships between volunteers and paid workers in an organisation also involve careful management of boundaries and are a potential source of conflict. In the first instance, paid workers may feel that their jobs are threatened by volunteers (Baines, 2004, p. 283). Indeed, in Canada, for example, labour unions often seek provisions in collective agreements to protect paid staff from being replaced by volunteers (Handy et al., 2008). But there are also some more complex issues about division of labour between paid workers and volunteers. As we alluded to earlier, several studies have found that service users tend to view volunteers very differently from paid workers. The former are often seen as selfless allies who really make a difference; the latter as uninterested, unavailable and judgmental. Natti Ronel's (2006) study gives some insight into the psychology of this response, but is that all there is to it? We believe that there may be significant organisational factors that make it harder for paid human service workers, particularly those working in public human service organisations, to act on the altruistic dimensions of their motivations.

Volunteer services are often set up to be more open-ended than professional or public services, both in the *amount* and *kind* of service offered. As shown in the previous section, the ideal of negotiating with service users to meet their own needs is likely to be difficult to achieve in public services, which have constrained budgets and which are typically mandated to serve all who meet a defined threshold of need. Public services are also those with statutory responsibilities for child protection, and other more control-orientated dimensions of human services. In particular, volunteer-based programs are much more likely to be orientated towards meeting needs for *social* support. Yet there are examples of programs offered by voluntary agencies in which both paid and volunteer workers provide services that include social support (McLeod et al., 2008). Further, a British study of the relationships between young people in care and their social workers found that those who reported good experiences with social workers had very much the same kinds of responses as the young people in Ronel's study with volunteers (McLeod, 2008). Such studies do *not* find that service users always respond differently to paid workers as compared to volunteers. Particularly where paid workers are able to offer more mutually negotiated social support, service users comment on how their relationship with workers was a crucial positive element of the service experience.

The final point we make in this section is that paid human service practitioners may themselves work partly as 'volunteers' in their employing organisations. Donna Baines (2004) has documented the growth of unpaid work in stressed social service NGOs in Canada. Under the impact of NPM, she argues, a 'continuum of compulsion/coercion exists in many social service workplaces in which unwaged labour is extracted from workers through a series of subtle and explicit expectations' (2004, p. 282). Some of the work is voluntary, in the sense that it includes tasks such as fundraising that fall outside an employee's work role. Other unpaid work is not voluntary, but undertaken in the form of lunchtimes skipped and unpaid overtime, simply to keep up with caseloads (2004, p. 283). It is significant to note that several of Baines' interviewees saw their unpaid overtime as a 'form of resistance to narrow, uncaring social agendas both within and outside the workplace' and that many 'felt compelled to stretch an uncaring system in order to ease suffering' (2004, p. 284). These findings suggest that the motives of paid and volunteer social service workers are likely to be more similar than different, and that their different organisational positions affect their approaches to, and capacities in, human services practice.

Service users as co-implementers of social policy

Social policy is not something that 'happens to' users of human services—although for some, in some situations, the experience may feel very much like that. Because service processes are interpersonal, how service users receive and participate in human services has an impact on the implementation of the service, and so on policy outcomes. This is not to say that if social policy is ineffective, service users are responsible. One of the principal messages of this book and this chapter is that interpersonal service processes are embedded in organisational and broader social contexts that shape and constrain the behaviour and orientations of the individuals involved. Our aim in this section is to discuss some of the organisational and discursive structures and changes in the social policy field that have affected how service users are conceptualised and integrated into human services practice.

Two key developments have propelled service users to the forefront of official social policy debates in recent decades. One is the already much discussed New Public Management. With its roots in the economic theory of individual choice, NPM conceptualises service users as consumers or customers in the human services system (Clarke, 2006; Vabø, 2006; Scourfield, 2007b). Some NPM-inspired policies such as direct payments to service users even turn them into employers and managers of service providers and 'entrepreneurs' in the service system (Clarke, 2006, pp. 433–34; Scourfield, 2007b, p. 116). The second is the emergence of participatory social movements of service users themselves, particularly of people with disabilities. These movements have sought to empower service users in human service systems, drawing on democratic ideals of autonomy and self-determination (Beresford and Campbell, 1994; Cooper, 1999). There is some overlap between these two discourses of the service user, which share an emphasis on choice and participation. Nevertheless, they are fundamentally different, partly because choice and participation are protean concepts that can be used to describe quite different practical actions. As Peter Beresford and Jane Campbell put it, NPM is based in the 'politics of the market', while user movements are based in the 'politics of liberation' (1994, p. 316).

As a result of these developments, social policies in Australia, the UK and elsewhere now increasingly offer or mandate new forms of service user choice and participation in human services delivery. The relative impact of each of the two discourses on human services differs between places and kinds of human services. There is a consensus, however, among many social policy analysts in the UK, where debate around these issues (and perhaps policy development) has proceeded furthest: that the NPM conceptualisation of the service user as a customer making choices has had the most impact (Clarke, 2006; Scourfield, 2007; Glendinning, 2008). In the remainder of this section, through some examples taken from recent research, we examine how 'choice' and 'participation' by service users are being framed and enacted in the process of implementing social policy.

The service user as customer: consumer choice in human services

One new way service users have become involved in human service provision is through the extension of different kinds of 'customer choice' or 'consumer choice' models, which are often linked to privatisation and the introduction of voucher systems. School choice in education (Campbell et al., 2009), choice of care for people with disabilities or older people (Glendinning, 2008; Gustafsson and Szebehely, 2009), and patient choice in healthcare (Greener, 2008) have been changing the human services landscape in many countries in recent years. Services previously offered by a single, public provider on a 'catchment' basis are now increasingly offered by a range of providers from which service users choose. The stated aim of consumer choice models is to increase the responsiveness of human service providers to the diverse wants, needs and desires of service users, and to give service users more control over the human services they receive (Clarke, 2006, p. 425; Glendinning, 2008, pp. 458–59). As we saw earlier, one term used to describe this framing of service systems is 'personalisation'.

A large body of research has emerged to explore the impact of consumer choice models for service users and service systems, and to interrogate the assumptions underlying this approach to social policy. We cannot comprehensively discuss this work here. Rather, we highlight three points that emerge as consistent concerns in the research.

First, it is not clear that service users want choice over all, or perhaps even most, dimensions of human services. On one hand, there is evidence that many projected benefits of consumer choice are experienced by some kinds of service users, for some kinds of services, under some kinds of choice models. Specifically, among older people and people with disabilities who choose to take them up, outcomes are generally positive for various 'cash for care' or voucher systems for personal care, which give service users significant control over what services they receive and from whom (Arksey and Kemp, 2008). On the other hand, the desire for more choice and the evidence of benefits are much less clear for other kinds of services, such as health and education. Analysing patient choice in healthcare in the UK, Ian Greener found that 'the scope of choices required by patients may be over-estimated by the present policy. Patients do want choices about when they are treated, but are reticent to take responsibility for choosing where they are treated or for choosing the treatment they will receive' (2007, p. 256). The study by Craig Campbell and colleagues (2009) of school choice in Australia found that many parents experienced anxiety and frustration under the manufactured competition that school choice policies have created. Overall, as John Clarke and colleagues point out, the public has 'a positive disposition towards choice as an abstract principle and more negative responses or anxieties when choice is concretised in various ways' (2006, p. 330).

Second, it is not clear that consumer choice, modelled on markets for consumer goods and services (such as breakfast foods or hairdressing), is appropriate or even achievable in publicly financed human services. In practice, many human services are funded by governments on the basis of needs, even if service users match themselves with service providers in consumer choice models, or have formal input into the needs assessment process. There is tension between what service users might 'want' or would like to 'choose' and what, on the basis of assessed needs, is actually on offer. This means that what consumers actually have choice over is often constrained by the rules of the human service system. In the 'consumer choice' model of Swedish elder care, for example, service users in many municipalities can choose their *provider* from a list of public and private organisations, but they cannot choose *what services* they will receive because these are determined by needs assessment. As we saw in the earlier discussion of research by Foster and colleagues (2006), even where there are attempts to systematically include service users in defining what their needs are, and so what the services will be, organisational factors, especially budgetary concerns, constrain the extent to which service users' personal choices are explored and met.

Third, across the spectrum of human services, from the needs based (such as disability care) to the universal (such as school education), there are some worrying dynamic impacts of the 'choice revolution', as Paula Blomqvist (2004) calls it. Increasing inequality in access to services and in the quality of services received is one major concern across all human services. Service users with more capital, whether financial, social or cultural, are more likely to have their needs met in consumer choice systems than those with less capital (Blomqvist, 2004, p. 152; Clarke, 2006, pp. 436–37). The problem here is the incompatibility between consumer choice, as actualised in quasi-markets, and the more solidaristic principles that gave rise to collectively funded welfare services in the first place (Glendinning, 2008, p. 465).

Participation in decision-making in statutory services

The idea of choice has become strongly associated with a market orientation in human services through its links to the idea of the service user as a customer. The idea of *participation* retains some connection to the emancipatory discourse of user movements, and with the idea of the service user as a citizen. Like choice, participation is increasingly mandated in human service policies around the world, including in statutory services, which also involve an element of compulsion. In this section, we briefly explore some issues in participation in statutory child welfare, both of young people in the care system and of parents.

The goals of participation by children and young people in statutory care are broadly the same as the goals of choice in other human services: improving service responsiveness and quality by giving voice to the service user. Further, just as advocates of consumer choice in care for people with disabilities or older people argue that the ability to choose is a good in itself, so do advocates of participation by children and young people in the child welfare system, maintaining that it offers a range of benefits to children (Carr, 2004, pp. 8–9; McLeod, 2007, p. 279).

So what do researchers find when they assess the success of policies mandating participation for children and young people? They find that children and young people are able to articulate their needs and show understanding of how services could better meet them (Carr, 2004). This confirms the practical worth of the participation agenda, alongside the values-derived imperative contained in the United Nations Declaration of the Rights of the Child, which underpins the move to enhance participation in many countries. However, there are significant barriers to achieving the goal of participation, because this goal challenges profoundly the taken-for-granted organisational and power structures in the child welfare system (McLeod, 2007; Gunn, 2008). Confronting these barriers can lead to disillusionment and withdrawal by young people, who often find participation strategies tokenistic or meaningless, in the sense that they cannot see results of their participation in the form of change in policy and practice (Carr, 2004, p. 10). Because the barriers are now well understood, there exists a range of guidance on how organisations need to change in order to genuinely engage young people as service users (NSW Commission for Children and Young People, 2004; Wright et al., 2006). Strategies focus on supporting children and young people to participate and on changing organisational cultures and practices to enable children's voices to be heard. The challenge to overcoming identified barriers remains significant. As Alison McLeod puts it, drawing on the language of 'listening', which is central in the participation discourse in the UK, 'It could be that the biggest barrier to effective listening is when adults do not really want to hear what children have to say' (2007, p. 285).

The issue of *parental* participation in the child welfare system is also a significant and challenging one, not least because constructively engaging parents is critical to ensuring the safety of children at risk in vulnerable families. However, as Karen Healy's (1998) path-breaking analysis shows, the ideal of parent participation needs to confront the realities of child protection work if participation is to be realised. Healy argues that a relatively unthinking opposition of paternalism and participation in the discourse about participation has meant that the complex power relationships in child protection work are obscured. Statutory child welfare work can require that practitioners exercise statutory power to protect children. They can use this power productively as well as coercively or paternalistically (see chapter 3). For example, practitioners may find there is a need to control one member of a family to mitigate the risks faced by others.

Recognising the internal power dynamics within families can show that it is unhelpful to uncritically oppose coercive statutory or professional power (bad) to participatory practice that renounces power (good). If practitioners do not feel able to use productive power, children might be endangered; if practitioners do use statutory power while holding views against its use, they may feel guilt and self-blame about 'their failure to effect the kinds of practice relations and change processes they think ideal' (1998, p. 906). Practice should be participatory, but on a model that values reflexive and respectful professional judgment: 'workers cannot avoid judgment, but a participatory ethos demands that these judgments are reflectively applied and that workers are accountable to the families who are the subject of them' (Healy, 1998, p. 912).

This brief overview of ways service users are involved in implementing social policy is by no means exhaustive. We discussed in chapters 2 and 3 various ways service users are involved in the process of making social policy. Service users can also make a significant contribution to human service evaluation (Cortis, 2007), and in chapter 8 we consider a model of evaluation that strongly emphasises participation. There are also opportunities for service users and human service workers to collaborate in campaigns to maintain and improve the quality of both services and jobs (Folbre, 2006). In this way, those on both sides of the front line can work together to change social policy for the better.

Conclusion

Changes to the way service users are positioned in the social policy process have implications for organisations and workers delivering social care services. The perhaps disappointing findings on choice and participation do not discredit the democratic ideals that underpin some ways of framing these values. Rather, organisational change is required to support their fuller enactment.

Trust in all kinds of organisations, the public sector, NGOs and the professions, has declined in recent decades. Yet there are risks in replacing bureaucrats and professionals with informal or commodified service provision based on ideal typical models of the 'citizen-volunteer' and 'sovereign consumer'. It is important that participation and professionalism are not seen as opposed, although they often are in theory and can be in practice. In a post-traditional world, professionalism remains an important ground for a values base in human services work. It takes significant skill and a strong values base to manage the often complex and competing needs and demands of service users, and to mediate these needs and demands within service systems.

A key lesson from this chapter is that practitioner commitment to high quality, service user-orientated practice is important, and professionalism can be one resource to support practitioner commitment. However, all human service practitioners need the opportunity to work in organisations that more unequivocally support high quality, service user-orientated practice goals. This suggests that organisational analysis and critique, and partnerships among practitioners and between practitioners and service users, are important dimensions of human services practice. In our next chapter, we consider the role of research in social policy.

CHAPTER 8

Evidence: the role of research in policy and practice

Introduction

Research is critically important in social policy practice. It can inform all stages of the policy process, from identifying problems and designing and comparing possible solutions to evaluating outcomes. Indeed, in recent decades, the 'evidence-based policy' movement has contended that research is perhaps *the* most important input into the policy process, on the assumption that it establishes a rational foundation for policy development, analysis and review. At the same time, research capacity within human service organisations is growing, and human service practitioners are increasingly expected to ground their practice decisions in 'the evidence', and to participate in research projects.

On the face of it, the increasing use of research in the social policy field seems to be an unalloyed good. Social policy intervenes in the lives of individuals, sometimes very intrusively in services such as child welfare and, as we saw in chapter 5, social spending commands a significant proportion of national resources in most rich democracies. Surely, then, using research to assess whether social policy interventions are as efficient and effective as possible is critical to good governance. However, as we show in this chapter, the goal of social policy based purely on rational scientific grounds has proved elusive. The reasons are complex. They touch on some of the most fundamental issues in the philosophy of science and the nature of human institutions.

In this chapter, we aim to give a sense of this complexity by examining the links between research, social policy and human service practice. We argue that although the idea of evidence is far more complex than often portrayed, research does play a crucial role in the social policy arena, as it should, and human service professionals can gain much by participating in research activity. To this end, we include an extended discussion of evaluation, which is the research activity that human service practitioners are most likely to engage in. However, we also argue that evidence does not, and perhaps cannot, replace politics in defining and alleviating social problems.

Evidence: why it has been promoted

As we have seen in chapter 2, technocratic policy-making, associated with the ethos of New Public Management, assumes that policy-making is a rational endeavour underpinned by scientific method (Stewart, 1999; Wells, 2007). This approach to policy has proved influential in the development of policy options and in decision-making processes. It has also led to the extension of the research capacity of government and non-government human service agencies and the proliferation of think tanks (see chapter 3). These research organisations, together with research consultants, not only work towards producing 'evidence', but also look at ways of linking 'evidence' to accountability, so that public funds can be seen to be well spent (Egan, 2008). Proponents of evidence-based *policy* see it as a key means of ensuring accountability, defined in terms of making the best possible use of public funds. Evidence-based *practice* is integrally related as a means of carrying this agenda forward into the field (MacDonald et al., 1992). However, at this stage, it is useful to unpack some of the underlying assumptions that surround the idea of 'evidence'.

Evidence: what is it and who decides?

One reason why research evidence cannot replace politics in the social policy field is that what constitutes evidence is itself contested. In some sense, therefore, the debate about the nature of evidence and the proper conduct of social policy research is itself political. One way of understanding the debate about what constitutes evidence is to envisage the various positions as lying along a continuum. At one end is a positivist, linear, rational framework that takes natural science as its model (see, for example, MacDonald et al., 1992). At the other end is a post-structural orientation, in which science and rationality are depicted as a form of discourse and evidence is understood as a reflection of the power-knowledge interplay operating in a particular situation (see, for example, Holmes et al., 2006). There are also, clearly, many positions in between.

There is much debate among researchers and within the human service professions about what counts as evidence. However, this diversity of positions is not reflected in official approaches to using research in policy and practice. Indeed, the idea that authoritative knowledge can only be produced by methods modelled on the natural sciences has become dominant among policy-makers over the last two decades. The Department of Health UK (1999), for example, sets out a clear hierarchy of evidence in 'The National Service Framework for Mental Health' in England and Wales. Type one, which is regarded as the most important, incorporates quantitatively orientated, randomised, controlled trials and systematic reviews. Type five, the least important, refers to expert opinion, which includes the views of service users and practitioners. In Australia, a recent paper by Andrew Leigh (2009), a member of the highly influential Social Policy Division of the Department of Treasury, discussed two such hierarchies in use by the UK Cabinet Office and the US government, with a view to advising Australian social policy-makers on what evidence they should use. Leigh comes to much the same conclusion as other technocratic policy advisers and researchers: systematic reviews or meta-analyses of multiple, randomised, controlled trials come at the top of the hierarchy and expert opinion and theoretical conjecture come at the bottom.

Thus, there is a sense in which, at least at the level of official definition, a clear account is given of what counts as 'good' evidence. Yet, as we shall see in the following sections, in practice the relationships between evidence and policy and evidence and practice are far from straightforward.

Politics and science in evidence-based policy

Nick Black (2001) points out that linear, rational perspectives tend to assume that research findings from meta-analyses, randomised controlled trials and large-scale observational studies can quite directly inform policy aims and outcomes. The broad span of linear, rational perspectives can be seen to encompass the technocratic approach to policy development and the rational policy process described in chapter 2.

A study by Christopher Jewell and Lisa Bero (2008) exemplifies this approach. Jewell and Bero examined the experiences of state legislators and administrators in the US to identify the 'facilitators' and 'hindrances' they faced in incorporating evidence into health policy-making. The barriers Jewell and Bero identified include competing sources of influence such as interest group pressure, limited budgets, political values and the difficulties involved in determining the usefulness and validity of different forms of evidence. The researchers do recognise that there are 'characteristics of the political setting that hinder evidence-informed decision-making' (2008, p. 183), including the role of political commitments and election promises in driving policy. They also highlight ways of addressing some of the barriers to the use of evidence, such as collaborative networking (2008, pp. 202–204) and 'evidence based skills training' for officials (2008, pp. 199–201). However, Jewell and Bero equate 'high quality information' with scientifically orientated research techniques such as randomised controlled trials, and continue to demonstrate the technocratic belief that there is an underlying rational relationship between certain research methodologies and good policy formulation. In this, it is implied that if only policy-making was not so political, and decision-makers were more like scientists, 'good' evidence would be produced and be available for use by policy-makers.

However, linear rational perspectives have been criticised by researchers who emphasise the *politics* of policy-making. Nick Black (2001) argues that there are too many competing ideas and interests for policy to be directly based on quantitative or even qualitative forms of research. In a similar vein, Alan France and David Utting (2005) refer to 'policy based evidence' rather than 'evidence-based policy' and argue that policy-makers have their own interests, which they will seek to support with available evidence. Alex Stevens (2007) uses a biological metaphor to explore the politics of the relationship between research evidence and social policy. Making an analogy with the process of evolution, he argues that a variety of ideas come from research and compete for attention in policy circles. He maintains that some of these will fit the interests of powerful groups and obtain strong support and some will not. He refers to this process as the survival of the 'fittest', with those findings that do 'fit' being translated into policy and those that do not withering away.

To illustrate his argument, Stevens refers to research carried out by Roger Zetter and colleagues (2003) as part of a Home Office study in the United Kingdom. Zetter and colleagues investigated the impact that asylum policies in different countries in Europe had had on the number of asylum seekers. They found that direct pre-entry measures, such as visas and sanctions on airlines, had the greatest impact on the number of asylum claimants, while responses, such as reception and detention centres and the withdrawal of welfare benefits, had a much more limited effect. They also discovered that, across the board, restrictive policies had consequences that included increased illegal immigration and the displacement of asylum seekers to other countries. Stevens (2007) points out that publication of this research was delayed for two years, and the findings were only selectively released by government officials. This approach allowed the least effective measures to be promoted by the government because they had the best 'fit' with the political priorities of the time.

Can research change policy?

The two positions we have just considered in the previous section—the technocratic and the political—are pessimistic about the role of research in policy-making in different ways. Those holding a technocratic view have an underlying belief in the power of science to inform rational policies, but lament the lack of skill and will among politicians to act on the best evidence. Those holding what we might call the 'strongly political' view are more likely to see power, ideological conflict and political expedience as overwhelming evidence in any particular situation. Wherever one might sit on the spectrum of approaches to what counts as evidence, it seems clear that research evidence, whatever the methodology used, is unlikely to be the *sole* determinant of policy change because there are too many agendas and influences operating.

However, this is not to suggest that research evidence cannot constructively influence major shifts in policy. There is a middle way, exemplified in a study by Carol Weiss (1979). Weiss argued that research has a cumulative rather than a direct influence on the climate of opinion in which decisions are made. She used a geological rather than a biological metaphor to describe this process, which she called the 'limestone effect', because evidence seems to seep into policy gradually and in unpredictable ways. As a result, she argued that different research studies and forms of research have influenced attitude change over time, in tandem with media interest, political movements and cause champions. A consequence of the limestone effect is that it is impossible to gauge which evidence informs which policy and the extent to which popular opinion influences policy or vice versa.

An historical example of the 'limestone effect' is Ann Oakley's ground-breaking study of housework, published in 1974. This case shows how one study, together with a range of divergent views coming from second wave feminism, equal opportunties debates and media commentary, had a significant effect on policy. Oakley's study examined women's feelings about housework, their orientation to the housewife role and the ways in which their feelings and orientation were mediated by social class. In relation to 'feelings about housework', it was notable that the majority of the 40 respondents talked about their dissatisfaction with the monotony of housework. Low status, loneliness and a long working week also featured as problems. The women valued the autonomy they experienced as housewives, but also imposed onerous standards and routines on themselves to make sense of the tasks involved.

A significant and influential aspect of Oakley's study was the way in which she linked her findings to the discipline of sociology and the position of women as a whole. She contested the male view of sociology as neutral and value free, drawing attention to the predominance of male-orientated values dressed up in objective clothing. She also highlighted the gendered division of work, both outside and inside the home, and focused on the operation of sexist practices. Oakley's findings and conceptual links may appear dated now, but this itself is testimony to the influence of the evidence and the impact that her research and analysis has had on changing views and policies.

Similarly, groundbreaking policy changes associated with equal opportunities and anti-racist agendas have resulted from a combination of research evidence, media interest and pressure group activity forging a climate in which such legislation became inevitable. However, it also needs to be acknowledged that policies regarded as progressive can be *subverted* by the selective use of research evidence and by media attention. The intervention in the Northern Territory in Australia in 2007, discussed in more detail in chapter 10, is a case in point. Here the influential report, *Ampe Akelyernemane Meke Mekarle*/Little Children are Sacred (Anderson and Wild, 2007) was used to justify the suspension of the Racial Discrimination Act (1975) so that punitive measures could be imposed solely on Aboriginal families living in the Northern Territory.

Policy change can also occur as a result of evidence coming from a variety of different sources. An example here is clinical research linking toxic stress and disruption in the architecture of the developing brain to causative factors such as poverty, physical or emotional abuse, chronic neglect and family violence (National Childhood Council on the Developing Child, 2007). These findings have served to strengthen policies aimed at intervention in the early years in disadvantaged communities. This research, clearly undertaken within the paradigm of the natural sciences, can be seen to have added to the evidence base and to have increased the pressure that has long been coming from a variety of directions, including human service professionals, for coherent policy-making and resources to be directed towards this area. Early intervention programs such as 'Families First' in New South Wales (The Office of Children and Young People, NSW, 2004) and 'Communities for Children' and 'Early Childhood—Invest To Grow', which operate Australia wide (FaHCSIA, n.d.), have subsequently been given priority in Australia.

Evidence-based practice: knowledge in the work of human service practitioners

As we noted earlier, calls for social *policy* to be more rigorously informed by the best evidence have come alongside calls for human services *practice* also to become 'evidence based'. Prominent exponents of evidence-based practice in the UK, Geraldine Macdonald and colleagues (1992), argue that rigorous, objective and empirically based studies serve as essential and effective counters to subjective assumptions and judgments informed by individual experience and ideology. They argue that a systematic approach to research and dissemination can produce effective, efficient practices and services that generate consistent results. This approach focuses on measuring quality and performance and, in line with rationally orientated policy perspectives, is attractive to policy analysts and policy-makers. Over recent years in the UK, this approach has featured significantly in child protection (Macdonald, 1998) and in mental health (DoH, 1999).

However, in a similar way to policy based on linear rational perspectives, evidence-based practice and the measurability of social processes and interventions by the application of scientific method has been subject to much critique. It has been argued that despite the prominence of the evidence-based practice movement with associated practice guidelines, most practice fails to follow an evidence-based format. This can be attributed to the complexities of practice, to continued contentions about what constitutes usable evidence, and to the capacity of the resource systems available to professionals (Clarke, 2007; Black, 2001). As a result, it can be maintained that while most of the hierarchies of evidence-based practice focus on research questions relating to effectiveness, this does little to help professionals engage in therapeutic or empowering relationships with service users or create enabling environments. Accordingly, the environment in which practitioners use evidence must be understood as complex, ambiguous, multifaceted and context-specific, and the nature of evidence itself has to be viewed broadly.

Stephen Webb (2001) is also critical of a narrow view of evidence-based practice based on scientific method. He draws attention to how prioritising quantitative evidence can entrap those working in the field into mechanistic forms of technical rationality, where only certain forms of action are considered legitimate. He argues that evidence-based practice, which has strong scientific undertones, assumes that human service workers engage in an epistemic process of sorting and prioritising information, which they then use to optimise practice to its best effect. He contests the underlying emphasis on rationality, logical decision-making and the axioms of a behavioural probability calculus, and maintains that complexity, differential interests and context play a critical role in practice decisions. He asserts that human service workers who operate in open and contingent environments cannot perform as logical, rational agents. They must use their own knowledge and experiences, as well as professional values and commonsense, to inform their decisions. As a result, these aspects should not be discredited by being contrasted to a methodology that is both unachievable and inappropriate.

It is clear that the nature of evidence and how it is constituted will continue to be much debated in the human services. Exponents of scientific, positivist and quantitative orientations will continue to challenge qualitative researchers for failing to provide measures of validity, reliability and generalisability. In turn, modernist ideals of scientific objectivity and positivism will continue to be criticised by post-structural and post-modern deconstructive analyses. In the human services, this is not to discredit the idea of evidence, nor to say that, in relation to evidence, anything goes. Rather, our aim is to draw attention to the need to interrogate critically the nature of the evidence provided in a situation, and ensure that the methodological process (which can be quantitative, qualitative or mixed method) is both transparent and justifiable.

Evaluation for practice: human service practitioners as researchers

As we have highlighted in this book, social policy operates at many different levels, which include the macro, meso and the micro. Social policy frameworks are developed within tiers of national and sub-national governments (which include state, provincial or local government), as well as within small-scale policy systems (including professional associations and social service organisations). Although what constitutes evidence is contested, and the connections between research evidence, policy and practice are not clear-cut, it is important to reinforce the message that research can influence policy at all levels, including the micro. It does so by drawing attention to policy gaps, deficits and ideological underpinnings, as well as to how well or otherwise a service or initiative is working. Thus, evidence will continue to play an important role in human services. Further, despite some reluctance to research their practice, human service professionals have a valuable part to play in the production of useful evidence. At this point, it is useful to provide a brief overview of the kinds of social policy and practice research that have the greatest relevance for those working in the human services.

Quantitative and qualitative orientations can characterise opposing positions and ideological stances, as seen earlier in this chapter. However, both are applicable in the human services if the evidence created is subject to ongoing critical scrutiny. Further, just as qualitative approaches vary from content analysis to phenomenology and discourse analysis, quantitative orientations also vary between studies conducted within a positivist, scientific frame and those that use statistical measures but do not claim neutrality or to be producing incontrovertible facts. In chapter 10, for example, we discuss how quantitative measures were used by the Labour government in the UK to determine the extent to which the educational targets for 'looked after' children had been met. This research, which looked at the number of children in the care system who obtained a specific educational qualification, clearly lent itself to statistical analysis. This analysis, in turn, enabled the outcomes of the care system to be clearly publicised and appraised. Mixed method research, which includes both qualitative and quantitative components, is also increasingly being seen as a valuable methodological strategy. Here people's views, understandings and meanings can be investigated qualitatively, using a quantitative statistical mapping of the area under review as a valuable complement (Cresswell, 2003; Bryman, 2006). Action research, where findings are continually used to inform the further development of a project or service, is also gaining ground (Fawcett, 2001). This form of research, which can easily be practitioner led, can enable human service professionals to obtain information on how services are operating and who the beneficiaries are. Further, many research projects in the human services, particularly those being carried out in the arena of disability, are emphasising the importance of participation so that the various stakeholders, including service users, are actively involved in carrying out the research (Moore et al., 1998; Beresford, 2006; Cortis, 2007).

Research frameworks can be devised in a variety of ways, but all should adhere to some key principles and tasks to ensure transparency and rigour in the conduct of the research, and to facilitate critical scrutiny of methods and findings. These principles and tasks include exploring the available literature or research findings on the area to be researched, considering ethical issues at the outset, deciding on a quantitative, qualitative or mixed method orientation, clarifying the research aim and related objectives, operating in accordance with the available resources, and clearly articulating and linking data collection methods and data analysis techniques to the research question.

Evaluations are essentially indistinguishable from other forms of research in terms of design, quantitative, qualitative or mixed method otientation, data collection methods and data analysis techniques (Bryman, 2008). However, evaluative research is research with a purpose, because it seeks to establish the value or worth of a service or initiative. As with evidence, power dynamics can affect evaluative research, in terms of who decides what constitutes value or worth. Those who conduct evaluations and use their findings need to pay attention to this possibility. There are also a number of different types of evaluative study. These include outcome evaluations, which focus on the extent to which specific objectives have been met; process evaluations that address 'what' and 'how' questions, such as how older people are being referred to a particular service, and evaluations of evaluations, where an existing evaluative report is looked at with fresh eyes to appraise what might have been missed, the robustness of the methodology used and the ways in which the findings have been interpreted.

Formative approaches can be linked to action evaluations by putting an evaluative framework in place at the start of a project and continually feeding the findings into the development of a project or service. By contrast, summative evaluations concentrate on reviewing whether the outcomes have been met at the end of a project. Another model is pluralistic or stakeholder evaluation, which recognises that different interest groups have different concerns, with different evaluative components being set up to address these. An example of a pluralistic model is an evaluation of a residential care home, where one aspect of the evaluation focuses on staff, another on residents and another on family members, with each aspect having a separate aim and set of associated objectives. After each aspect has been evaluated, the various findings are then compared and contrasted to produce the overall evaluation (Robson, 2002; Bryman, 2008).

Action evaluation: a model for human service practitioners

Action evaluation can be seen as a way of enabling human service practitioners to evaluate their practice constructively (Fawcett, 2001). Although, as discussed in the previous section, there are many forms of evaluation, this section presents an example of a form of action evaluation drawn up by one of the authors that has been successfully used in human service agencies (Fawcett, 2003). The intention here is to illustrate a staged methodological approach that can be easily adapted for use by human service professionals.

Action evaluation is a form of formative evaluation that enables findings to continually feed into and inform policy, practice and service developments. It is inclusive, in that all stakeholders are involved in deciding the extent and nature of their involvement. It is also 'bottom up', in that it is concerned with what is happening on the ground. As with all approaches to research and evaluation, there are clearly positive and negative features of action evaluation. Problems can emerge if the findings are moulded to fit expectations, or taken out of context to justify sweeping changes or used to 'show' that an evaluation is taking place without any intention of paying attention to process or outcomes. Participation can also be tokenistic, and inadequate resources can result in an evaluation failing to deliver to any significant extent. However, the stages outlined below do give human service professionals a framework for action, which can play a part in bringing about change in both social policy and human services practice.

Table 8.1   Action Evaluation Framework

Involve	All those connected to the project
Clarify	The level of involvement in the evaluation
Produce	An ethical statement for all participants in the evaluation
Outline	The current situation in the project
Specify	The available resources for the evaluation The overall aim and the specific objectives of the project The long-term outcomes and time scale The medium-term outcomes and time scale The short-term outcomes and time scale
Link	Each long-term, medium-term and short-term outcome to each specific objective of the project
Detail	The rationale for the project
Monitor	The activity and the processes involved in the project
Review	The progress (or lack of it) towards the specified long-term, medium-term and short-term outcomes
Detail	Why progress (or lack of it) has occurred in the project
Review	The objectives and specified outcomes of the project
Document	The changes to the objectives and the specified outcomes of the project
Feed	The findings of the evaluation into the development of the project
Complete	The evaluation by finalising the report

Action evaluations may be carried out in several different ways (Hart and Bond, 1995), but the framework given here operates as both an evaluative plan and a checklist to facilitate practitioner-orientated evaluative research activity. This framework focuses on involving practitioners, managers and service users. Those with experience of a service have the most to contribute to any evaluation, although ways of involving service users have to be carefully thought through. This necessitates paying considerable attention to the practical questions of participation, including the funding of travel expenses, childcare, training and so on. It also has to be emphasised that service users need to be involved in ways that are meaningful to them and which avoid jargon and organisationally standardised ways of operating. In a similar manner, the level and extent of involvement needs to be discussed and clarified, because involvement can mean many different things, from being consulted about key aspects, to full participation in the planning and operation of all the evaluative stages. As well as carefully thinking through how to involve key participants, the production of an ethical statement at the outset highlighting how an action evaluation is to be conducted is also important. This needs to be short and to the point, but has to include assurances of confidentiality that take on board the need for action if the evaluation identifies an area requiring immediate attention. Examples could be a human service professional whose practice appears to differ from that expected, or a service user whose personal issues make continued involvement in the evaluation inappropriate.

In any evaluation, baseline information relating to the situation at the start of the evaluation is essential. This enables developments to be tracked and, as it highlights key areas of activity or concern, helps to shape the future direction of the service or project. Both quantitative and qualitative information can be collected at this point. Quantitative information can include, for example, the number of women and men using a particular service or project, with relevant details being collected about ethnicity, cultural background, age, residential location and so on. Qualitative information can focus on how the service or project has been experienced, what works and what does not work so well, where the gaps are and how these can best be met. It may also be useful for those involved in carrying out the action evaluation to visit similar or related services or projects, so that ideas and information can be obtained to inform discussion with service users about the sort of service they would like to see developed. Attention has also to be paid to the resources available to carry out the evaluation. These include human resources and overall capacity as well as money. Evaluations often fail because there are insufficient resources to implement the evaluative plan.

Action evaluations facilitate the appraisal or the drawing up of the aim, linked objectives and outcomes of a service or project. The aim refers to the broad overall purpose, which is then clearly broken down into a set of associated objectives. The objectives can, in turn, be linked to long-term, medium–term and short-term outcomes. So, if the overall aim is to improve services for older people from culturally and linguistically diverse backgrounds, linked objectives could be to develop an advocacy service and produce outreach materials in appropriate languages. Each objective can then be matched to the outcome that is expected at the end of a given time frame. For example, the long-term outcome could be set as '40 volunteer advocates to be working with older people from culturally and linguistically diverse backgrounds by the end of year two'. Medium-term outcomes are then designed to make and ensure progress towards this longer-term objective. For example, the outcome for the end of year one could be set as 'the creation of a volunteer advocacy network with associated training and support networks'. Working back yet again, at the end of the first six months the outcome could be to produce information about how other agencies have created volunteer advocacy networks. In some action evaluations, only the objectives, not the accompanying outcomes are specified, because the project or service is new or exploratory and so to specify outcomes at the start of the evaluation could limit the developmental nature of the project or service. Changes may need to be made as a result of inadequate resources or altered circumstances, but it is important to always be clear about the overall aim, specific objectives, outcomes and associated time frames at any particular point. This ensures that the evaluation does not lose its clarity and its potential to influence policy.

As part of the action evaluation process, it is also useful to include and continue to update an accompanying rationale within the overall evaluative framework. This relates to the reasons why the aim, objectives and outcomes of the project or service were decided upon, and the grounds for any changes that may have occurred. This ensures that what is being evaluated and the accompanying reasons remain clear to all concerned so that the evaluation retains its overriding relevance. Monitoring activity—what happens after the gathering of baseline information—is carried out by the regular collection of quantitative and qualitative information. Quantitative material can be collected by the establishment of systematic monitoring mechanisms to keep a record of key aspects of the project. In this, it is important not to try to collect too much data and to disentangle significant from interesting but not crucial material. This also prevents practitioners from feeling overwhelmed with paperwork and helps to sustain interest in the evaluation. The information then needs to be collated and entered in a database regularly. Qualitative information also needs to be regularly collected and analysed. Once a decision has been made by those involved in the evaluation about what information to collect, this can be obtained by means of diary sheets, 'pro forma' data collection devices, interviews or a combination of these.

An action evaluation would then continue to review progress towards the long, medium and short-term outcomes and the matched objectives, highlighting any blocks or difficulties encountered. This ensures that the activity is set within its overall context and facilitates the production of reports reviewing the data and relating it to the project or service. These reports can be discussed with all those involved and be used to develop the project or service further. It also enables the overriding aim and specific linked objectives and outcomes to be reviewed regularly to ascertain their continued relevance and viability.

With regard to the service they are involved in, this practical example of an action evaluation framework enables practitioners, service users and managers to obtain a clear picture of what is going on, what is or is not working well, and why. Although exponents of positivist quantitative orientations would argue that those involved in a project or service cannot be involved in an evaluation of it because they cannot be objective, the argument is rapidly losing credibility as, despite the influence of technocratic opionion, it becomes increasingly difficult to justify scientific claims of objectivity in the social sphere. As Bryman (2008) highlights, provided an evaluation is carried out in a transparent, structured, comprehensive and reflexive manner, the findings can be seen to provide evidence which can then be used to influence policy at a range of levels.

How practitioners can communicate research

To make a difference to social policy at the micro, meso or macro levels, the findings of social policy and evaluative research findings need to be effectively disseminated. As highlighted in this chapter, findings can be selectively used or ignored if they contradict major policy platforms, but even if this does happen, the evidence produced can be used to open up areas for discussion and to generate debate. As indicated in chapter 3, one key way of doing this is to engage the media and ensure that journalists specialising in social policy and human services are aware of research or evaluative research projects and their implications. Producing and distributing accessible and regularly updated bulletins to a range of significant players can also assist in effective dissemination, as can the strategic involvement of agency media or public relations officers.

It is also important to note that changes in policy at the micro or meso levels can be brought about by including senior agency personnel, together with influential external figures, in a project from the outset. This can serve to put in place key building blocks for change, including consideration of the processes necessary to achieve change within organisations. Where relevant, major funding bodies, such as national charities or government research councils, can also be brought into the frame to support and publicise findings.

Conclusion

Clearly, 'evidence' is a contested concept, and its relationship to policy and practice is such that it is rarely possible to identify a direct connection. Nevertheless, it is possible to assert that research and evaluation have a valuable contribution to make in the field of human services. Of course, as we have highlighted throughout this chapter, all 'evidence' has to be subject to critical scrutiny in terms of its production and use. In this, human service professionals have a role to play both in initiating and carrying out research and evaluative research projects, so that they can produce, utilise, justify and scrutinise the production of evidence for themselves. This enables human service practitioners and organisations to make a strong case for change to policy and practice, for governments and organisations to take a proactive rather than a reactive stance and for increased resources to be made available to meet the needs of vulnerable citizens.

In chapters 9, 10 and 11, we engage in critical policy analysis to investigate several potential paths for social policy development: reorientation, radical reform and re-invigoration.

CHAPTER 9

Changing social policy: reorientation through social inclusion?

Introduction

'Social inclusion' has become a core framework that governments in the British and Australian welfare states are using to reorientate social policy. As we mentioned in chapter 5, the concept of social inclusion has emerged as one of several new ways of thinking about social and economic disadvantage. Its conceptual distinctiveness and utility have been related to the way it broadens conventional frameworks that link disadvantage and inequality to poverty, and define poverty narrowly as lack of resources. It has been suggested that a social inclusion framework provides an important bridge between discussions of poverty, equality and citizenship, and provides a basis for understanding social and economic differences between groups and individuals in nations (Jones and Smyth, 1999). The framework does this through its focus on the extent to which individuals and social groups are able to participate in the economic, social, political and cultural life of their society.

In this chapter, we argue that in the UK and Australia, the social inclusion agenda needs to be considered as closely intertwined with another highly influential approach to social policy: the welfare-to-work or 'workfare' agenda. The two are coupled because the dominant way that social inclusion has been enacted in policy has been by framing *economic* participation as the path to full social participation. In the context of these dual agendas, a primary goal of social inclusion policy has been increasing the level of employment among adults of working age who, in the past, might have been outside the labour market and been reliant on income support. Underpinning the social inclusion framework is a dominant and often unquestioned assumption that paid employment for all is the route to inclusion and therefore the solution to achieving greater equality.

The chapter explores the discourses of social inclusion and social exclusion, and describes how they have been taken up in contemporary contexts. We examine the implications of this new framework for the people who are the target of social inclusion policies, and the human service practitioners who mediate or deliver social policies. Our aim is to show, through critical policy analysis, how human service practitioners can be assisted to work towards positive change by understanding the conceptual underpinnings and practical consequences of shifts in the ways social policy frames social problems and their solutions.

Reorientating the social policy framework: the rise of 'social inclusion'

The shift from neo-liberal or neo-conservative governments to labour (or social liberal) parties in power in countries such as Australia, New Zealand and the UK has been accompanied by a reorientation of social policy around the concept of social inclusion. The policy concept of social inclusion has several sources. However, it clearly emerged from the idea and understanding of social *exclusion*. The social exclusion concept is often cited as emerging in the 1970s, when a member of the French Government observed that one in ten people were among '*les exclus*' or outcast from mainstream French society, and argued for the state taking responsibility for remedying this situation, particularly for people suffering major disabilities, addictions or other health problems (Davies, 2005, p. 4; Beall, 2002, pp. 44–45). A core aspect of this conceptualisation was not only the recognition that excluded people who suffered poverty, but also that they were alienated from broader national political and social processes and goals.

'Social exclusion' captures the ways in which some groups and individuals are excluded from the ordinary living patterns, customs and activities of the broader community. The concept has been built on an extensive foundation of scholarly literature that began describing how neo-liberalism created social exclusion (Sen, 1997; 2000; Cousins, 1998; Silver, 1994), and was concerned with how groups such as women, ethnic minority groups or people with disabilities, as well as different social classes, were included in or excluded from different welfare regimes and across different nation states. Peter Whiteford's reminder that 'Not all low-income people are excluded from society, nor do all excluded people have low income' (2001, p. 66) underscores the significance of this concept.

This kind of analysis of disadvantage has led to demands for social policies that enhance social inclusion and social participation (Bittman, 1998, p. 1). It has also led to the development of new measures of disadvantage. Within a social inclusion framework, for example, a broad range of factors is considered relevant, such as experience of social connectedness, access to services, social integration, political engagement, capacity to overcome personal crises, various health, housing and education measures, as well as access to paid work and income (Richardson and Le Grand, 2004; Atkinson et al., 2002). However, despite this more broad-ranging approach to measuring disadvantage, social inclusion strategies often remain focused on the idea of *economic* participation as the path to full social participation.

Doug Porter and David Craig argue that social inclusion has its roots in a global movement for a new liberalism, a post free-market liberalism that they see as emerging from two distinct dimensions (2004, p. 390). The first dimension is a reactionary one in response to neo-liberalism's lack of durability, repeated global economic crises in the past two decades, the failure to address world poverty, violent protests against globalisation and the 'collapse of social service delivery' (Porter and Craig, 2004, pp. 390–391). The second dimension, they argue, is more pro-active, based on 'an expansion of inclusions', which can be seen as a 're-framing and reconstitution of society and political economy' and a way of connecting many liberal spheres of interests, programs and groups (Porter and Craig, 2004, p. 391). They write, 'whereas a previous neo-liberalism would have left [the poor, the marginal, the child] to sink or swim in the frank market, "inclusive" liberalism won't let them get away so easily. Their right to be included comes with an obligation' (2004, pp. 392–93)—an obligation to work, or to work towards working.

Porter and Craig argue that 'expanding inclusions' is a way of creating order where society has become increasingly fractured or factionalised between the 'haves' and the 'have-nots', those who had a job and were part of the neo-liberal project and those who did not have a job and were excluded from the neo-liberal project. This positioning of social inclusion as a global political and ideological trend is important for understanding the broader context of national policy-making. However, for most human service professionals, the social inclusion framework is most relevant at the national or local level, and we focus primarily on these levels in this chapter.

Social exclusion and inclusion in the United Kingdom

Social inclusion in the national context began its governmental career in the UK in the diagnosis of the problem to which it would be the solution: social *exclusion*. In 1997, the Blair Labour Government established an interdepartmental Social Exclusion Unit, initially to develop new approaches to the 'problems of the worst housing estates' (Social Exclusion Unit, 1997, p. 2). The unit then went on to develop a range of policy initiatives and a much broader 'social exclusion agenda'. In the UK, social exclusion and poverty are devolved responsibilities and the Social Exclusion Unit was a strategy for England. Similar bodies, however, were established in Scotland (The Social Inclusion Strategy), Wales (Building an Inclusive Wales) and Northern Ireland (Targeting Need in Northern Ireland).

Following its establishment, the Social Exclusion Unit identified three 'strands' in its response to social exclusion. The first comprised the 'New Deals' for unemployed people, lone parents and disabled people. The second comprised new funding programs to support the regeneration of poor neighbourhoods, and the third aimed at developing a 'joined-up' approach of cross-departmental groups to ensure access to services and to improve the way governments at all levels responded to social exclusion (Percy-Smith, 2000). Related policy and program developments included the introduction of welfare-to-work programs, tax and benefit changes to address low-income poverty, increased funding to schools and early years services in the poorest areas, the introduction of individual payments for social care, and the introduction of community regeneration and neighbourhood renewal strategies in disadvantaged public housing estates.

These strategies were developed in response to the following 'problem definition' by the Social Exclusion Unit (2001, p. 10), which described social exclusion as:

a short–hand term for what can happen when people or areas have a combina-tion of linked problems, such as unemployment, discrimination, poor skills, low incomes, poor housing, high crime and family breakdown. These problems are linked and mutually reinforcing. Social exclusion is an extreme consequence of what happens when people don't get a fair deal throughout their lives, often because of disadvantage they face at birth, and this disadvantage can be transmit-ted from one generation to the next.

As Grover (2006) notes, there was some recognition by the Labour Government (at that time, relatively new) that social exclusion is multi-dimensional and that the social and economic circumstances that exclude individuals from mainstream society are interconnected. He argues, however, that in its political use, the social exclusion framework was reduced to concerns with exclusion from paid employment. This focus leads to a problem construction and policy response that 'individualises exclusion rather than taking seriously its embeddedness in social and economic practices' (Grover, 2006, p. 78). Along with a raft of other critics, Grover is particularly concerned with the centrality of work activation policies in the British Government's social exclusion and social inclusion agendas. The New Deals for young people and for unemployed people, for example, included mandatory 'intensive activity periods' (a 13-week period of training and/or work placements). The scope of claimants expected to take part in work-focused activities has since increased: from 2006, all people making new claims for social assistance, sickness and disability-related benefits, bereavement benefits and benefits for carers are compelled to participate in work–focused interviews as a condition of their eligibility. In addition, there has been a shift in orientation towards groups such as lone mothers and sick and disabled people; where once they had a 'protected' status outside of paid employment, they are increasingly being defined as unemployed labour and are being drawn into 'voluntary' and mandatory work activation activities.

In 2009, the Social Exclusion Unit was disbanded. It was replaced by a Communities and Local Government structure, under the responsibility of government ministers but governed by a board made up of central and local government members and officials, and supported by quasi-government organisations (Communities and Local Government, 2009) and a Social Exclusion Task Force in the Cabinet Office (Social Exclusion Task Force,

2009). Although the social policy infrastructure had been transformed and the strategic response realigned to community building, the definition of social exclusion remains.

Social inclusion and 'a stronger, fairer Australia'

The concept of social exclusion was articulated in welfare discussions during the latter part of the decade of the Howard Liberal–National Coalition Government (1996–2007), and it developed a strong presence in Australian social policy scholarship during this time. However, with the election of the Australian Labor Party government at the end of 2007, the social inclusion framework became the social policy catchcry. Conforming to Porter and Craig's analysis (2004), the new Labor Government presented social inclusion as a way of softening the harsh impact of 11 years of the previous conservative government. As a point of what we might call 'product differentiation', the new government also chose to use the term 'inclusion' rather than 'exclusion'

Philip Mendes has argued that the Australian Labor Party has maintained an adherence to a broad social justice agenda by promoting a role for the state protecting and supporting those who face disadvantage, and this principle is embodied in its social inclusion agenda (2008, pp. 173–175). Responding to ample evidence of growing social and economic division in Australia (discussed in chapter 5), particularly of increased poverty and persistent disadvantage among specific geographical and social groups such as Aboriginal and Torres Strait Islander communities, the Rudd election campaign promised to create a new inclusive Australian community.

Acting on this framework immediately, Prime Minister Rudd opened the first sitting of parliament in 2008 with an apology to indigenous Australians for past wrongs. This was a powerful and long awaited symbolic gesture of social inclusion (Peatling, 2008). The next symbolic gesture of inclusion was to call a summit, at which around one thousand diverse people from around the country met with the new government. The aim of the 'Australia 2020' Summit, held at Parliament House, was to 'shape a long-term strategy for the nation's future' (Australian Government, 2008a). One of the 10 major challenges addressed at the summit was 'strengthening communities, supporting families and social inclusion' (Australian Government, 2008b, p. 1). The final report from the 2020 summit had 35 sections referring to or discussing social inclusion, demonstrating a highly successful assertion of the framework. Social inclusion was a key theme of the summit, which proposed many possible social policy initiatives to promote a more inclusive society (Australian Government, 2008b).

The Australian Government proceeded to establish a social inclusion infrastructure with the creation of a portfolio held by the deputy prime minister and the setting up of a cross-government bureaucracy, on very similar lines to the previous Labor Government's approach to social justice. A Social Inclusion Board has been established, as a representative cross-section of high-level stakeholders, including human service professionals, CEOs of the largest welfare NGOs, consumer representatives, research academics and so on. The board is to have a role in scrutinising social policy and budgets across the range of related governmental agencies, with a view to auditing and modelling policy that would satisfy the social inclusion framework. This is a familiar social policy strategy that Australian Labor governments used during the 1980s for women's policy audits, and during the late 1980s and early 1990s for social justice audits.

Creating a broad social policy framework such as 'social inclusion' allows a government to package change neatly, create a discourse of consistent social policy goals and create benchmarks for achievements in its broad social agenda and in reporting problem-solving outcomes. For the human services sector, social inclusion policy offers a framework for alignment of and participation in shared goals or, if the government is seen to be failing to meet its social policy commitments, a focus of criticism. This is a lesson that can be learned from the UK experience under the Blair Government, where social exclusion became an important framework within which researchers and practitioners could engage with policy. Indeed, they had to learn 'social exclusion speak' to become effective or influential (Saunders, 2003, p. 16).

The Australian Government's social inclusion strategy has been promoted as creating opportunities for work and participation and a platform from which 'to launch a new era of governance to mainstream the task of building social inclusion so that all Australians can share in our nation's prosperity' (Australian Government, 2008a). The philosophy and politics of social inclusion has tended to paint an idealised gloss over some aspects of social policy under the Rudd Government. For example, the previous government had enacted a series of 'welfare-to-work' reforms to income support policy under the rubric of 'Mutual Obligation' (which we discuss in more detail later in this chapter), and had undertaken the 'Northern Territory Intervention', which involved suspending the Racial Discrimination Act. These punitive policies have been continued by the Rudd Government, without being tested against the principles of social inclusion. This raises questions about the value of social inclusion as a big picture framework for social policy.

Welfare-to-work: framing 'inclusion' in the social inclusion framework

It is important to understand the social inclusion agenda in the context of other social policy developments, most obviously those aimed at increasing 'activation' and economic participation through welfare-to-work initiatives. In particular, we need to consider how well the objectives and strategies of policies with different underlying goals fit together when they share a 'target population'. In Australia, as in the UK, there is a significant overlap between people who are on income support, people who are poor and people who are socially excluded. Thus, reforms to income support programs will have their most profound impact on people already experiencing profound disadvantage.

As we discussed in chapter 5, one enduring debate in the social policy field has been over the economic costs of the welfare state. Many conservative social policy analysts and economists have argued that social spending is a 'drain' on the economy. Specifically, they argue that social spending redirects resources *away* from productive uses in well-meaning but self-defeating programs that encourage 'dependency'. Accordingly, one proposed response to these criticisms is to reframe social spending as 'investment' and reorientate social programs in ways that make them 'productive', 'enabling' or focused on 'activation' (Dingeldey, 2007, p. 823). Reorientation of the welfare state in this direction has been a key focus of most rich democratic governments since the rise to dominance of the economic paradigm in social resource allocation. The extent of reorientation ranges from adjustments around the edges of welfare states, trimming the costs of welfare, to what some perceive as 'major revisions in the principles and philosophies of social protection' (Gilbert, 2004, p. 9).

Nations around the world have developed various policy responses to the shared ideological underpinnings of activation programs that are now 'pandemic' in rich democracies (Goodin 2001, p. 189). These concerns are essentially that the passive receipt of welfare will undermine responsibility, self-reliance and other desirable attributes of citizenship. International institutions, such as the

OECD and EU, support activation agendas, emphasising the importance of supporting participation in member countries, especially by improving work incentives (OECD, 1996). On this view, previous social policies, as much as anything else, created social exclusion by demanding too little from 'passive recipients' of 'welfare'. In Australia, under Howard's neo-liberal administration, the response was framed by another umbrella social policy framework referred to as Mutual Obligation, a framework in which citizen 'responsibilities' were emphasised over citizens' rights.

Despite common pressures, such welfare reorientation objectives and design vary in different contexts, with programs needing to mesh with other arrangements, including tax systems, labour market regulations, and immigration policies as well as umbrella social policy frameworks such as social inclusion. Thomas Lorentzen and Espen Dahl point out six dimensions along which activation policies can differ: (1) whether systems use 'work first' requirements versus human capital development and job creation initiatives to promote participation; (2) whether programs are compulsory or voluntary (and for whom); (3) what kinds of sanctions and rewards are attached to participation; (4) which additional support services are available; and (5) which groups are targeted. Context also matters, including the norms on which policies and programs are built, as well as business cycles and labour market conditions (2005, p. 29).

There is debate about the extent to which welfare states have become reorientated away from protective towards productive functions (Gilbert, 2004; Vis 2007; Hudson and Kühner, 2009). However, the discourse of social policy has changed in many countries. In some, policies towards key 'dependent' populations of working age have changed significantly. The emergence of 'welfare-to-work' or 'workfare' policies has been one critical dimension of this kind of policy reorientation in Australia, the UK and the United States. In Australia and the US, a 'work first' approach has been taken. This approach emphasises punitive measures to push people off income support and into the labour market, and pays little attention to the quality of jobs and the levels of support some very disadvantaged people need to enable them to participate in society, including in paid work. A key question raised by this form of reorientation is, how do these policies mesh with the 'softer' agenda of social inclusion?

In Australia, the origin of welfare-to-work programs can be traced to the tightening of job search requirements in the 1990s, and the introduction of

Work for the Dole for 18 to 24 year olds who had been unemployed for six months or more in 1998 (Dapré, 2006, p. 431). Compulsory job search and workforce participation have since expanded, under principles of Mutual Obligation. In 2000, Work for the Dole became compulsory for people under 40 who had been on unemployment benefits for six months or more (Yeend 2004). Changes announced in the 2005–2006 Australian Federal Budget further extended workforce participation requirements and associated compliance systems. From 1 July 2006, eligibility for the Disability Support Pension (DSP) and Parenting Payment Single (PPS) were also narrowed. For DSP, qualification criteria were tightened by reducing the work capacity test and requiring those assessed as able to work 15 hours a week to seek work, whereas previously, only those able to work 30 hours a week were required to look for work. Sole parent pensioners could previously remain income support beneficiaries, fulfilling their unpaid care responsibilities without having to look for paid work until their youngest child turned 16. Under the new rules, when their youngest child turns eight, sole parents become defined by their unemployed rather than caring status, and are transferred to Newstart Allowance (NSA) or unemployment benefit, with its lower payment rate and tighter income and activity tests.

Associated with the increasing conditionality of income support payments are mandatory compliance mechanisms, which include benefit withdrawal and benefit control. Where benefit withdrawal would impact adversely on dependants or vulnerable recipients, benefit control may apply. Benefit control in the form of 'welfare quarantining' or 'income management' was introduced from 1 July 2006, and was extended to all welfare recipients (both Indigenous and non-Indigenous) in 'prescribed communities' in the Northern Territory as part of the Intervention (see chapter 10). In 2009, the Rudd Labor Government ensured that it was extended nationally when it made a further policy commitment for welfare quarantining. With the policy objective of reducing intergenerational welfare dependency, parents on income support payments welfare quarantining lost discretion over a portion of their payment if their child or children were deemed by state authorities to be at risk of neglect or if they failed to attend school regularly (FACSIA 2007a; 2007b).

Evidence suggests that in Australia, the impact of welfare-to-work programs has been harsh on some of the most vulnerable members of the community. Exploratory research undertaken with practitioners in two large Sydney NGOs revealed significant concerns about their service users, many of whom have complex needs and so are most at risk of serious social exclusion (Bellamy and Cowling, 2008). Two principal concerns emerged from the research. First was the clash between the demands of the new income support rules and other human service systems with which service users interacted, including child welfare, education, vocational training and childcare. A simple example starkly illustrates the problem. Some service users are parents whose children have been notified to the statutory authorities as at risk of abuse or neglect, and are undertaking parenting courses, attending meetings and counselling sessions and generally attempting to be more available to their children, in order to meet the demands of the child welfare system. This can limit their capacity to meet the activity requirements designed to promote their inclusion in the labour market. According to the researchers, 'Caseworkers report that parents in this situation can feel that they are forced to choose between being breached (under the welfare-to-work system) and losing benefits for up to eight weeks or losing access to their children (under the child protection system)' (Bellamy and Cowling, 2008, p. 3). Second was that very disadvantaged members of the community need significant personal, social and educational support to enable them to make the transition to the labour market—support at a level much higher than that currently on offer under the 'work first' model (Bellamy and Cowling, 2008, p. 7).

This mismatch between welfare-to-work and social inclusion did not need to have been so stark. Mendes (2008) suggests three clear areas in which the Labor Government could have adopted distinctly different directions from the previous government's policies. These include adopting different names for programs such as 'Work for the Dole' to reflect a social inclusion approach, reviewing the extent and nature of penalties for the failure to comply to work participation rules for the unemployed, and including local community-based unemployed people in current Job Network provider offices to represent the interests of the unemployed (Mendes, 2008, p. 177). This list could be extended, drawing on work such as that of John Bellamy and Sally Cowling (2008) discussed above. At the time of writing this book, we are not in a position to say whether the social inclusion social policy framework in Australia is an effective umbrella policy. However, as the analysis of welfare-to-work policies suggests, a 'work first' approach to 'activating' excluded members of the community is likely to have as many costs as benefits for participants.

Social inclusion and cultural diversity

So far our focus has been on documenting and evaluating how policies related to economic inclusion, which act on a person's class status, affect their social inclusion. Yet there are other social organising principles that impact on the inclusion of individuals and groups, such as gender and ethnicity. In this section, we consider the challenge of social inclusion of ethnic minorities who are often, but not always, relative newcomers to societies with the stated aim of being inclusive.

In many rich democracies, ethnic differences are central to the processes that create inclusion and exclusion. Refugee and migrant groups often arrive with automatic exclusion markers such as their forms of dress, appearance, religion and language (Research Intelligence, 2006; Council of Europe, 2008). It has been suggested that a new kind of racism has emerged in the twenty-first century that is rooted in ethnocentric, even xenophobic, hostility towards migrant workers and asylum seekers (Research Intelligence, 2006, p. 3). Exploring the *reasons* for the social exclusion of migrant workers and asylum seekers can lead to the need to acknowledge racism as a structural cause of social exclusion. This is not an easy social problem to address but it is under keen focus by the European Parliament, for example, where it is recognised as a fundamental barrier to social cohesion all across Europe (Council of Europe, 2008).

The political consequences of the social policy problem of 'inclusion' of migrant workers and their families, asylum seekers and refugees, have been highlighted in Denmark, a rich democracy renowned for its universalistic, citizenship-based welfare state (Hedetoft, 2006). The problem of addressing the social exclusion of non-European settlers has posed a major threat to a well-established universalistic social policy framework in Denmark. It has been seen to divide both the public and political parties' views, 'threatening the consensus which has been a hallmark of Danish politics since World War II' (Hedetoft, 2006). According to Ulf Hedetoft, even the Social Democratic party with its universalistic orientation has had a struggle in trying to establish a 'clear, coherent, and united political position, partly because their membership, like the population at large, has been split between a tolerant/international and an inward-looking/patriotic approach to the presence of non-Western foreigners' (2006, p. 7). Given that the number of non-Western country settlers increased by 520 per cent between 1980 and 2005, compared to a 19.8 per cent increase of Western immigrants in the same period, inclusion of new minorities has become a significant social policy problem (Hedetoft, 2006, p. 3).

Traditionally, Denmark has relied on 'successful integration' as a benchmark for the social inclusion of newcomers, expecting 'acculturation to the mores of Danish life'. The Danish system does not officially recognise minorities, which creates an obstacle to immigrants with distinctive ethnic and cultural identities and needs (Hedetoft, 2006, p. 6). The Danish Government has introduced many technical, legal constraints on family immigration and citizenship to deter this burgeoning immigrant group but has also relied on a social inclusion framework that uses labour market integration as its major means of addressing exclusion. However, given the scale of non–European immigration, there is a clear need to address the specific problem of a direct conflict between the Danish commitment to an inclusive, but culturally homogeneous society and the inevitably different needs of immigrants with distinct ethnic and cultural identities.

Remedying racism or indeed other structural manifestations of exclusion is, as suggested above, an important challenge for human service workers. Addressing the processes of exclusion requires a focus on how certain groups are positioned by politicians, by policies, by the media and by wider social attitudes and discourses. There are laws against racism in most rich democracies, but the actual work of countering social exclusion must be done at all the points of exclusion, in everyday encounters and in the full gamut of social roles and locations. The elusiveness of changing entrenched prejudices makes the broader project of framing social policy through the concepts of social exclusion or inclusion far more challenging. To take problems like racism into account, responses need to go well beyond promoting employment, improving access to education or building more houses. Such concrete objectives are important, but their impact on exclusion can be undermined by a lack of social cohesion, especially if it is understood that the experience of social exclusion is not *exclusive* to people living in poverty.

Questioning the social inclusion framework

We argue that if welfare-to-work has economic participation as its primary goal, and social inclusion has social participation as its distinct objective, it is important to consider the role of equality. As discussed in chapter 5, there is substantial evidence that poverty is only effectively addressed where equality is also addressed. This brings into question the logic of a social inclusion framework as an effective way of addressing social exclusion. For example, the principle of access to services such as education can only make an individual equal in a contemporary competitive employment market if the level and quality of education they gain access to is equal to the best education on offer in the same market. Making the quality of education equally high across geographical and class divides comes back to a review of how wealth is distributed, redistributed and played out in a particular social protection model in national and local contexts. Given that Australian governments have regularly cut income and other taxes in recent years, the potential for the redistribution of wealth has been reduced and it will remain reduced. Such self-imposed constraints on redistribution pose a significant challenge for the government's ability to realise the goals of the social inclusion agenda.

Human service providers need to engage critically with the idea of social inclusion to ensure that, in the process of providing support or social inclusion services, it does not continually focus on the status of service users as excluded, which only serves to create a self-perpetuating cycle. The Micah Projects in South Brisbane are run by a Christian NGO that provides services to families and communities, with a focus on improving childhood and adolescent health. As Kris Olsson (2008) observed of the Micah Projects, social inclusion has been integral to their services for some time. 'Micah's mission has always been to respond to the needs of anyone who experiences exclusion; through poverty, social isolation, disability, mental illness or homelessness' (Olsson, 2008, p. 8). This includes programs such as the 'Young Mothers, Young Women' program, which provides support and early intervention for women under 24 with children under eight, and the Mental Health and Disability unit that provides support for people in hostels and boarding houses (Olsson, 2008, p. 8.) According to the then project leader, Mark Reimers, Micah focuses on disadvantaged and marginalised people in a non-judgmental way. However, he expressed concern that strategies aimed at addressing social inclusion also need to address the structural issues around poverty and marginalisation in ways that are 'not punitive and that bring an understanding of trauma … as most of us don't want to 'fess up to poverty, or to mental illness, so we come up with other strategies to cope' (cited in Olsson, 2008, p. 8).

Through this critical engagement with the social inclusion agenda, Reimers recognises how social inclusion strategies, through the focus on identifying who the socially excluded are, can indeed construct individual users negatively. He also observed that there is often an attitude of punishment in 'interactions with those on the margins' (Olsson, 2008, p. 9).

A key problem with broad social policy frameworks in contemporary governments, such as social inclusion, is that they tend to be aimed at solving visible problems that are in many ways perennial. Rather than reflect a substantial shift in approaches to social policy, they are often created as an umbrella for the short-term political agenda of a government. For example, the Australian social inclusion agenda is concerned with 'coordinating policies across national, state and local governments to ensure no Australian is excluded from meaningful participation in the mainstream economic and social life of the country' (Gillard, 2008a, p. 13). This is to be achieved through everyone getting a job, gaining access to services, being part of networks, having an ability to deal with personal crises and having their voice heard (Gillard, 2008a, p. 13).

Achieving such goals in Australia confronts some of the challenges we discussed in chapter 3, that is, multiple levels of government with divergent responsibilities and sometimes, divergent political agendas. Further, if participation is integral to inclusion, the current form of democracy in Australia may need to be reformed. As Iris Marion Young observed, the way that democracy functions is often counter to ideals of inclusion: we have a political system that elects an elite of decision-makers and makes it difficult to forge connections between the ideas and interests of ordinary citizens and power elites (or elected political leaders) (Young, 2000, p. 173).

In calling the '2020 Summit', Prime Minister Rudd seemed to demonstrate that he had a sense of the shortcomings of executive rule of policy in the current system. But developments following his public apology to Indigenous Australians, also under the umbrella of social inclusion, have not been particularly promising. The key to the new approach in Indigenous affairs is the 'Closing the Gap' strategy (FAHCSIA 2009), which purports to be a reorientation, but is more likely a repackaging (Altman et al., 2004). Indeed, many Indigenous Australians affected by the Northern Territory (NT) Intervention have expressed disappointment at the lack of effective change in the targeted communities. For example, a coalition of people affected by the Intervention distributed an open letter to the government. It stated:

> You talk about 'closing the gap' between Indigenous and non-Indigenous people. But we want to close the Gap our way, on our terms—not like past assimilation policies ... How can we trust your government? You are pushing out the NT Intervention, which is racist to the hilt. Your policies are hammering down on us on all sides. They are making it harder to get food, live on traditional lands and live day to day. Children are being punished through this Intervention. All it has given us is heartache (The Prescribed Area People's Alliance delegation to Canberra, 2009).

This commentary reflects a key flaw in social inclusion as a broad policy framework; it is similar to the problems highlighted in the response of the Danish Government to non-European immigrants. In this case, the idea of 'inclusion' is based on a fundamental assumption that the way dominant white middle Australia lives sets the benchmark to which all Australians aspire; in other words, everyone should desire to be included in such a model for living in 'the mainstream economic and social life of the country' (Gillard, 2008a, p. 13). Setting the mainstream as a benchmark suggests that an inclusive society means assimilation of all into the mainstream model. Yet the kind of investment that would result in equal choice to be part of the mainstream has not been made and governments have failed to include the citizens in the NT communities in their own shift towards 'inclusion'.

Jonathon Davies, in an analysis of the UK's New Labour social inclusion approach, raised a similar concern when he stated that 'while the government has a sophisticated approach to social inclusion, offering a conditional pass to common membership of society, it remains unproven, and, moreover, it represents a departure from traditional socialist and social democratic thought' (2005, pp. 3–4). It seems that, to be realised, governments' broad social policy frameworks need to be pushed towards a set of 'big' questions, including the structural causes of exclusion from work and mainstream social standards of living and engagement, and where the views of the excluded fit in defining the meaning of inclusion.

Conclusion

Overarching social policy discourses like those concerning social inclusion can significantly reorientate the nature and scope of social provisioning. These discourses position individuals in relation to the state in different ways to past welfare state models. They also affect the kinds of social policy and service provision practices human service workers are involved in.

The major aim of this chapter has been to provide a critical insight for human service workers into how understandings of broad social policy frameworks can be utilised to improve, or perhaps to homogenise, the experience of service users. We conclude by encouraging human service workers to engage in productive ways with the social inclusion agenda, while retaining a critical perspective on its impact. In our next chapter, we continue this discussion by considering the ways in which radical social policy change can result in innovative or reactionary responses.

CHAPTER 10

Changing social policy: radical and reactionary social policies

Introduction

Social policy interventions can bring about social change in a variety of ways. Often a number of competing perspectives inform subsequent action. In this chapter, we consider two examples of radical interventions in social policy. The first is the approach taken by the Labour Government in England towards 'looked after' children or children in the care system during the period between 1997 and 2002. The second is the Howard Liberal-National Coalition Government's (1996–2007) 'shock and awe' campaign to take over Aboriginal policy in the Northern Territory in 2007. Although these policies have very different underpinning rationales and consequences, we draw attention to both interventions being centrally directed, having a universal application and being directed towards groups grappling with marginalisation and the consequences of entrenched social exclusion. In this chapter, we examine how these radical interventions came about, the consequences, the lines that can be drawn between reactionary entrenchment and significant advancement and the implications for human service professionals.

Background to the interventions

Looking first at 'looked after' children, the Labour Government in the UK came to office in 1997 with a reforming agenda and emphasised social investment from the outset. The underpinning rationale was provided by the Beveridge lecture given by the then Prime Minister, Tony Blair, in 1999. In this address, he emphasised the need to encourage independence, initiative and enterprise over passive welfare dependency, and maintained that a central platform was 'investing in children'. This approach was derived in part from the work of sociologist Anthony Giddens (1998), who drew attention to the importance of investing in human capital rather than in the direct provision of economic maintenance or welfare payments (Fawcett et al., 2004). The Labour Government promoted this approach in England and Wales by initiating schemes such as 'Sure Start'. This was first introduced in 1998 and provided a range of measures for parents and children under four. The overarching aim was improving the overall well-being and the later attainments of children by providing a good start in life. However, despite the centrality afforded to this policy platform, there have been criticisms of a social investment approach to children. A key reservation is the priority this approach gives to what children will *become* rather than what they are now. However, a social investment approach to social policy has proved persuasive and the Rudd Government, which took office in Australia in November 2007, has promoted it.

The British Labour Government's social investment policies are, from one perspective, exemplified by their response to 'looked after' children. The legacy of state neglect and abuse, and the recommendations for change following a series of inquiries, clearly showed the need for action. Such inquiries included the 'Pindown' inquiry in Staffordshire, which found that children in the care system had been subject to abuse (Levy and Kahan, 1991), and the inquiry into the controversy over child physical and sexual abuse in North Wales in the 1990s (Waterhouse, 2000). Policies were introduced in England and Wales to try to prevent further abuses in the care system by ensuring that all children had an effective voice and easy access to complaint mechanisms. These incorporated the setting of clear targets for educational standards and the re-drafting of local authority responsibilities, the bodies responsible for the care of 'looked after' children in their area.

While the Labour Government's targeting of 'looked after' children in the UK took place at the beginning of its term in office, the intervention by the Howard Government in the Northern Territory marked the final significant act of almost 12 years in power. The underpinning rationale for this intervention has variously been attributed to cynical electioneering (Downer, 2007), providing a flagging government with the opportunity to demonstrate leadership and decisive action (Dodson, 2007), a means of re-exerting control of Aboriginal land as a result of valuable mineral deposits (Stott Despoja, 2007), and a much needed response to family violence in Aboriginal communities (Gordon in Jopson, et al., 2007). John Howard justified the calling of a 'National Emergency' following the receipt of a report entitled *Ampe Akelyernemane Meke Mekarle/ Little Children are Sacred*. This report followed the establishment of a board of inquiry led by Patricia Anderson and Rex Wild QC to examine the extent and nature of child sexual abuse in the Northern Territory and to consider how the Northern Territory Government could help support communities to address identified problem areas effectively. Commissioned by the presiding chief minister of the Northern Territory in 2006, the report was presented to the Northern Territory Government at the end of April 2007. In June 2007, after having only one week to review the report, the Howard Government accused the Northern Territory Government of inaction and instituted a 'crackdown' (Howard, 2007a) on Aboriginal townships in the Northern Territory.

The Northern Territory Emergency Response Act (2007) that ratified the government's policy came into effect in August 2007. The Rudd Labor Government, which took office in November 2007, formally apologised on 13 February 2008 to Aboriginal people for the events of the stolen generation. They also instituted a review of the intervention, which was carried out by Peter Yu, and reported to the Australian Government on 13 October 2008 (Commonwealth of Australia, 2008). The review committee made it clear that urgent action was needed to address the unacceptably high levels of disadvantage and social dislocation experienced by Aboriginal communities in the Northern Territory. The government was also advised to re-establish their relationship with Indigenous people on the basis of genuine consultation, engagement and partnership. However, the Rudd Government, while appearing to agree with the overall message, rejected the specific recommendations contained in the report. This serves as an example of how a new government can continue to adhere to the policies of the preceding government, while appearing to take a different direction.

From the outset, the 'National Emergency' initiated by the Howard Government in June 2007 was characterised by the use of highly emotive and military language. Appeals to help save vulnerable children from abuse were interspersed with statements about 'securing and stabilising' up to 73 Aboriginal communities, bringing in substantial numbers of police to enforce a 'law and order crackdown', making 'security a first priority', establishing an externally mandated emergency task force and 'mobilising the armed forces' (ABC, 2007). It is notable that the accompanying media release contained few references to children or to child sexual abuse and used terms such as 'enforcing', 'acquiring', 'banning' and 'restricting'. One of the few times child abuse is mentioned is in the evocative title 'The National Emergency Response to Protect Aboriginal Children in the Northern Territory' (Brough, 2007).

Reactions to the calling of the 'National Emergency' have varied. Noel Pearson, an Aboriginal leader from Cape York in Queensland, has been such a strong supporter of the policies that the measures have been referred to as the Pearson model (Landis, 2007). However, it is indicative of reactions from Indigenous people outside Australia that Hone Harawira, a Maori member of parliament in New Zealand, commented that the action taken was punitive, racist and being imposed on a people who could not fight back (Small et al., 2007).

The policies introduced in the Northern Territory specifically related to Aboriginal people. The measures included the introduction of compulsory health checks for all Aboriginal children, the quarantining of welfare payments for all Aboriginal recipients in the Northern Territory and the introduction of market-based rents and more stringent public territory housing arrangements for all Aboriginal tenants. Enforced school attendance for the children of all families living on Aboriginal land, with meals at school paid for by their parents, was also mandated. In addition, alcohol and pornography bans for all Aboriginal communities were introduced and provision was made for the Australian Government to take over Aboriginal townships in the Northern Territory on enforced five-year leases.

It is clear that Aboriginal communities in the Northern Territory have to contend with a lack of infrastructure resources such as health, education, housing and employment. There is also entrenched disadvantage, impoverishment and endemic discrimination (Altman and Hinkson, 2007). Anderson and Wild (2007) make it clear that the cumulative effects of poverty, deprivation, poor education, training and general disempowerment have led inexorably to family and other violence for some members of the targeted communities. However, as Tom Calma (2007) and Bill Fogarty and Marisa Paterson (2007), among others, point out, there are many examples of constructive and successful community initiatives and responses to identified problem areas. One of these is the Maningrida Community Action Plan Project, co-ordinated by Aboriginal women, which adopts a strengths-based approach. The women work with other organisations to address the under-reporting of child sexual abuse and operate a women's safety patrol to keep the streets safe. They also formed a pivotal liaison point between local community members and health agencies. Another example is the Kurdu-Kurdu Kurlangu Childcare Centre at Yuendumu. This started in 2005 at the local school as a play centre for preschool children and then developed to become a comprehensive childcare centre. The centre provides real jobs and accredited training of a national standard to 14 local Aboriginal women as well as operating as a valuable community childcare resource (Gosford, 2008).

Patricia Anderson (2007), one of the authors of the *Ampe Akelyernemane Meke Mekarle*/Little Children are Sacred report, has made it clear that Aboriginal people have the answers to stamp out child sexual abuse but are being ignored by the government (Anderson and Wild, 2007).

The intervention in June 2007, rather than supporting successful projects and facilitating the further development of others, bypassed existing community initiatives and gave executive powers to members of an externally mandated task force. The associated scrapping of Community Development Employment Projects (CDEP), which enabled Aboriginal community members to take on valued, paid roles within communities, has also made it increasingly difficult for schemes to continue. The Kurdu-Kurdu Kurlangu Childcare Centre described above looks likely to be a casualty of the new funding model. Rudd pledged to reinstate the CDEP scheme when he took office, but it appeared that, during his first year at least, 'work for the dole' schemes and the universally applied quarantining measures have taken priority.

The consequences of radical interventions

In relation to 'looked after' children', the legislation produced during the period from 1997 to 2002 was considerable. This included the 'Quality Protects' initiative, the Children (Leaving Care) Act 2000, part of the Care Standards

Act 2000 and the Adoption and Children Act 2002, as well as further guidance on the education of 'looked after' children. The Quality Protects initiative was particularly important and set key objectives for local authorities. These were linked to the imperative of protecting children in regulated services from harm and poor care standards and included maximising life chances with regard to education, health and social care, facilitating and ensuring the making of secure attachments to appropriate carers and putting measures in place to enable care leavers to participate socially and economically in society. The meaningful involvement of children and young people in planning services and tailoring individual packages of care, as well as the availability of accessible and effective complaints mechanisms, were also prioritised. In turn, these objectives were linked to targets that focused on reducing the numbers of looked after children having three or more placement moves per year, reducing the percentages of children who had missed more than 25 days schooling in the previous year, and increasing to at least 50 per cent by 2001 the proportion of children leaving care at 16 or later with a General Certificate in Secondary Education (GCSE) or General National Vocational Qualification (GNVQ), with this rising to 75 per cent by 2003. A target that was brought in slightly later focused on increasing the proportion of care leavers aged over 16 leaving school with five GCSE grades in the A to C range by the year 2004 (DoH, 2003a). Within schools, each 'looked after' child was also required to have a mandatory Personal Education Plan. Money was provided for improvements in the targeted areas and this was linked to a detailed Management Action Plan (MAP) that had to be produced by each local authority.

The action taken by the British Labour Government clearly required compliance by local authorities. It also involved controversial measures, such as changes to the benefit system for 16 to 18 year olds, which was seen by some as an infringement of civil liberties (Calder, 2000). Because of the changes, all young people in the 16 to 18-year age group who had chosen to live independently from the care system or from their parents were unable to claim benefits. The rationale presented was that this reform would counteract the growing tendency for young people to leave care at 16 and move on to benefits, absolving local authorities from a duty to provide further support. It was argued that by removing this 'perverse financial incentive' and providing strengthened leaving care arrangements (which included local authorities having responsibility for providing aftercare support until the age of 21 and putting in place leaving care plans and personal advisers), local authorities would have to produce extended interagency resources (such as those associated with housing, leisure, education, training and social support). It was made clear that the continuation of support would apply even if a young person moved outside the area of the local authority that had taken responsibility for their care arrangements.

Overall, the targets set by the British Government's policy achieved varying results. The number of children leaving care with one GCSE or GNVQ rose by 31 to 41 per cent between 2000 and 2002. The target of five or more GCSEs in the A to C grades rose from four per cent in 2000 to five per cent in 2002 (DoH, 2003). Although these achievements do not look impressive when compared to the 'not in care' population, the fact that there was an upward trajectory for a group routinely viewed as non-achievers is not to be dismissed. Nevertheless, it is notable that the government's response was to change the targets rather than put in place additional measures to enable the targets to be met. The new targets focused on 90 per cent of care leavers sitting but not necessarily passing a GCSE exam by 2006, with 15 per cent obtaining five or more GCSEs. With regard to the provision of ongoing support for young people leaving care, the figures show that local authorities remained in touch with 75 per cent of those leaving care, until their nineteenth birthday (DoH, 2003). Again, although not a groundbreaking statistic, it does demonstrate positive movement in an area traditionally beset by poor contact and an absence of support measures (Fawcett et al., 2004).

In relation to the intervention by John Howard's Australian Government in the Northern Territory in 2007, the deficit model employed focused attention on all Aboriginal families requiring highly policed compliance-orientated measures to address externally identified problem areas. Despite the evidence of a pervasive lack of infrastructure and resources, the consequences have been not only to pathologise Aboriginal individuals and communities further, but also to prioritise centrally directed and controlled action. As a result, compulsory health checks can render clinics places of surveillance and compliance rather than supportive community resources. Penalising parents for their children having three unexplained absences from school by holding back 50 per cent of welfare payments and 100 per cent of family assistance for up to 12 months, not only fails to view schools as focal points for community action but also asks more of Aboriginal families than is expected of non-Aboriginal Australians, who generally have much higher incomes and greater resources to draw from.

Targets can, as shown in the case of 'looked after' children in England and Wales, serve to raise the baseline and increase, albeit incrementally, both results and expectations. However, if a program emphasises the meeting of targets by the implementation of punitive, exclusive and non-negotiable measures, the building blocks for effective long-term social change tend not to be put in place. Regarding the intervention in the Northern Territory, Calma (2008), the Aboriginal and Torres Strait Islander Social Justice Commissioner, draws attention to the imperative to include all stakeholders in order to determine the nature of issues to be addressed and to set targets and take action on the agreed items. He points to the need for any measures taken to recognise human dignity, worth and social justice and for such measures to be underpinned by human rights principles. Fred Chaney (in Anderson and Wild, 2007), a retiring member of the National Native Title Tribunal, also cites the need for locally based, resourced and controlled action and highlights that centrally driven systems are inflexible, non-inclusive and cannot be invested in by local community members. He emphasises the importance of educational projects being managed within communities, with attention being paid to outcomes that community members want to achieve.

The lines between reactionary entrenchment and significant advancement

Although the British Labour Government's approach to children's rights in England and Wales has not been comprehensive, it can be argued that it has been at its most positive with regard to 'looked after' children. This has resulted from the combination of poor past performance, scandals within the public sector and a reappraisal of local and national government responsibilities in this area. Embedding the meaningful involvement of children in planning services, in producing individually tailored packages of care and in ensuring the effective operation of complaints measures, within initiatives such as 'Quality Protects' and legislation such as the Children Leaving Care Act 2000, has also played a significant part. Indeed, the emphasis on participation singles out these policies from many others, and provides a stark contrast with the activities of the Howard Government under the 'National Emergency' in 2007.

The top-down nature of policy intervention in the Northern Territory has meant that consultation with Aboriginal parents and Aboriginal communities has not been prioritised. Although the report used to justify the intervention strongly emphasised the need to work in partnership with Aboriginal communities to build on strengths and tackle systemic disadvantage, the Howard Government failed to consult or even inform Aboriginal communities about what was happening. In this, it appears that consultation continued to be viewed as an ineffective way of working with Aboriginal people. Wesley Aird (2008), a former Indigenous adviser to the Howard Government, commented in an article entitled the *Great Aboriginal Con*, 'The paralysing effect of consultation is yet another problem on the list of con jobs that must be managed ... Granted, there are plenty of instances when consultation will improve the effectiveness of a project, however there needs to be a balance between the legal or business outcomes and the benefit of imposing additional time and costs' (Aird, 2008, p. 8). The policies enacted by the Howard Government caused the Tangentyere Council near Alice Springs to issue a media release entitled *Work with us, Not Against Us,* and the *Sydney Morning Herald* quoted Dodson as saying, 'It's heavy handed and certainly without consultation. There has been no consultation—not even with the Northern Territory Government' (Jobson et al., 2007).

Attention has also to be paid to the ways in which the policies rolled out by the Howard Government in 2007 created tensions with previous policies. The intervention was only possible because of the suspension of the Australian Racial Discrimination Act (1975). As the Australian Human Rights and Equal Opportunity Commission (2007) point out, according to the legislation, 'special measures' have to be cited if one particular group is to be treated differently from other Australians. This involves effective consultation with the intended group and the obtaining of general consent. It is clear that in 2007, the Howard Government did not comply with the special measures criteria and that a policy directed solely towards Aboriginal recipients rode roughshod over a policy intended to ensure human rights for all Australians.

The issue of the rights of Aboriginal communities in Australia and the ways that these might best be met in policy terms remains the subject of considerable controversy. In April 2008, Prime Minister Kevin Rudd called a summit to help shape a long-term strategy for the nation's future and to tackle the long-term challenges confronting Australia by thinking in new ways. However, in the stream that considered 'Options for the Future of Indigenous Australia', prevailing divisions resurfaced. In relation to Indigenous governance, one submission suggested a treaty or compact of recognition and understanding between the Australian Government and Indigenous Australians similar to agreements in place in the US, Canada and New Zealand. Proposals were also put forward for regional governance structures run by Indigenous leaders to operate in parallel with mainstream authorities. This sparked a clear oppositional response, with another group emphasising the need to focus on children without politics getting in the way. The latter group saw the foregrounding of constitutional and treaty issues as a manoeuvre for Indigenous groups to re-enter the national conversation, accompanied by a denial of the issues confronting Indigenous children. However, Jackie Huggins, the co-chair of the summit's Indigenous stream, cut across this divide to assert, 'to be on par, to have parity with other Australians, to close the gap in all areas—is very fundamental to where we want to head in the future' (Robinson and Rintoul, 2008, p. 7).

When comparing and contrasting the two policy platforms discussed in this chapter, it is clear that in both instances the achievement of social change was linked to the taking of universal, centralised action by governments. However, although the 'looked after' children initiative emphasised hearing the voices of children in the care system and putting in place participatory and inclusive strategies, the intervention in the Northern Territory was, by contrast, exclusive and non participatory. Sue Gordon (cited in Karvelas, 2008, p. 6), the leader of the task force appointed by Howard, has highlighted that the all-embracing nature of the measures required change for those who were clearly able to manage their finances and care for their children. She commented before the Yu Committee presented its report to the Australian Government in October 2008, 'I think I would like to see those people who are very good not to be income managed after 12 months' (cited in Karvelas, 2008, p. 6). Nonetheless, the effects of placing families in a position where they are subject to punitive sanctions without recourse to appeal, even when they are operating appropriately, has not been taken on board and no changes have been made. Further, allegations of child sexual abuse appear not to have been substantiated. Although figures are hard to obtain, it was reported in May 2008 that of 7433 Aboriginal children examined by doctors as part of the National Emergency, only 39 had been referred to the authorities for suspected abuse, and of these, only four cases had been taken further (Pilger, 2008). Again, in the Katherine region of the Northern Territory, only eight arrests and three convictions were reported at the end of the first year (ABC, 2008). This leads to speculation either that the claims relating to the extent of the child sexual abuse were exaggerated, or that the intervention has been singularly ineffective in addressing these issues.

This discussion can lead to the conclusion that a target-orientated stance can work for a government looking to improve the educational and social circumstances of 'looked after' children, but it appears to continue the historical legacy of colonialism and racism when applied to a specific population group. Throughout the intervention, Prime Minister Howard denied charges of racism and claimed that the policies constituted an important watershed in Indigenous policy in Australia (Howard, 2007b). However, others, such as Jon Altman and Melinda Hinkson (2007), Mick Dodson (in Jopson et al., 2007) and Tom Calma (2007; 2008) have viewed the intervention as a highly charged political act and challenged the utilisation of such an important issue as child sexual abuse to further erode individual and community rights and further entrench discrimination (Calma, 2007; Dodson, 2007). The fact that this action was taken by a democratic nation that subscribes to international human rights treaties emphasises that the forces of regression and reaction can continue to provide a viable option for governments embarking on 'radical' social policy initiatives.

Regarding the implications for human service professionals, it can be argued that the ways in which different groups within societies are viewed informs both the actions taken and the outcomes experienced. An emphasis on vulnerability can result in paternalism and control to the exclusion of voice, consultation and participation. Similarly, focusing on perceived irresponsibility can prioritise regulation and oversight, and deny agency. Professional training, ethical statements, agency protocols and national and state policy imperatives provide the framework for action, but often it is *process* considerations relating to how action is taken, how participants are responded to and how inclusive features are incorporated, that determine both the effects and the legacy of the policies enacted.

In relation to Indigenous Australians in particular, Sue Green and Eileen Baldry (2008) maintain that human service professionals working within Indigenous communities, have to critically appraise power relationships, deconstruct colonising discourses and focus on social justice, human rights, self-determination and anti-oppressive and anti-discriminatory practice. They argue that social work (and work undertaken by human service professionals generally) is not about prescriptive practice, but about shifting modes of thinking about respectful partnerships and dialogues and, above all, about valuing the frameworks and capacities of Indigenous Australians.

Conclusion

Radical interventions in social policy have both innovatory and reactionary potential. Although political ideology clearly plays a part in how such interventions are interpreted, what is promoted as progressive can either put in place the building blocks for long-term social change or serve to mirror past injustices and perpetuate appropriating practices. The British Labour policy focus on 'looked after' children in England and Wales did not achieve outstanding results against its own set targets, but it did lay the foundations for further constructive developments and establish effective building blocks for significant long-term social change. The intervention in the Northern Territory in Australia and its outcomes are likely to remain controversial. However, it is possible to assert that the lack of consultation, investment in community strengths and supported and sustainable solutions is far more likely to leave a legacy of regressive retrenchment than to result in significant advancement for the communities involved. In chapter 11, we use examples of community capacity building projects and programs to discuss the traps and opportunities that the 'return to community' presents to human service organisations and practitioners working for social change.

Changing social policy: reinvigoration through the community?

Introduction

In many rich democracies *and* in many developing nations, policy-makers are re-emphasising the role of communities and community participation in a range of social policy areas. This shift has been heralded as an important element in the reinvigoration of a host of areas of social provision, signifying a renewed commitment to social policy for positive social change. In chapter 1, we described how social policy can be conceptualised in terms of the state intersecting with the spheres of the market, the family and the community, and that the community sphere consisted of diverse organisations, associations and relationships that make up 'civil society'. We also introduced the recent shift in social policy whereby government action has become more focused on the role of civil society in addressing social and political problems. In chapters 6 and 7, we explored some implications of these developments for NGOs and volunteers, both crucial in the discourse of civil society and its role in social policy. This chapter develops these ideas and issues in more detail, and provides concrete examples of the possibilities and limitations of reinvigorating social policy through 'community' policies and practices.

In a range of social policy contexts, 'community' has re-emerged as the sphere of society that can and should be harnessed to manage social and economic inequalities and what have come to be regarded as 'intractable' social problems. This new view of community as an appropriate foundation for policy-making is most evident in the explosion of activities across nations that are based on concepts such as social capital, partnerships, and community engagement, regeneration, renewal and capacity building. In order to explore the traps and opportunities that the 'return to community' presents to human service organisations and practitioners working for social change, the chapter focuses on the policies, projects and practices that have emerged under the banner of one of these concepts: community capacity building.

Community governance

Internationally, a new discourse concerned with changing the relationships between the state, the market and civil society has emerged. In this discourse, governmental strategies and actions aimed at strengthening the role of civil society have been accorded a great deal of legitimacy in some areas of social policy. Rather than civil society simply being regarded as 'the realm we create ourselves', positioned outside of government activity (Barber, 1998), or the arena that responds to issues when the state is unwilling or unable to (Beck, 1992; Howes et al., 2004), governments are taking an active and explicit interest in fostering the development and activities of some sectors of civil society. This in itself represents a reconfiguration of state power and constitutes a new style of governance: community governance (Newman, 2005). Community governance involves government action 'at a distance', where the state subtly defines the boundaries, characteristics and activities of civil society. In some quarters, this type of government action has been referred to as *enabling* activity, in which the state's role is to 'enable communities to exert choice and control and to integrate activities into community settings' (Armstrong and Francis, 2004). As such, community governance is a qualitative shift away from approaches to social policy, which emphasise either the state or the market as the most appropriate provider of social provisions.

Interestingly, the community governance approach to social policy, and the practices that flow from it, has diverse bases of support. It resonates with neo-liberal, communitarian and even radical democratic approaches to state–market–civil society relations (Giddens, 2000, p. 62; Botsman and Latham, 2001). In broad terms, the neo-liberal position sees community governance as a way of providing a solution to market failures by using voluntary community action to replace many state and market services. In this way, local communities are seen as capable of both reducing social service budgets and filling gaps in service provision. In line with anti-state sentiments, communities are seen as not only providing a cheaper alternative to public provision, but also as a qualitatively 'better' way of producing social policy outcomes, predominantly because they are thought to approximate the goals of self-reliance and self-support. More cynically, community governance can also be seen as 'shifting the burden' of cost, decision-making and risk away from governments to communities. On the other hand, communitarians and some radical social movements have embraced community governance, but they focus on its potential to reinvigorate collective and democratic approaches to social policy. They emphasise the place of civil society in economic development and social cohesion, and the use of 'bottom-up' approaches to social and economic development. The employment of self-help solutions for community problems is regarded as an attempt to empower citizens and community groups, and reinsert marginalised groups back into broader national and global decision-making processes in ways that the market and state institutions have been unable to. The communitarian and radical democratic ideas about the significance of community are, of course, not new and have underpinned community development and community empowerment practices for a long time. What is new is the legitimacy they have been accorded in social policy.

The strategic application of community as a central social policy tactic has emerged in a wide range of national settings, arising out of diverse conditions. It takes a variety of forms. In the UK and the European Union, community governance forms part of a broader governance agenda, known as the Third Way. A central plank of the Third Way is the devolution of social services to local community groups and associations in order to redress 'social exclusion', defined as the exclusion of individuals from the economic, political and cultural life of the nation (see chapter 9 for an extended discussion of social inclusion and exclusion). In this formulation, it is argued that community-centred provisions are capable of producing social inclusion and active citizenship in ways that state provisions cannot. In addition, social policies should be based on the premise that institutions—public, private and not-for-profit—can be encouraged to co-operate with one another in constructive partnerships rather than competing with one another.

In Canada, Australia and New Zealand, community governance appears primarily as state sponsoring of 'community strengthening' or 'community capacity building' activities. In Australia, almost all state governments now have policy units or even whole departments devoted to community development, which do things like 'measure social capital', develop indicators of community strength and employ 'place managers'—workers whose role is to help local communities identify their own needs and solutions. At the national level, governments have introduced community strengthening funding programs to replace a raft of traditional family, community and children's services (Randolph, 2004; Verity, 2007). In addition, some Indigenous community leaders, arguing that the welfare state has been heavily implicated in Indigenous social and economic disadvantage, have advocated for social policy approaches that enable Indigenous communities to take responsibility for their economic and cultural futures (Pearson, 2001). Indeed community governance has become a key theme in the politics of Indigenous social policy. Janet Hunt (2005), for example, argues that Indigenous community governance discourses in Australia and elsewhere derive from political concepts relating to human rights, self-determination and Indigenous nation-building, all of which require fundamental changes in the relationship between governments and Indigenous civil society, including the devolution of power and resources.

In many of the nations of Latin America, South-East Asia and Africa, community governance has become the mainstay of social policy. Following the post-Washington consensus, the World Bank and the International Monetary Fund have positioned the fostering of pre-existing social capital (which has been somehow constructed as particularly endogenous to these societies) in opposition to state support as the key to managing social and economic inequalities (Molyneaux, 2002). In Thailand, for example, this primarily means that the main form of state support for people in poverty is through community-based micro-financing projects, called 'community savings groups' (Senanuch, 2008).

Mike Geddes (2005), drawing on Esping-Andersen's comparative welfare regime typology, suggests that community governance is much more likely to be found in liberal or residual welfare regimes than in the social democratic or corporatist states. Geddes (2005, p. 16) suggests that an emphasis on local community regeneration and partnership building is consistent with the emphasis on private provision of public services and targeted mechanisms for the allocation of resources. But there are, as always, some exceptions. For example, Eva Jeppson Grassman's work (2003) suggests that community governance is evident in Sweden in what she calls the 'informalisation of social services', by which communities are being encouraged to undertake 'informal helping'. Her research shows that while there is a long, solid tradition of volunteering in Sweden, volunteers did not work in the provision of social services until the 1990s when Sweden experienced its 'welfare state crisis'.

In the US, there is a long tradition of community development activity and a history of voluntary social service provision, but the discourse of governing through community is not dominant. However, the ideas of US theorists have been significant in the development of community governance. For example, the ideas of Osbourne and Gabler (1992), in their book *Reinventing Government*, justified the move of governments across the globe out of service provision 'to steer, not row', and to empower communities to solve their own problems. The work of Amitai Etzioni (1993) has also been significant. His articulation of communitarianism has been used explicitly in rationales for developing active communities and the Third Way, in the UK in particular (Giddens, 1998; 2000). Finally, the work of Robert Putnam (2000) re-popularised the idea of social capital in his portrait of declining social capital in the US in *Bowling Alone*. Putnam's book has also been significant in bolstering arguments for state actions that shape, support and sponsor activities in civil society.

In the following section, we describe the ways in which these ideas have been put into practice, specifically through the social policy focus on 'community capacity building'. As Fiona Verity (2007) notes, the words community capacity building have increasingly become part of the policy and program language in health, social welfare, family and community services, education, environment, local government, rural and regional services and social and urban planning. In these areas, community capacity building has become the focus of a huge volume of reports, studies, projects, planning documents, best practice tools and evaluation frameworks produced by governments and civil society organisations. The widespread uptake of community capacity building means that human service professionals in a range of contexts are increasingly expected to understand, analyse, work alongside and participate in community capacity building policies and programs.

Community capacity building policies and programs

Community capacity building has become a central objective in a wide range of public policies and programs. In many senses, the ideas behind it are not new. The term 'community capacity building' came to attention in the 1990s, but must be regarded as part of a longstanding tradition of approaches with 'community' as a prefix, where community refers to any medium-sized grouping of people united by a common identity, location or goal. These include community development, community organising, community empowerment and community action (Hounslow, 2002; Raeburn et al., 2006). Many of the aspirations, processes and strategies of community development are also found in the current manifestations of community capacity building, as are many of the principles of community action and health promotion. As a result, community capacity building is sometimes regarded as 'old wine in a new bottle' (Wong, 2003). Other writers suggest that a distinction between community development and community capacity building does exist, and the differences relate to the degree to which the approaches focus on investing in capacities, capabilities and resources within communities. For example, Smith, Littlejohns and Thompson (2001, p. 33) define community capacity as 'the degree to which a community can develop, implement and sustain actions which allow it to exert greater control over its physical, social, economic and cultural environments'. In a similar vein, Howe and Cleary (2000) suggest that community capacity is 'the ability of individuals, organisations and communities to manage their own affairs and to work collectively to foster and sustain positive change'. Both these definitions emphasise self-determination and sustainability; intrinsic to most descriptions of community capacity are ideas and practices of community participation.

While community capacity building, as both a concept and a strategy, has relevance to all communities and to society as a whole, it is most commonly applied to communities and population groups regarded as disadvantaged. In part, this is an acknowledgment that recent global economic, cultural and social trends have had a differential impact on communities within nations, benefiting some individuals and communities and disadvantaging others (Gleeson and Carmichael, 2001). Despite high levels of economic growth in rich democracies in the past two decades, economic and social transformations have resulted in more deeply entrenched pockets of disadvantage. These impacts are particularly stark when they are concentrated in certain geographic areas, such as the new regional population centres outside cities, which were formed by the migration of lower and middle-income earners in search of affordable housing. These rapidly developed localities tend to be characterised by a lack of local employment and infrastructure, resulting in a large commuter workforce, poor transport infrastructure, a scarcity of cultural and leisure facilities, few training and employment opportunities, and limited neighbourhood facilities for families. In addition, communities that develop in this way are prone to having poor networks for social support and so residents experience high degrees of social isolation. So, while some geographic areas benefited immensely during the period of economic growth, one of the costs has been new spatial concentrations of disadvantage.

Community capacity building policies and programs are concerned with issues of social cohesion as well as social disadvantage. Blaxter and colleagues (2003) argue that the public policy legacy of the 1980s and 1990s was one of increased individualism, which led to the dislocation and fragmentation of families and communities. The changes have produced communities where people are disconnected from one another, they feel unsafe and insecure and are disengaged from decisions that impact upon them. It has been argued that violent crime, vandalism, personal isolation, racism and populations divided by age, ethnicity and class are symptomatic of this alienation (Lane and Henry, 2001). At the policy level, there has been an acknowledgment that new forms of social conflict, along with the emergence of concentrated disadvantage, require new and more effective interventions.

In this context, governments are increasingly aware of the importance of local citizens and local communities developing their capacities to produce security and well-being (Adams and Hess, 2000; Herbert-Cheshire, 2000; Everingham, 2001). In turn, local citizens and local communities are becoming increasingly concerned about ensuring that social development is something that communities 'do themselves', rather than 'have done to them'. In other words, social interventions are not the result of top-down processes, but are propelled from within the local community, from 'the ground up' (Simpson et al., 2003). Indeed, current research argues that the sustainability and effectiveness of projects aimed at reducing social disadvantage and increasing social cohesion depend on extensive and authentic community participation and partnerships (Smith et al., 2007).

In the following sections, we describe some of the key ideas and practices that are central in community capacity building policies and programs. These include a holistic or system-based approach to social needs, a focus on geographic communities, concentration on cross-sectoral and co-ordinated approaches to meeting social needs, emphasis on assets rather than deficits, the re-positioning of professionals, and attention to program sustainability and self-management.

A system-based or 'holistic' approach to social needs

The community capacity building approach, in theory at least, recognises the multi-faceted nature of social problems and social needs and represents a shift away from policies and programs designed to achieve specific outcomes (for example, programs designed to prevent child abuse and neglect, youth homelessness or substance abuse). In the health policy arena, for example, the community capacity building approach shifts the focus away from just specific disease impacts to the 'overall well-being' of individuals in their communities. Here, it is argued that intervening in specific health and social welfare issues at the community rather than the individual level is crucial. In this sense, community capacity building fits with the social determinist framework central to public health understandings of health inequalities, as well as with social justice approaches to social inequalities.

As a result, community capacity building provides a rationale for policy-makers and service providers in discrete areas to concentrate on 'system' issues such as educational or employment opportunities or social ties. For example, community capacity building provides health promotion workers with a rationale for focusing on the development of human and social capital rather than a specific 'health issue', and housing workers with a rationale for focusing on social networks and neighbourliness rather than 'rents and repairs'. In addition, many practitioners and analysts argue that community capacity building is desirable as an end in itself because it contributes to the creation and maintenance of active citizenship and social trust—sometimes called social capital. It is important to point out, however, that while community capacity building has become an important discourse in *most* social policy arenas and social program contexts, 'top down', 'individualised' and 'pathology' approaches to social needs remain dominant (Raeburn et al., 2006). As such, many human service professionals are operating in a field of contradictory discourses where attention to systemic needs and issues can be overwhelmed by pressures to produce tangible outcomes around specific issues.

A geographic or 'place-based' approach to social needs

While the concept 'community' refers to groups based on a diverse range of associations—religion, ethnicity, gender and other forms of identity—community capacity building policies and programs predominantly target geographic communities. This focus on place or location rests on a specific understanding of the relationship between locality and social disadvantage and between locality and social conflict. In many countries, governments have introduced programs targeted at a range of spatial scales and location contexts, from neighbourhoods, sub-areas of cities, to local regions in recognition of what Bill Randolph (2004) calls the 'geography of disadvantage'. This is the idea that not only can disadvantage be concentrated in particular places, but that neighbourhoods might have a compounding effect on disadvantage.

In Australia, the contours of the geographical distribution of disadvantage have been systematically mapped by Tony Vinson, most recently in the report *Dropping Off the Edge: The Distribution of Disadvantage in Australia* (2007). In that report, Vinson identifies a strong geographical correlation with a complex web of indicators of inter-generational disadvantage, such as low income, limited computer and internet access, early school leaving, physical and mental disabilities, long-term unemployment, prison admissions and confirmed child maltreatment. The Jesuit Social Services, which sponsored the report, argue that '(w)hen social disadvantage becomes thus concentrated, it can be impervious to the broad policy instruments of health, education and macro-economic growth—in such cases, general policies need to be supplemented by locality-specific ones. Place-based policy thus needs to be continued' (Jesuit Social Services, 2008, p. 2).

Place-based policies have had considerable appeal to people working with residents of public housing neighbourhoods. Community regeneration and community renewal strategies have been implemented in public housing neighbourhoods in Europe, England, Scotland and Wales, and more recently in Australia. Increasingly, people living in public housing estates have seen their basic quality of life decline because of economic and social change, and this has had a range of social and health consequences. With the reduction in available housing and an increase in prioritising tenants according to needs other than low income, public housing bodies are increasingly accommodating families and single people with complex problems. This has led to a concentration of vulnerable families and individuals in public housing (Randolph and Wood, 2003). Because these individuals and families often need and use social and human services, it has been argued that such concentrations tend to create social drain in areas where the community's own capacity to address and ameliorate social problems is seriously depleted (Vinson et al., 1996).

In Australia, community regeneration of public housing neighbourhoods has been a priority since the 1990s, with a focus on improving the condition of homes and design of neighbourhoods, preventing crime, developing resident employment and training, diversifying the social mix in estates, increasing resident participation in decision-making, improving access and co-ordination of services and building communities and social networks. Since then, community renewal priorities have included involving residents in decisions affecting the management of estates, adopting a flexible, localised approach to resident consultation and involvement in decision-making processes, and building residents' skills to contribute more effectively to their community (Hoatson, 2001; Arthurson, 2003).

New research reviewing the effectiveness of taking a place-based community capacity building approach in public housing neighbourhoods suggests positive outcomes. The evaluation of the Community Renewal strategy in Victoria, Australia, for example, suggests that more residents are participating in the governance of estates and community events, highly disadvantaged people have gained employment, some neighbourhoods are developing business enterprises, volunteering has increased, local streetscapes and community facilities have been improved, and external funding for the communities has been leveraged (Ferrie, 2008). In the UK, the evaluation of the first four years of the English neighbourhood renewal action plan has identified positive changes in disadvantaged communities, including improving educational attainments, increases in employment rates, growth in social and community cohesion and a reduction in levels of crime. These changes have been primarily attributed to the active involvement of local communities and collaboration between services and the community.

Some researchers, however, are wary about the negative impacts of place-based policies on disadvantaged people. Zoë Morrison (2008) argues that the concentration of poor people and particular social groups within the one place ensure that particular neighbourhoods and 'communities' have become convenient tools and powerful metaphors for government to express their commitment to social inclusion. The evocation of disadvantaged or excluded neighbourhoods or localities, she argues, 'reinforces negative stereotypes about poorer people, and disregards the cultural harm such stereotypes can cause' (Morrison, 2008, p. 6). This can have real consequences, including physical avoidance of these places by people who do not live there, contributing to the isolation and stigmatising of the residents who do.

The view that solutions to problems are best developed and implemented by those closest to the problem is succinctly expressed in the phrase 'local solutions to local problems'. Viewed from this perspective, community capacity building, neighbourhood regeneration and community renewal are the latest manifestations of decentralisation in social policy. One of the mechanisms popular with government to address disadvantaged localities is 'place management', which marries community capacity building with social planning. Place management programs restore the 1970s approach of community needs assessment feeding into rational planning procedures. Of significance to human service professionals is the way that place management attempts to replace conventional systems of program-focused management, whereby health, education and training, social welfare and community services are designed and delivered through silos that eradicate the significance of local connections and contexts. It is in this context that local human service workers are being encouraged to work inter-sectorally and in partnership with other providers, and for policy-makers to see social needs as 'joined-up' problems.

A cross-sectoral and co-ordinated approach to social needs

The community capacity building approach places great emphasis on cross-sectoral approaches to tackling social and economic issues, and on including business and the private sector in economic and social development. Indeed, the focus on local economic development as a central plank for social development has injected an element of 'market-based' solutions to some social welfare needs. As a result, a new form of welfare organisation, the 'social enterprise', has emerged. The place-based approach discussed above provides an opportunity to break down segmentation in social, economic and health arenas and to co-ordinate the activities of different government portfolios and spheres of government, such as local, state and national. It also provides an opportunity to link up the activities of government and non-government agencies with the activities of business, community and the philanthropic sectors. Here, concepts such as 'joined-up' governance, 'partnerships' and 'collaboration' come to the fore.

Although, in theory, community determined processes are the core of community capacity building, there are frequently professionals and government officials involved, and the extension of relationships with business means there is often corporate involvement. Thus, community capacity building policies and programs provide a range of new positions for human service workers. New occupations include place manager, community builder, community engagement worker, collaborations manager and partnership manager. These positions may be located in government, non-government, philanthropic or private sector organisations. (Some large insurance companies, for example, have employed community builders, on the basis that strong communities have low property crime rates, thus reducing insurance payouts.) Community capacity building, therefore, involves a range of operational activities, only some of which involve direct work with disadvantaged or socially isolated people in communities.

An assets-based approach

The concept of capacity building is also predicated on the conviction that all communities, whether geographic communities or communities of interest, have strengths or 'assets'. This is emphasised to counterbalance the 'deficit' prism through which disadvantaged people and communities are usually viewed. The assets approach challenges what is understood as a form of paternalism inherent in many public policies and programs and in the ways that 'professionals' often work with communities. It also recognises that 'interventions which take into account and build upon existing community capacities are more likely to be successful in accomplishing desired change than those which are adopted in a more traditional top-down manner' (Smith et al., 2001, p. 37).

Asset-Based Community Development (ABCD) is a model for working with communities that has emerged over the past decade in the US, where it has been used extensively in communities often described as 'disadvantaged'.

Asset-Based Community Development uses a process to identify and mobilise the assets available in a particular community, using a broad definition of assets that encompasses individuals, associations, institutions, physical assets and the local economy (Foster and Mathie, 2001; Mathie and Cunningham, 2003). Assets approaches have been contrasted to traditional models of community development, which emphasise the importance of identifying and addressing needs and gaps experienced by communities. The ABCD model holds that a community development process that begins with needs and deficits ends with communities being defined as powerless and reliant exclusively on help from outside. Further to this, needs-based models of community development can entrench power in the hands of 'helpers' who have a strong interest in keeping that power away from communities. In contrast to this, identifying and building on local assets and strengths shifts power back into the hands of community members by building community 'from the inside out' (Kretzman and McKnight, 1993).

The strengths and assets focus of some community capacity building approaches potentially changes the role and nature of the work of human service professionals. The kinds of activities community building workers engage in include the mapping of skills, resources and networks of individuals in communities, the mapping of physical resources (such as parks, halls, buildings, meeting rooms, etc.), and the mapping of economic and cultural resources or assets available in the community. Given that conventionally human service professionals have engaged in social policy processes in order to politicise, interpret and address social needs and social problems, the strengths or assets-based approach produces quite different ways of participating in social policy for social change.

The re-positioning of professionals

Building community capacity through community empowerment is a fundamental change, a paradigm shift, in assumptions and values about managing and addressing social problems. In the emerging paradigm, the values of stakeholder participation and empowerment, community integration and community access to resources, shifts power from those who are professionals and traditional decision-makers to those who are affected by the problems. The community capacity building approach places a great deal of emphasis on the community identification of needs and outcomes; that is, on the community initiating action rather than being mobilised to act (Smith et al., 2001). Thus, there is an emphasis on local democracy, whereby bottom-up initiatives take priority over solutions imposed from outside. Indeed, it is argued that the multiple and layered social and physical issues in disadvantaged communities will only be addressed successfully with genuine resident engagement and involvement (Arthurson, 2003; Berg et al., 2003). Where human service professionals are involved, their role becomes one of facilitation, consultancy and advocacy. In the ideal form, community members only use professionals when they need to. Thus, human service professionals are re-positioned in relation to individuals in the community.

The position of human service professionals working in community capacity building programs in relation to organisational context is more complex. Often they are employed, funded or sponsored by government organisations, a private sector organisation or a non-government organisation. Organisations bring with them demands for accountability and legitimation of the activities undertaken. Community capacity builders are therefore often impelled to meet performance indicators, measure and map social change and conduct program evaluations. These types of activity have become central to human service workers in disadvantaged localities, and they could be regarded as a field of practice in themselves.

An attention to program sustainability and self-management

A key emphasis of capacity development is on achieving and *sustaining* outcomes. This has important implications for social policy. Many capacity development initiatives fail, or have not been successfully sustained, because of the conditions and time limitations of government funded capacity building projects. In some accounts, community members have reported decreased local or community capacity due to 'burn-out' and cynicism, especially in the face of short-term funding, high expectations and unresponsive institutions (Verity, 2007). While successful at the time, government funded programs are often not sustained once the community building funding finishes. In addition, the goal of creating projects that will be managed by the community rather than by professionals sometimes relies on an overstatement of the skills, resources and interest available in many communities. One way that governments seek to redress these problems is to fund programs for longer periods. Community capacity building programs in Scotland, for example, are often funded for 10 years. Referring to the community capacity building programs in Australia, Martin Mowbray (2005, p. 264) argues that if governments are generally concerned with empowering communities, rather than '… strengthening central governmental agendas', they would 'embark on whole-hearted socio-economic reform' and support practices that are long term, well funded and have devolved decision-making.

Conclusion

Many analysts and practitioners in the human services field regard the re-centralising of community as a social policy development that will lead to positive social change. This chapter has provided a discussion of one of the most visible manifestations of community governance, community capacity building. The exploration suggests that community capacity policies and programs provide opportunities to approach social needs in new ways and develop new ways of working with and for communities. For instance, community capacity building recognises the systemic nature of social problems, the significance of place and the importance of cross-agency collaborations, citizen participation, community strengths and sustainable program development. It is clear, however, that community capacity building also poses dilemmas for human service professionals, and may not be a panacea for the complex social issues that have arisen in contemporary rich (and poorer) democracies. There appear to be some obvious problems with the prevailing views of community as the appropriate foundation for social policy, which human service professionals should keep in mind:

First, current community initiatives, across nations, tend to focus exclusively on geographic communities, or communities of place. The construction of policy responses around local communities draws attention to the spatial distribution of disadvantage, but there are problems with constructing disadvantage as spatial. For instance, the approach constructs communities of place as though they are undifferentiated (everyone who lives there has similar or equivalent needs or interests), yet the 'community' is not a single or homogeneous entity. The emphasis on community consensus or coherence may be at the expense of dissenting voices. In addition, where there is local community consensus, this may be in conflict with the equity or social cohesion goals of the wider national community. As such, governments may have an important role beyond enabling local communities.

Second, there are not always local solutions to social problems, regardless of the strength of a community's 'capacity'. Some problems require state or national (or even international) level changes in policies, political approaches and resource allocations. Community governance also produces problems for the ideal of universal citizenship, particularly in relation to equal political and social rights. It cannot guarantee, or even offer, citizens across communities the same access to political participation or to standardised and universal social services.

Finally, community governance discourses, such as community capacity building, partnerships and place management have become very popular and have provided leverage for some organisations, associations and individuals to access assistance, resources and support from governments and from one another. However, this is only one part of the community politics story. Another part concerns the more independent, often unruly efforts of civil society actors who come together to press claims for a better deal from governments and markets. For these reasons, human service providers need to consider whether government efforts to shape civil society need to be resisted, rather than supported, at particular times.

CHAPTER 12

Conclusion

From the start, this book set out to revisit social policy as a key component of the broad field of human services. The topics covered in the various chapters reflect key perspectives and fields of knowledge that are considered central to the process of making social policy an instrument for social change. They also indicate points of interception and engagement for human service practitioners, a perspective that has made this book unusual in social policy literature. Although it has drawn on important fields of knowledge that are consistently part of social policy and welfare state scholarship, it has, by using contemporary and historical examples, shifted the perspective of these well-worn scholarly paths. This fresh perspective includes dynamic links between understanding the big picture as a framework for local change, accepting complexity as a key characteristic of human services practice, encouraging flexibility as a compass for navigating the contemporary world and using knowledge about context as a tool for being effective in influencing social policy for social change.

Throughout the book, we have drawn from a wide range of examples of social policies, mainly from within what we have called 'rich democracies'. Rich democracies fall into groups based on shared social, cultural and economic experiences and relationships. Generally, we have drawn from examples in rich democracies that have also undergone many similar transformations in their welfare states and have similar sets of players in the social policy field. The examples of how social policy has been adopted, formed or produced, and the roles of the various stakeholders in the process in different countries are also distinctive, owing to the specific political, social and economic trajectories of change that shape each nation's institutions.

The fact that rich democracies have experienced different *and* similar ways of pursuing, engaging or developing social policy at different times raises interesting questions about social policy. Is social policy a matter of adopting and trying out different ideas that have been tried somewhere else? Do governments learn from the failure of social policy to 'solve' social policy problems? Is social policy so intrinsic to its context that external experiences can only present possible ideas to work from? Is social policy such a political process that the parallels between the approaches of different countries are actually drawn from shared ideologies and political objectives?

Clearly, part of the purpose of this book has been to plough the field from which these questions arise and plant seeds of thought that may find purchase in the minds of students, practitioners and scholars engaged in the business of social policy. Responding to such questions is not simple and the complexities that arise in trying to answer them could indeed *be* the answers. Social policy in complex societies is itself complex. Responding to and intervening in social policy can only be effective if there is sufficient flexibility to cope with that complexity.

However, the prime purpose of this book is to make sense of the complexity of social policy. In this, we can all be considered to receive welfare so that discussions about social policy affect all of us. A further point is that social policies provide generalised responses that serve specific groups and categories rather than individuals. As a result, some will benefit more than others will, and those whose problems are not captured well by social policy generalisations may lose out. Further, human service practitioners, as well as service users, are directly affected by the design and organisation of social policies. Social policies provide the substantive framework for service provision. We argue that all human service professionals play a part in policy processes and can guide change in a whole variety of ways.

We also suggest that knowledge and understanding of the complexity of social policy development and implementation is central to the capacity to use or engage with it as an effective process for positive social change. As we have seen throughout the book, social policy is shaped by politics, economics, values, social movements and research. Although often enhancing the complexity of interests in the social policy process, none of these factors is in itself straightforward. The book gives many examples of competing claims that are played out in different ways. As we highlighted in chapter 2, the policy process is fluid but not chaotic, and ambiguous but not muddled. Social policy can be seen as the structured commitment of important resources, where various players try to shape outcomes in ways consistent with their own agendas. This occurs by means of the creation and utilisation of discourses, both within and against prevailing organisational structures.

There are many ways of understanding social policy. One view we have highlighted is that social problems and social policies are best understood not as given, factual entities with linear, rationally orientated connections, but as the interaction of interpretive processes and resource conflicts. Accordingly, what is identified as an issue requiring attention and the resulting social policy responses is influenced by shifts in understandings and by a range of actors with varying perspectives and resources coming together to bring about social change. Fraser's (1989) identification of three moments or phases can serve as a useful example of the process of social policy formation. Here, as highlighted in chapter 2, an initial struggle to establish or deny the political status of any given need is followed by contestation over the interpretation and contention about the ongoing satisfaction of 'identified' needs.

The central project of this book has been to establish a framework for thinking about social policy as a tool for or facilitator of social change. Like the concept of social policy, social change has been viewed from a range of political, ideological, social and academic perspectives, which themselves reflect and develop contemporary values and influencing factors. As we have emphasised, social change can happen as an all-encompassing process, generated by large-scale events such as economic crises or war, or by means of gradual processes that reflect shifting values, ideologies and changes in social and economic structures. However, most importantly we have sought to explore the possibility that social policy is a means of bringing about positive social change.

Even though what constitutes social change is itself changeable, varying over time and in different societies, it is important to note that, in the contemporary context, the ideal of social justice has wide-ranging support, evident in the emergence of human rights as an internationally accepted priority. For human service professionals, as we have seen, the achievement of social change is often measured against a set of positive ideas and values about what a better state of being or standard of living might be for service users. As highlighted above, human service professionals at a range of levels and in a variety of capacities contribute to the development of improvements for the well-being, resources and quality of life of all, especially the most vulnerable. Human service professionals together with other members of society shape values, determine what is acceptable or unacceptable, legitimate or illegitimate, and support or contest policies rolled out by governments. At a more local or organisational level, human service practitioners influence the policies of agencies and professional organisations. Some human service practitioners will participate in the design of policy frameworks, some will exert pressure for change and all, by involvement in even relatively small-scale research and evaluation projects, can ensure that policy and practice remain live, relevant and responsive.

As a final statement in this book, it seems important to present a message about the future of social policy as an instrument for social change. If we reflect on recent history, both in rich democracies and in emerging welfare states in Asia (Kwok, 2008; Ku, 2007; Yu, 2006), we can conclude that social policy continues to be seen as an instrument for the betterment of people's lives. This broad sentiment towards positive social change is unlikely itself to change, even if the many configurations of the way social policy is formed and carried out do. For example, reflecting on a world rife with risk and on the potential to 'democratise welfare', Tony Fitzpatrick suggests that what is required of social policy is not to 'develop a once-and-forever series of welfare institutions that will protect us from external hazards, but to create a social culture of experimental diversity that allows quick, flexible and transnational management of risks whenever they arise' (2002, p. 12). It is clear that as the world becomes more integrated in its need to respond to global social problems, the way we manage responses to those problems will have to be more collective and more flexible. It is hoped that those who are part of human services will find a parallel message in this book for the future of social policy within their own countries or communities, and look forward to continued participation in the project of social policy for social change.

References

ABC (Australian Broadcasting Corporation) 2007, *7.30 News Report*, 22 June.

ABC 2008, *The Intervention: Katherine in the Northern Territory*, 9.30pm, 30 October.

ABC (Australian Broadcasting Corporation) 2008, 'Binge drinking violence rising: Survey', ABC News, 15 April, viewed 21 April 2008, <www.abc. net.au/news/stories/2008/04/15/2217120.htm>.

ABC Learning 2008, Australian Government information site for parents 'mychild.gov.au', 26 November and 10 December, viewed 18 February 2009, <www.mychild.gov.au/abc.htm>.

ABC Radio, 2001, 'Liberal Party charges $7,500 fee for policy development', *The World Today Archive*, Reporter: Alexandra Kirk, Friday, 16 March, viewed 16 March 2009, <www.abc.net.au/worldtoday/stories/s261350.htm>.

Abrahamson, P, 1999, 'The welfare modelling business', *Social Policy and Administration*, vol. 33, no. 4, pp. 394–415.

ABS 2001, *Community Services, Australia, 1999–2000*, Cat. No. 8690.0, Australian Bureau of Statistics, Canberra.

ABS 2007a, *Household Income and Income Distribution, Australia, 2005–06*, Cat. No. 6523.0, Australian Bureau of Statistics, Canberra.

ABS 2007b, 'Low income low wealth households', *Australian Social Trends 2007*, Cat. No. 4102.0, Australian Bureau of Statistics, Canberra.

ABS 2007c, 'One-parent families', *Australian Social Trends 2007*, Cat. No. 4102.0, Australian Bureau of Statistics, Canberra.

ABS 2007d, *Voluntary Work, Australia*, Cat. No. 4441.0, Australian Bureau of Statistics, Canberra.

ABS 2008, *Not-for-profit Organisations, Australia, 2006–7*, Cat. No. 8106.0, Australian Bureau of Statistics, Canberra.

Ackerman, DJ 2006, 'The costs of being a child care teacher: Revisiting the problem of low wages', *Education Policy*, vol. 20, no. 1, pp. 85–112.

ACOSS 2007, 'Open letter to the Hon Mal Brough MP', in B. McDermott (ed), *A Collection of Initial Responses to the Howard Government's Intervention in the Northern Territory*, Indigenous Law Centre, University of NSW, Sydney.

Adams, D and Hess, M 2001, 'Community in public policy: Fad or foundation?' *Australian Journal of Public Administration*, vol. 60, no. 2, pp. 13–23.

Adema, W and Ladaique, M 2005, *Net Social Expenditure, 2005 Edition: More Comprehensive Measures of Social Support*, OECD Social, Employment and Migration Papers No. 29, OECD Publishing, Paris.

Ahmed, S and Potter, D 2006, *NGOs in International Politics*, Kumarian Press, Bloomfield, USA.

AIHW (Australian Institute of Health and Welfare) 1998, *Australia's Health 1998*, Australian Institute of Health and Welfare, Canberra.

AIHW 2007a, *Australia's Welfare 2007*, Australian Institute of Health and Welfare, Canberra.

AIHW 2007b, 'Child protection in Australia 2002–2006', *Child Welfare Series*, No. 40, AIHW, Cat. No. CWS 28, AIHW, Canberra.

AIHW 2008, *Australia's Health 2008*, Australian Institute of Health and Welfare, Canberra.

Aird, W 2008, 'Great Aboriginal con', *The Australian*, 28 April, p. 8.

Alampay, P and Ong, C 2007, 'Kapwa Ko, Mahal Ko Foundation' in Carino, Ledivina V. and Delores D. Gaffud (eds). What They Contribute. *Case Studies on the Impact of Nonprofit Organizations*, Center for Leadership, Citizenship and Democracy, Quezon City, Philippines.

Alber, J 1995, 'A framework for the comparative study of social services', *Journal of European Social Policy*, vol. 5, no. 2, pp. 131–149.

Albrecht, G and Seelman, K 2003, *Handbook of Disability Studies*, Sage, Thousand Oaks.

Alcock, P, Glennerster, H, Oakley, A, and Sinfield, A (eds) 2001, *Welfare and Well-being: Richard Titmuss's Contribution to Social Policy*, The Policy Press, Bristol.

Altman, JC, Biddle, N and Hunter, B 2004, *Indigenous Socioeconomic Change 1971–2001: A Historical Perspective*, Discussion Paper No. 266/2004, Centre for Aboriginal Economic Policy Research, Australian National University, Canberra.

Altman, J and Hinkson, M (eds) 2007, *Coercive Reconciliation*, Arena Publications, Melbourne.

Anderson, P and Wild, R 2007, 'Ampe Akelyernemane Meke Mekarle'/'Little Children are Sacred', *Report of the Northern Territory Board of Inquiry into the Protection of Aboriginal Children from Sexual Abuse*, Northern Territory Government, Darwin.

Andrews, GJ, Gavin, N, Begley, S and Brodie, D 2003, 'Assisting friendships, combating loneliness: Users' views on a "befriending" scheme', *Ageing & Society*, vol. 23, no. 3, pp. 349–62.

Andrews, K and Edwards, B 2004, 'Advocacy organizations in the US political process', *Annual Review of Sociology*, vol. 30, pp. 479–506.

Anttonen, A and Sipilä, J 1996, 'European social care services: Is it possible to identify models?' *Journal of European Social Policy*, vol. 6, no. 2, pp. 87–100.

Arksey, H and Kemp, PA 2008, 'Dimensions of choice: A narrative review of cash-for-care schemes', *Social Policy Research Unit Working Paper No. DHP2250*, University of York.

Armstrong, A and Francis, R 2004, 'The role of community governance in public sector programs and initiatives', in Integrated Governance: Linking up Government, Business & Civil Society, 25–26 October (unpublished), Prato, Italy.

Arthurson, K 2003, 'Neighbourhood regeneration: Facilitating community involvement', *Urban Policy and Research*, vol. 21, no. 4, pp. 357–37.

Arts, WA and Gelissen, J 2002, 'Three worlds of welfare capitalism or more? A state-of-the-art report', *Journal of European Social Policy*, vol. 12, no. 2, pp. 137–158.

Atkinson, AB 1999, *The Economic Consequences of Rolling Back the Welfare State*, MIT Press, Cambridge, Massachusetts.

Atkinson, AB, Atkinson, T, Marlier, E and Nolan, B, 2002, *Social Indicators: The EU and Social Inclusion*, Oxford University Press, Oxford.

Atkinson, J 2007, 'Indigenous approaches to child abuse', in J. Altman, and M. Hinkson, (eds) 2007, *Coercive Reconciliation*, Arena Publications, Melbourne.

Australian Government 2007, *Australian Institute of Health and Welfare — Health and Ageing Portfolio Agency*, Department of Health and Ageing, Australian Government, Canberra.

Australian Government 2008a, 'Social inclusion', *Social Inclusion Website*, Australian Government, Canberra, viewed 12 December 2008, <www.socialinclusion.gov.au/>.

Australian Government 2008b, *Australia 2020 Summit, Final Report*, Australian Government, Canberra, viewed 12 December 2008, <www.australia2020.gov.au/final_report/index.cfm>.

Australian Human Rights and Equal Opportunity Commission 2007, *HREOC Submission to the Australian Senate Legal and Constitutional Committee on the Northern Territory National Emergency Response Legislation*, 10 August, Canberra, Australia.

Australian, The 2008, 'Indigenous kids trampled in summit race for treaty', 22 April, pp. 1 and 7.

Ayre, P 2001, 'Child protection and the media: Lessons from the last three decades', *British Journal of Social Work*, vol. 31, no. 6, pp. 887–901.

Bacchi, C 1996, *The Politics of Affirmative Action: 'Women', Equality and Category Politics,* Sage, London.

Bacchi, C 1999, *Women, Policy and Politics: The Construction of Policy Problems,* Sage, London.

Bacchi, C 2008, 'The ethics of problem representation: Widening the scope of ethical debate', *Policy & Society*, vol. 25, no. 2, pp. 3–22.

Bagilhole, B 1996, 'Tea and sympathy or teetering on social work? An investigation of the blurring of the boundaries between voluntary and professional care', *Social Policy and Administration*, vol. 30, no. 3, pp. 189–205.

Baines, D 2004, 'Caring for nothing: Work organization and unwaged labour in social services', *Work, Employment and Society*, vol. 18, no. 2, pp. 267–295.

Baines, D 2008, 'Neoliberal restructuring, activism/participation, and social unionism in the nonprofit social services', *Nonprofit and Voluntary Sector Quarterly*, OnlineFirst, published 19 December as doi:10.1177/0899764008326681.

Baldock, JN, Manning, N and Vickerstaff, S (eds) 2007, *Social Policy,* 3rd edn, Oxford University Press, Oxford.

Bambra, C 2005, 'Worlds of welfare and the health care discrepancy', *Social Policy and Society*, vol. 4, no. 1, pp. 31–41.

Banks, S 2006, *Ethics and Values in Social Work*, 3rd edn, Palgrave Macmillan, Basingstoke.

Banks, S 2008, 'Critical commentary: Social work ethics', *British Journal of Social Work,* vol. 38, no. 6, pp. 1238–49.

Barber, B 1998, *A Place for Us: How to Make Society Civil and Democracy Strong*, Hill and Wang, New York.

Barnes, M, Newman, J, Knops, A and Sullivan, H 2003, 'Constituting "the public" in public participation', *Public Administration*, vol. 81, no. 2, pp. 379–399.

Barr, N 1992, 'Economic theory and the welfare state: A survey and interpretation', *Journal of Economic Literature*, vol. 302, pp. 741–803.

Baudrillard, J 1998, *Live: Selected Interviews*, M. Gane (ed), Routledge, London/ New York.

Bauman, Z 1992, *Intimations of Postmodernity*, Routledge, London.

Bauman, Z 1993, *Postmodern Ethics*, Blackwell, Oxford.

Bauman, Z 1998, *Work, Consumerism and the New Poor,* Oxford University Press, Buckingham.

Beall, J 2002, 'Globalization and social exclusion in cities: Framing the debate with lessons from Africa and Asia', *Environment and Urbanization* vol. 4, no. 1, pp. 41–51.

Beck, U 1992, *Risk Society,* Sage, London.

Beers, S 1969, *Modern British Politics,* Faber, London.

Bellamy, J and Cowling, S 2008, 'The lived experience of welfare reform: Stories from the field', paper presented to ARACY ARC/NHMRC Research Network supported Workshop on the Impact of Welfare-to-Work and Workplace Reforms on Young People and Children at Risk, University of Sydney, 13 February.

Beresford, P 2005, 'Redistributing profit and loss: The new economics of the market and social welfare', *Critical Social Policy*, vol. 25, no. 4, pp. 464–82.

Beresford, P 2006, Developing inclusive partnerships: User defined outcomes, networking and knowledge—A case study, *Health and Social Care in the Community*, vol. 14, no. 5, pp. 436–444.

Beresford, P and Campbell, J 1994, 'Disabled people, service users, user involvement and representation', *Disability and Society*, vol. 9, no. 3, pp. 315–25.

Beresford, P and Croft, S 2004 'Service users and practitioners re-united: a key component for social work reform', British Journal of Social Work, vol. 34, no. 1, pp. 53–68.

Berg, L van den, Meer, J van der and Pol, PMJ 2003, 'Organising capacity and social policies in European cities', *Urban Studies*, vol. 40, no. 10, pp. 1959–1978.

Bergman, S 2008, 'Women-friendly Nordic societies?' *Euro Topics*, Federal Agency for Civic Education 31 March, viewed 10 March 2009, <www.eurotopics.net/en/magazin/gesellschaft-verteilerseite/frauen-2008-3/artikel_bergman_frauen_norden/>.

Bernard, P and Boucher, G 2007, 'Institutional competitiveness, social investment, and welfare regimes', *Regulation and Governance*, vol. 1, no. 3, pp. 213–229.

Bertone, C 2003, 'Claims for child care as struggles over needs: Comparing Italian and Danish women's organization', *Social Politics: International Studies in Gender, State & Society,* vol. 10, no. 2, pp. 229–255.

Billis, D and Glennerster, H 1998, 'Human services and the voluntary sector: Towards a theory of comparative advantage', *Journal of Social Policy*, vol. 27, no. 1, pp. 79–98.

Bittman, M 1998, 'Social participation and family welfare: The money and time costs of leisure', paper presented at the Changing Families, Challenging Futures, *6th Australian Institute of Family Studies Conference*, Melbourne, 25–27 November, viewed 24 April 2006, <http://aifs.gov.au/institute/afrc6papers/bittman.html>.

Black, N 2001, 'Evidence based policy: Proceed with care', *British Medical Journal,* vol. 323, pp. 275–21.

Blau, J and Abramovitz, M 2007, *The Dynamics of Social Welfare Policy*, 2nd edn, Oxford University Press, New York.

Blaxter, L, Farnell, R and Watts, J 2003, 'Difference, ambiguity and the potential for learning—Local communities working in partnership with local government', *Community Development Journal*, vol. 38, no. 2, pp. 130–139.

Blomqvist, P 2004, 'The choice revolution: Privatization of Swedish welfare services in the 1990s', *Social Policy and Administration*, vol. 38, no. 2, pp. 139–155.

Bochel, C, Bochel, P, Somerville, P and Worley, C 2007, 'Marginalised or enabled voices? User participation in policy and practice', *Social Policy and Society*, vol. 7, no. 2, pp. 201–210.

Bode, I 2007, 'New moral economies of welfare: The case of domiciliary elder care in Germany, France and Britain', *European Societies*, vol. 9, no. 2, pp. 201–227.

Botsman, P and Latham, M (eds) 2001, *The Enabling State: People Before Bureaucracy,* Pluto Press, Sydney.

Bowles, W, Collingridge, M, Curry, S and Valentine, B 2006, *Ethical Practice in Social Work,* Allen & Unwin, Sydney.

Bradley, G 2003, 'Administrative justice and charging for long-term care', *British Journal of Social Work,* vol. 33, no. 5, pp. 641–57.

Brady, D, Fullerton, A and Cross, JM 2008, 'Putting poverty in political context: A multi-level analysis of working-aged poverty across 18 affluent democracies', Luxembourg, *Working Paper*, no. 487, Luxembourg Income Study, Brussels.

Brady, D and Kall, D 2008, 'Nearly universal but somewhat distinct: The feminization of poverty in affluent Western democracies, 1969–2000', *Social Science Research*, vol. 37, no 3, pp. 976–1001.

Bredgaard, T and Larsen, F 2007, 'Implementing public employment policy: What happens when non-public agencies take over?' *International Journal of Sociology and Social Policy*, vol. 27, no. 7/8, pp. 287–300.

Bredgaard, T and Larsen, F 2008, 'Quasi-markets in employment policy: Do they deliver on promises?' *Social Policy and Society*, vol. 7, no. 3, pp. 341–352.

Brennan, D 1998, *The Politics of Australian Child Care: Philanthropy to Feminism and Beyond*, revised edn, Cambridge University Press, Melbourne.

Brennan, D 2007, 'The ABC of child care policy', *Australian Journal of Social Issues*, vol. 42, no. 2, pp. 213–225.

Bridgman, P and Davis, G 2007, *The Australian Policy Handbook,* 4th edn, Allen & Unwin, Sydney.

Brinkerhoff, J, Smith, S and Teegen, H 2007, 'The role of NGOs in health, education, environment, and gender: Application of the theoretical framework', in J. Brinkerhoff, S. Smith and H. Teegen (eds), *NGOs and the Millennium Development Goals, Citizen Action to Reduce Poverty*, Palgrave Macmillan, New York, pp.149–188.

Brough, M 2007, 'National emergency response to protect Aboriginal children in the Northern Territory', *Ministerial Media Release,* 21 June, Canberra.

Brown, KA and Keast, RL 2005, 'Social services policy and delivery in Australia: Centre-periphery mixes', *Policy and Politics*, vol. 33, no. 3, pp. 505–518.

Bryman, A (ed) 2006, *Mixed Methods*, Sage, London.

Bryman, A 2008, *Social Research Methods,* 3rd edn, Oxford University Press, Oxford.

Bryson, L 2001, 'Australia: The transformation of the wage earners' welfare state', in P. Alcock and G. Craig (eds), *International Social Policy*, Palgrave, Basingstoke, Hampshire.

Burch, H 1998, *Social Welfare Policy Analysis and Choices*, Haworth Press, New York.

Burgess, J and Strachan, G 2005, 'Integrating work and family responsibilities: Policies for lifting women's labour activity rates', *Just Policy*, vol. 35 (March), pp. 5–12.

Burgmann, V 2003, *Power, Profit and Protest: Australian Social Movements and Globalisation,* Allen & Unwin, Sydney.

Busse, R and Riesberg, A 2004, *Health Care Systems in Transition, Germany,* World Health Organization, Copenhagen, viewed 24 April 2006, <www.euro. who.int/observatory/ctryinfo/ctryinfo>.

Burton, J and van den Broek, D 2008, 'Accountable and countable: Information management systems and the bureaucratization of social work', *British Journal of Social Work,* Advance Access published 26 April, 2008, doi:10.1093/bjsw/ bcn027.

Byrne, J and Davis, G 1998, *Participation in the NSW Policy Process: A Discussion Paper for the Cabinet Office,* NSW Cabinet Office, Sydney.

Cabinet Office 2009, 'Context for social exclusion work: What do we mean by social exclusion?' Cabinet Office Social Exclusion Task Force Website, viewed 17 March 2009, <www.cabinetoffice.gov.uk/social_exclusion_task_force/ context.aspx>.

Cahill, D 2002, 'Funding the ideological struggle', *Overland*, vol. 168, pp. 21–26.

Calder, A 2000, 'Financial support for care leavers', *Poverty*, no. 106, pp. 11–13.

Calma, T 2007, 'Comment', *Sydney Morning Herald*, 10 July, p. 1.

Calma, T 2008, 'The role of social workers as human rights workers with Indigenous people and communities', paper presented at the Australian Catholic University, 12 February.

Campbell, C, Proctor, H and Sherrington, G 2009, *School Choice: How Parents Negotiate the New School Market,* Allen & Unwin, Sydney.

Carey, M 2003, 'Anatomy of a care manager', *Work, Employment and Society*, vol. 17, no. 1, pp. 121–35.

Carney, T and Hanks, P 1994, *Social Security in Australia*, Oxford University Press, Melbourne.

Carr, S 2004, 'Has service user participation made a difference to social care services?' *Social Care Institute for Excellence Position Paper No. 3*, The Policy Press, Bristol.

Casey, J and Dalton, B 2006, 'The best of times, the worst of times', *Australian Journal of Political Science,* vol. 41, no. 1, pp. 23–38.

Casey, J, Dalton, B, Onyx, J and Melville, R 2008, 'Advocacy in the age of compacts: Regulating government—community sector relations: International experiences', *Centre for Australian Community Organisations and Management,* Working Paper Series No. 76, February.

Caspar, S and O'Rourke, N 2008, 'The influence of care provider access to structural empowerment on individualized care in long-term-care facilities', *Journal of Gerontology: Social Sciences*, vol. 63B, no. 4S, pp. 255–65.

Castles, F 1985, *The Working Class and Welfare*, Allen & Unwin, Sydney.

Castles, F 2004, *The Future of the Welfare State: Crisis Myths and Crisis Realities*, Oxford University Press, Oxford.

Castles, F and Mitchell, D 1992, 'Identifying welfare state regimes: The links between politics, instruments and outcomes', *Governance*, vol. 5, no. 1, pp. 1–26.

Castles, F and Obinger, H 2007, 'Social expenditure and the politics of redistribution', *Journal of European Social Policy*, vol. 17, no. 3, pp. 206–222.

Castles, F (ed) 1993, *Families of Nations: Patterns of Public Policy in Western Democracies*, Dartmouth, Aldershot.

CBS News 2008, 'Emergency room death sparks outrage', *CBS News Web Site*, New York, 2 July, viewed 28 November 2008,<www.cbsnews.com/stories/2008/07/02/national/main4227468.shtml?source=RSSattr=U.S._4227468>.

Chambers, DE and Wedel, KR 2005, *Social Policy and Social Programs: A Method for the Practical Public Policy Analyst,* 4th edn, Allyn and Bacon, Boston.

Chappell, L 2001, 'Federalism and social policy: The case of domestic violence', *Australian Journal of Public Administration*, vol. 60, no. 1, pp. 59–69.

Chappell, L 2002, *Gendering Government, Feminist Engagement with the State in Australia and Canada*, UBC Press, Vancouver.

Cheetham, J, Fuller, R, McIvor, G and Petch, A 1992, *Evaluating Social Work Effectiveness*, Open University Press, Buckingham.

Cheverton, J 2005, 'Past their peak? Governance and the future of peak bodies in Australia', *Australian Journal of Social Issues*, vol. 42, no. 3, pp. 427–436.

Clarke, J 2006, 'Consumers, clients or citizens? Politics, policy and practice in the reform of social care', *European Societies*, vol. 8, no. 3, pp. 423–442.

Clarke, J 2007, 'It's not like shopping: Citizens, consumers and the reform of public services', in M. Blair and F. Trentmann (eds), *Governance, Citizens and Consumers, Agency and Resistance in Contemporary Politics*, Palgrave, Basingstoke.

Clarke, J and Newman, J 1997, *The Managerial State: Power, Politics and Ideology in the Remaking of Social Welfare*, Sage, London.

Clarke, J, Smith, N and Vidler, E 2006, 'The indeterminacy of choice: Political, policy and organisational implications', *Social Policy and Society*, vol. 5, no. 3, pp. 327–336.

Cloke, P, Johnsen, S and May, J 2007, 'Ethical citizenship? Volunteers and the ethics of providing services for homeless people', *Geoforum*, vol. 38, no. 6, pp. 1089–1101.

Cochrane, A 2000, 'new Labour, new urban policy', *Social Policy Review*, vol. 12, pp. 184–202.

Colebatch, HK 2000, *Policy,* Open University Press, Buckingham.

Colebatch, HK (ed) 2006, *Beyond the Policy Cycle: The Policy Process in Australia*, Allen & Unwin, Sydney.

Colebatch, HK 2007, *Doing Policy, Doing Analysis: Accounting for Policy in Australia*, Department of Public Policy and Administration, University of Brunei Darussalam.

Commonwealth of Australia 2008, *Report of the Northern Territory Emergency Response Review Board*, chaired by Peter Yu, released 13 October, Canberra, Australian Government.

Communities and Local Government 2009, Communities and Local Government Website, viewed 17 March 2009, <www.communities.gov.uk/corporate/about/who/>.

Connell, R 2008, 'Good teachers and hungry markets', Paper presented at Sisters of Sisyphus? Human Service Professions and the New Public Management Academy of the Social Sciences Workshop, University of Sydney, 2–3 October.

Cooper, M 1999, 'The Australian disability rights movement lives', *Disability and Society*, vol. 14, no. 2, pp. 217–26.

Cornes, M, Manthorpe, J, Huxley, P and Evans, S 2007, 'Developing wider workforce regulation in England: Lessons from education, social work and social care', *Journal of Interprofessional Care*, vol. 21, no. 3, pp. 241–50.

Cortis, N 2007, 'What do service users think of evaluation? Evidence from family support', *Child and Family Social Work*, vol. 12, no. 4, pp. 399–408.

Council of Europe 2008, 'European Muslim communities confronted with extremism', *Opinion, Committee on Migration, Refugees and Population*, viewed 13 March 2009, <http://assembly.coe.int/Main.asp?link=/Documents/WorkingDocs/Doc08/EDOC11575.htm>.

Cousins, C 1998, 'Social exclusion in Europe: Paradigms of social disadvantage in Germany, Spain, Sweden and the United Kingdom', *Policy & Politics*, vol. 26, no. 2, pp. 127–146.

Cresswell, JW 2003, *Research Design, Qualitative, Quantitative and Mixed Method Approaches*, 2nd edn, Sage, London.

Dalton, T, Draper, M Weeks, W and Wiseman, J 1996, *Making Social Policy in Australia, An Introduction*, Allen & Unwin, Sydney, Australia.

Daly, M 2003, 'Governance and social policy', *Journal of Social Policy*, vol. 32, pp. 113–128.

Dapré, B 2006, 'A compendium of legislative changes in social security 1983–2000 Part 2: 1994–2000', *Occasional Paper No. 13*, Department of Family, Canberra, Community Services and Indigenous Affairs.

Davidson, B 2009, 'For-profit organizations in managed markets for human services', in D. King and G. Meagher (eds), *Paid Care in Australia: Politics, Profits, practices*, Sydney University Press, Sydney, pp. 43–79.

Davies, C 1995, 'Competence versus care? Gender and caring work revisited', *Acta Sociologica*, vol. 38, no. 1, pp. 17–31.

Davies, C 1996, 'The sociology of professions and the profession of gender', *Sociology*, vol. 30, no. 4, pp. 661–78.

Davies, J 2005, 'The social exclusion debate: Strategies, controversies and dilemmas', *Policy Studies*, vol. 26, no. 1, pp. 3–27.

Deakin, N 2001, *In Search of Civil Society*, Palgrave, London.

Dean, H 2006, *Social Policy*, Polity Press, Cambridge.

Dearing, E 2008, 'Psychological costs of growing up poor', *Annals of the New York Academy of Science*, vol. 1136, pp. 324–332.

Department of Health (UK) 1999, *National Service Framework for Mental Health: Modern Standards and Service Models*, The Stationery Office, London.

Department of Health (UK) 1999, LAC (99) 33, *The Quality Protects Programme 2001/02 Transforming Children's Services*, The Stationery Office, London.

Department of Health (UK) 2000, *The Care Standards Act 2000*, The Stationery Office, London.

Department of Health (UK) 2002, *The Adoption and Children Act 2002*, The Stationery Office, London.

Department of Health (UK) 2003, 'Care leavers, year ending 31 March 2002, England', Department of Health Statistical Bulletin, London.

Department of Health (UK) 2005, 'Health reform in England: Update and next steps', UK Department of Health, viewed 25 March 2009, <www.dh.gov.uk/en/Publicationsandstatistics/Publications/PublicationsPolicyAndGuidance/DH_4124723?IdcService=GET_FILE&dID=8715&Rendition=Web>.

Denemark, D 2005, 'Mass media and media power in Australia', in S. Wilson, G. Meagher, R. Gibson, D. Denemark and M. Western (eds), *Australian Social Attitudes: The First Report*, UNSW Press, Sydney, pp. 220–239.

Dingeldey, I 2007, 'Between workfare and enablement—The different paths to transformation of the welfare state: A comparative analysis of activating labour market policies', *European Journal of Political Research*, vol. 46, no. 6, pp. 823–851.

Dodson, M 2007, 'Bully in the playground: A new stolen generation', in J. Altman and M. Hinkson (eds), *Coercive Reconciliation*, Arena Publications, Melbourne, pp. 21–29.

Downer, A 2007, ABC Television News, 7.30pm 25 November.

Drake, R 2009, *The Principles of Social Policy*, Houndmills, Basingstoke, Hemshire: Palgrave.

Drakeford, M 2006, 'Ownership, regulation and the public interest: The case of residential care for older people', *Critical Social Policy*, vol. 26, no. 4, pp. 932–44.

Dustin, D 2007, *The McDonaldization of Social Work*, Ashgate, Aldershot.

Edebalk, PG 2000, 'Emergence of a welfare state—Social insurance in Sweden in the 1910s', *Journal of Social Policy,* vol. 29, no. 4, pp. 537–551.

Egan, S 2008, 'Research for practice in small human service organizations', in D. Bottrell and G. Meagher (eds) *Communities and Change: Selected Papers,* Sydney University Press, Sydney, pp. 303–317.

Eliasson-Lappalainen, R and Nilsson Motevasel, I 1997, 'Ethics of care and social policy', *International Journal of Social Welfare*, vol. 6, no. 2, pp. 189–96.

Ellis, K 2007, 'Direct payments and social work practice: The significance of "street-level bureaucracy" in determining eligibility', *British Journal of Social Work*, vol. 37, no. 3, pp. 405–422.

England, P, Budig, M and Folbre, N 2002, 'Wages of virtue: The relative pay of care work', *Social Problems*, vol. 49, no. 4, pp. 455–473.

Esping-Andersen, G 1990, *The Three Worlds of Welfare Capitalism*, Polity Press, Cambridge.

Esping-Andersen, G 1999, *Social Foundations of Postindustrial Economies,* Oxford University Press, Oxford.

Esping-Andersen, G 2002, *Why We Need a Welfare State*, Oxford University Press, New York.

Etzioni, A (ed) 1969, *The Semi-Professions and their Organization: Teachers, Nurses and Social Workers*, The Free Press, New York.

Etzioni, A 1993, *The Spirit of Community*, Crown Books, New York.

Evans, T and Harris, J 2004, 'Street-level bureaucracy, social work and the (exaggerated) death of discretion', *British Journal of Social Work*, vol. 34, no. 6, pp. 871–895.

Everingham, C 2001, 'Reconstituting community: Social justice, social order and the politics of community', *Australian Journal of Social Issues*, vol. 36, no. 2, pp. 105, 123.

Exworthy, M and Halford, S 1999, *Professionals and the New Managerialism in the Public Sector*, Open University Press, Buckingham.

FACSIA (Department of Family and Community Services and Indigenous Affairs) 2006, 'Income support customers: A statistical overview 2004', *Statistical Paper No. 3*, Department of Family, Community Services and Indigenous Affairs, Canberra.

FACSIA 2007a, 'Welfare payments reform: Helping children at risk of neglect', *Fact Sheet,* viewed 31 January 2008, <www.facsia.gov.au/internet/facsinternet.nsf/via/families/$file/welfare_reform_factsheet2.pdf>.

FACSIA 2007b, 'Welfare payments reform: Enhancing parental responsibility for school attendance', *Fact Sheet*, viewed 31 January 2008, <www.facsia.gov.au/internet/facsinternet.nsf/via/families/$file/welfare_reform_factsheet1.pdf>.

FaHCSIA (n.d.), 'Early childhood—invest to grow' and 'Communities for children', viewed 7 May 2009, <www.fahcsia.gov.au/sa/families/progserv/Pages/default.aspx>.

FaHCSIA 2009, *Closing the Gap on Indigenous Disadvantage: The Challenge for Australia,* viewed 20 March 2009, <www.fahcsia.gov.au/indigenous/closing_the_gap/default.htm>.

Farrell, C and Morris, J 2003, 'The "neo-bureaucratic" state: Professionals, managers, and professional managers in schools, general practices and social work', *Organization*, vol. 10, no. 1, pp. 129–56.

Fawcett, B 2001, 'Action evaluation', *Social Work Review*, Spring 2001, vol. 12, no. 3, pp. 37–41.

Fawcett, B 2003, 'An action evaluation as a tool to engage users and practitioners', in S. Ramon (ed), *Users Researching Health and Social Care: An Empowering Agenda*, Venture Pressa, Birmingham, pp. 57–71.

Fawcett, B and Featherstone, B 1998, 'Quality assurance and evaluation in social work in a postmodern era', in J. Carter (ed), *Postmodernity and the Fragmentation of Welfare*, Routledge, London, pp. 67–82. Fawcett, B,

Featherstone, B and Goddard, J 2004, *Contemporary Child Care Policy and Practice,* Palgrave, Basingstoke.

Fawcett, B and Karban, K 2005, *Contemporary Mental Health: Theory, Policy and Practice*, Routledge, London.

Fenech, M, Sumsion, J and Goodfellow, J 2006, 'The regulatory environment in long day care: A "double-edged sword" for early childhood professional practice', *Australian Journal of Early Childhood,* vol. 31, no. 3, pp. 49–58.

Fenna, A 2004, *Australian Public Policy,* 2nd edn, Pearson Longman, Frenchs Forest.

Ferrie, D 2008, 'Social inclusion and place based disadvantage: What we have already done that is valuable for the future', in *Social Inclusion and Place Based Disadvantage Workshop Proceedings*, 13 June, Brotherhood of St Laurence and the Department of Planning and Community Development, Victoria.

Fincher, R 1995, 'Women, immigration and the state: Issues of difference and social justice', in A. Edwards and S. Magarey (eds), *Women in a Restructuring Australia: Work and Welfare,* Allen & Unwin, Sydney.

Fine, M and Shaver, S 1995, 'Social policy and personal life: Changes in state, family and community in the support of informal care', in *Towards a National Agenda for Carers,* Aged and Community Care Service Development and Evaluation Reports, No. 22, Department of Human Services and Health, AGPS, Canberra, pp. 19–36.

Fitzpatrick, T 2002, 'In search of a welfare democracy', *Social Policy & Society,* vol. 1, no. 1, pp. 11–20.

Fitzpatrick, T, Manning, NP, Kwon, H, Midgley, J and Pascall, G (eds) 2006, *International Encyclopedia of Social Policy*, Routledge, London.

Flynn, JP 1992, *Social Agency Policy: Analysis and Presentation for Community Practice*, Nelson-Hall, Chicago.

Fogarty, B and Paterson, M 2007, *Constructive Engagement: Impacts, Limitations and Possibilities During a National Emergency Intervention*, PIA Consultancy, Commissioned by Bawinanga Aboriginal Corporation, NT, Australia.

Folbre, N 2006, 'Demanding quality: Worker/consumer coalitions and "high road" strategies in the care sector', *Politics and Society*, vol. 34, no. 1, pp. 11–31.

Foster, M and Mathie, A 2001, *Situating Asset-Based Community Development in the International Development Context,* New and Evolving Ideas Series, Coady International Institute, St Francis Xavier University, Nova Scotia, Canada.

Foster, M, Harris, J, Jackson, K, Morgan, H and Glendinning, C 2006, 'Personalised social care for adults with disabilities: A problematic concept for frontline practice', *Health and Social Care in the Community*, vol. 14, no. 2, pp. 125–35.

Foucault, M 1981, 'Question of method: An interview with Michel Foucault', *Ideology and Consciousness*, vol. 8, pp. 1–14.

Foucault, M 1984, 'On the genealogy of ethics: An overview of work in progress', in P. Rabinow (ed), *The Foucault Reader*, Penguin, Harmondsworth.

France, A and Utting, D 2005, 'The paradigm of risk and protection focused prevention and its impact on services for children and families', *Children and Society*, vol. 19, no. 2, pp. 77–90.

Frankel, B 2001, *When the Boat Comes In*, Pluto Press, Annandale.

Fraser, A 2008, 'A plan turned sour: The rise and fall of Eddy Groves', *The Australian*, 4 October, viewed 18 February 2009, <www.theaustralian.news.com.au/story/0,25197,24472714-5018061,00.html>.

Fraser, N 1989, *Unruly Practices: Power, Discourse and Gender in Contemporary Social Theory*, Polity Press, Cambridge.

Frey, B 1998, 'Institutions and morale: The crowding-out effect', in Avner Ben-Ner and Louis Putterman (eds), *Economics, Values and Organization*, Cambridge University Press, Cambridge, pp. 437–460.

Fung, A 2006, 'Varieties of participation in complex governance', *Public Administration Review*, vol. 66, no. s1, pp. 66–75.

Gardner, H and Barraclough, S 2007, *Analysing Health Policy: A Problem-oriented Approach*, Elsevier, Melbourne.

Geddes, M 2005, 'International perspectives and policy issues', in P. Smyth, T. Reddel and A. Jones (eds), *Community and Local Governance in Australia*, UNSW Press, Sydney.

Giddens, A 1998, *The Third Way: The Renewal of Social Democracy*, Polity Press, Cambridge.

Giddens, A 2000, *The Third Way and Its Critics*, Polity Press, Cambridge.

Gilbert, N 2004, *Transformation of the Welfare State, The Silent Surrender of Public Responsibility*, Oxford University Press, Oxford, New York.

Gilbert, N 2005, 'The "enabling state"? From public to private responsibility for social protection: Pathways and pitfalls', *OECD Social, Employment and Migration Working Papers No. 26*, Organization for Economic Co-operation and Development (OECD), Paris.

Gillard, J 2007, 'The economics of social inclusion' [Address to The Sydney Institute on 12 July], *Sydney Papers*, vol.19, no. 3, pp. 102–112.

Gillard, J 2008a, *Media Release*: 'Majority of ABC Learning childcare centres to remain open in 2009', 26 November, viewed 21 February 2009, <www.deewr.gov.au/Ministers/Gillard/Media/Releases/Pages/Article_081128_145026.aspx>.

Gillard, J 2008b, 'Federal Government Social Inclusion Agenda' [Speech to ACOSS Conference, 10 April], *Impact*, Autumn, pp. 12–15.

Gilroy, P 1992, 'The end of racism', in J. Donald and A. Rattansi (eds), *'Race', Culture and Difference*, Open University Press/Sage, London.

Ginsburg, N 1992, *Divisions of Welfare: A Critical Introduction to Comparative Social Policy*, Sage, London.

Gleeson, B and Carmichael, C 2001, *Thinking Regionally, Acting Locally: Lessons for Australia from Overseas Housing and Regional Assistance Policies*, Australian Housing and Urban Research Institute, University of New South Wales.

Glendinning, C 2008, 'Increasing choice and control for older and disabled people: A critical review of new developments in England', *Social Policy and Administration*, vol. 42, no. 5, pp. 451–469.

Goddard, C and Liddell, M 1995, 'Child abuse fatalities and the media: Lessons from a case study', *Child Abuse Review*, vol. 4, no. 5, pp. 356–364.

Goldstein, L 2008, 'Kindergarten teachers making "street-level" education policy in the wake of no child left behind', *Early Education and Development*, vol. 19, no. 3, pp. 448–478.

Goodin, R, Headey, B, Muffels, R and Dirven, HJ 1999, *The Real Worlds of Welfare Capitalism*, Cambridge University Press, Cambridge.

Goodin, RE 2001, 'False principles of welfare reform', *Australian Journal of Social Issues*, vol. 36, no. 3, pp. 189–205.

Goodwin, S 2003, 'States, communities and individuals', in G. McFee (ed.), Communities and Their Capacity to Tackle Disadvantage, *ACOSS Paper 30*, pp. 12–17.

Goodwin, S 2005, 'Community and social inclusion', in P. Smyth, T. Reddel and A. Jones (eds), *Community and Local Governance in Australia*, UNSW Press, Sydney.

Goodwin, S 2006, 'Working from the outside in: The NSW Women's Advisory Councils', in D. Brennan and L. Chappell (eds), *No Fit Place for Women?: Women and Politics in New South Wales 1856–2006*, UNSW Press, Sydney.

Gordon, D, Levitas, R, Patsios, D and Townsend, P 2000, *Poverty and Social Exclusion in Britain*, Joseph Rowntree Foundation, York, viewed 18 November 2008, <www.jrf.org.uk/node/1718>.

Gottschalk, M 2000, *The Shadow Welfare State*, ILR Press, Ithaca and London.

Gray, G 2004, *The Politics of Medicare*, University of New South Wales Press, Sydney.

Greener, I 2007, 'Are the assumptions underlying patients choice realistic? A review of the evidence', *British Medical Bulletin*, vol. 83, no. 1, pp. 249–58.

Greener, I 2008, 'Towards a history of choice in UK health policy', *Sociology of Health and Illness*, Advanced Access, published 3 December, 10.1111/j.1467-9566.2008.01135.x.

Greer, G 2007, 'Worlds apart', *The Guardian*, 3 July.

Grover, C 2006, 'Welfare reform, accumulation and social exclusion in the United Kingdom', *Social Work and Society,* vol. 4, no. 1, pp. 78–91.

Gunn, R 2008, 'The power to shape decisions? An exploration of young peoples' power in participation', *Health and Social Care in the Community,* vol 16, no. 3, pp. 253–261.

Gustafsson, RÅ and Szebehely, M 2009, 'Outsourcing of eldercare services in Sweden: Effects on work environment and political legitimacy', in D. King and G. Meagher (eds) *Paid Care in Australia: Politics, Profits, Practices,* Sydney University Press, Sydney, pp. 81–112.

Hancock, L 2006, 'Bringing in the community sector: Partnerships and advocacy', in H. K. Colebatch (ed) 2006, *Beyond the Policy Cycle: the Policy Process in Australia,* Allen & Unwin, Sydney, pp. 42–65.

Handy, F, Mook, L and Quarter, J 2006, 'Organisational perspectives on the value of volunteer labour', *Australian Journal of Volunteering,* vol. 11, no. 1, pp. 28–36.

Handy, F, Mook, L and Quarter, J 2008, 'The interchangeability of paid staff and volunteers in nonprofit organizations', *Nonprofit and Voluntary Sector Quarterly,* vol. 37, no. 1, pp. 76–92.

Hart, E and Bond, M 1995, *Action Research for Health and Social Care: A Guide to Practice,* Open University Press, Buckingham.

Hasenfeld, Y and Garrow, E 2007, 'The welfare state, the non-profit sector and the politics of care', paper presented to *Dead Sea Conference for Third Sector Research,* Israel, 14–15 March.

Healy, J 1998, *Welfare Options: Delivering Social Services,* Allen & Unwin, Sydney.

Healy, K 1998, 'Participation in child protection: The importance of context', *British Journal of Social Work,* vol. 28, no. 6, pp. 897–914.

Healy, K and Meagher, G 2004, 'The reprofessionalization of social work: Collaborative approaches for achieving professional recognition', *British Journal of Social Work,* vol. 34, no. 2, pp. 243–60.

Healy, K, Lyons-Crew, C, Michaux, A and Gal, I 2008, 'Change in volunteering roles: Managing change to build volunteer capacity', *Australian Journal of Volunteering,* vol. 13, no.1, pp. 5–16.

Healy, K, Meagher, G and Cullin, J 2009, 'Retraining novices to become expert child protection practitioners: Creating career pathways in direct practice', *British Journal of Social Work,* vol. 39, no. 2, pp. 299–317.

Hedetoft, U 2006, 'Denmark: Integrating immigrants into the homogeneous welfare state', *Migration Information Source,* Migration Policy Institute, Washington DC, USA, viewed 12 March 2009, <www.migrationinformation. com/Profiles/print.cfm?ID=485>.

Heffernan, K 2006, 'Social work, New Public Management, and the language of the "service user"', *British Journal of Social Work*, vol. 36, no. 1, pp. 139–147.

Henderson, P and Thomas, DN 1987, *Skills in Neighbourhood Work*, 2nd edn, Allen & Unwin, London.

Herbert-Cheshire, L 2000, 'Contemporary strategies for rural community development in Australia: A governmentality perspective', *Journal of Rural Studies*, vol. 16, pp. 203–215.

Himmelweit, S 1999, 'Caring labor', *Annals of the American Academy of Political and Social Science*, vol. 561, pp. 27–38.

Himmelweit, S 2007, 'The prospects for caring: Economic theory and policy analysis', *Cambridge Journal of Economics*, vol. 31, no. 4, pp. 581–99.

Hoad, P 2002, 'Drawing the line: The boundaries of volunteering in the community care of older people', *Health and Social Care in the Community*, vol. 10, no. 2, pp. 239–246.

Hoatson, L 2001, 'Public housing redevelopment: Opportunity for community regeneration?' *Urban Policy and Research*, vol. 20, no. 4, pp. 429–441.

Hogan, M 1996, 'Advocacy and Democratic Governance', in A. Farrar and J. Inglis (eds), *Keeping it Together: State and Civil Society in Australia,* Pluto Press, Sydney.

Holden, C 2005, 'Organizing across borders: Profit and quality in international-ized providers', *International Social Work*, vol. 48, no. 5, pp. 643–653.

Holmes, D, Murray, S, Perron, A and Rail, G 2006, 'Deconstructing the evidence-based discourse in health sciences: Truth, power and fascism', *International Journal of Evidence-based Healthcare*, vol. 4, no. 3, pp. 180–186.

Holstein, JA and Miller, G (eds) 2003, *Challenges and Choices: Constructionist Perspectives on Social Problems,* Aldine Transaction, New York.

Hounslow, B 2002, 'Community capacity building explained', *Stronger Families Learning Exchange Bulletin,* vol. 1, Autumn, pp. 20–22.

Howard, C 2007, *The Welfare State Nobody Knows, Debunking Myths About US Social Policy*, Princeton University Press, Princeton and Oxford.

Howard, J 2007a, *Indigenous Communities Joint Press Conference* (with the Hon Mal Brough, Minister for Families, Community Services and Indigenous Affairs), Parliament House, Canberra, 21 June.

Howard, J 2007b, 'Concession speech', *Electoral Coverage,* Australian Broadcasting Corporation, 24 November, Sydney.

Howe, B and Cleary, R 2000, *Community Building: Concepts and Strategies for the Victorian Government*, report commissioned for the Victorian Government, Australia.

Howes, M, Lyons, K and Bryant, S 2004, 'Civil society revisited: Possibilities for increasing community collaboration in a competitive world', *Australian Political Science Association Conference Proceedings,* University of Adelaide.

Howlett, M and Ramesh, M 1995, *Studying Public Policy: Policy Cycles and Policy Subsystems*, Oxford University Press, Toronto.

Hudson, J and Kühner, S 2009, 'Towards productive welfare? A comparative analysis of 23 OECD countries', *Journal of European Social Policy*, vol. 19, no. 1, pp. 34–36.

Hunt, J 2005, 'Capacity building in the international development context: Implications for Indigenous Australia', *Discussion Paper No 278*, Centre for Aboriginal Economic Policy Research, Australian National University, Canberra.

Hwang, GI 2006, *Pathways to State Welfare in Korea, Interests Ideas and Institutions*, Ashgate, Hampshire.

Hywood, G 2004, 'The unelected groups we should scrutinise', *Sydney Morning Herald*, June 24.

Ife, J 1997, *Rethinking Social Work: Towards Critical Practice*, Longman, Melbourne.

Ife, J 2008, *Human Rights and Social Work: Towards Rights-Based Practice*, revised edn, Cambridge University Press, Cambridge.

International Gender Budgeting Projects, no date, viewed 3 February 2009, <www.wbg.org.uk/GBA_Inter.htm>.

Isgro, K 2005, 'Unsanctioned (bedroom) commitments: The 2000 US Census discourse around cohabitation and single motherhood', in S. Meagher and P. Diquinzio, (eds), *Women and Children First, Feminism, Rhetoric and Public Policy*, State University of New York Press, Albany, pp. 37–55.

Jaensch, D 1992, *The Politics of Australia*, Macmillan, Melbourne.

James, N 1992, 'Care = organisation + physical labour + emotional labour', *Sociology of Health and Illness*, vol. 14, no. 1, pp. 488–507.

Jeppson Grassman, E 2003, *Anhörigskapets uttrycksformer* (The nature of informal care), Studentlitteratur, Lund.

Jesuit Social Services 2008, 'Leading nationally—responding locally: Building social inclusion in localities on the edge', *Issues Paper*, Catholic Social Services, Melbourne.

Jewell, C and Bero, L 2008, 'Developing good taste in evidence: Facilitators of and hindrances to evidence-informed health policymaking in state government', *Milbank Quarterly*, vol. 86, no. 2, pp. 177–208.

Johns, G and Roskam, J 2004, *The Protocol: Managing Relations with NGOs, Report to the Prime Minister's Community Business Partnership*, Institute of Public Affairs, Melbourne.

Jones, A and Smyth, P 1999, 'Social exclusion: A new framework for social policy analysis?' *Just Policy*, vol. 17, pp. 11–21.

Jones, K, Netten, A, Francis, J and Bebbington, A 2007, 'Using older home care user experiences in performance monitoring', *Health and Social Care in the Community*, vol. 15, no. 4, pp. 322–332.

Jones, P and Cullis, J 2003, 'Key parameters in policy design: The case of intrinsic motivation', *Journal of Social Policy*, vol. 32, no. 4, pp. 527–547.

Jopson, D, Gibson, J and Chandler, J 2007, 'Leader's lament: It's a knee-jerk step back', *Sydney Morning Herald*, 22 June, p. 7.

Jordan, B 2006, *Social Policy for the Twenty-First Century*, Polity Press, Cambridge, MA.

Joyce, B and Nash, F 2006, *The National Senators' Dissenting Report*, Senate Standing Committee on Environment, Communications, Information Technology and the Arts, Broadcasting Services Amendment (Media Ownership) Bill 2006, Commonwealth of Australia, <www.aph.gov/au/Senate/committee/ecita_completed_inquiries/2004-07/cross_media/report/d01.pdf>.

Judd, B and Randolph, B 2006, 'Community renewal and large public housing estates', *Urban Policy and Research*, vol. 8, no. 1, pp. 91–104.

Jupp, J 2005, 'Immigration and multiculturalism', in C. Aulich and R. Wettenhall (eds), *Howard's Second and Third Term,* UNSW Press, Sydney, pp. 173–188.

Kähkönen, L 2005, 'Costs and efficiency of quasi-markets in practice', *Local Government Studies*, vol. 31, no. 1, pp. 85–97.

Kaiser Commission, n.d., 'Myths about the uninsured', *Myths and Facts Fact Sheet #7307*, Kaiser Commission on Medicaid and the Uninsured, Washington DC, viewed 20 March 2009, <www.kff.org/uninsured/7307.cfm>.

Kang, E 2007, 'The health, economic, and policy implications of the ageing Korean society', in R. Phillips (ed), *Generational Change and New Policy Challenges, Australia and South Korea*, Sydney University Press, Sydney, pp. 192–205.

Karvelas, P 2008, 'Welfare quarantine rules may be eased', 17 April, p. 6.

Kelly, J 2007, 'Reforming public services in the UK: Bringing in the third sector', *Public Administration*, vol. 85, no. 4, pp. 1003–1022.

Kenway, J 2006, 'Education policy, markets and society', in A. McClelland and P. Smyth (eds), *Social Policy in Australia: Understanding for Action*, Cambridge University Press, Melbourne.

King, D 2007, 'Rethinking the care-market relationship in care provider organisations', *Australian Journal of Social Issues*, vol. 42, no. 2, pp. 199–212.

Komblut, A 2008, 'Measured response to financial crisis sealed the election', *Washington Post*, 5 November, p. A01, <www.washingtonpost.com/wpdyn/content/article/2008/11/04/AR2008110404531.html?sid=ST2008110403463&s_pos>.

Korpi, W 1985, 'Economic growth and the welfare state: Leaky bucket or irrigation system?' *European Sociological Review*, vol. 1, no. 2, pp. 97–118.

Korpi, W and Palme, J 1998, 'The paradox of redistribution and strategies of equality: Welfare state institutions, inequality and poverty in Western countries', *American Sociological Review*, vol. 63, no. 5, pp. 661–687.

Kretzman, J and McKnight, J 1993, *Building Communities from the Inside Out: A Path Toward Finding and Mobilizing a Community's Assets*, Center for Urban Affairs and Policy Research, Neighborhood Innovations Network, Northwestern University.

Ku, I 2007, 'Social welfare reform since the 1997 economic crisis in Korea: Achievement, limits, and future prospects', *Asian Social Work and Policy Review*, vol. 1, no. 1 pp. 21–35.

Kulik, L 2006, 'Burnout among volunteers in the social services: The impact of gender and employment status', *Journal of Community Psychology*, vol. 34, no. 5, pp. 541–61.

Kwok, J 2008, 'Regional perspective from Asia: Social work and social development in Asia', *International Social Work*, vol. 51, no. 5, pp. 699–744.

Lake, D 2002, 'Critical social numeracy', *The Social Studies*, vol. 93, no. 1, pp. 4–9.

Lake, M 1999, *Getting Equal: The History of Australian Feminism*, Allen & Unwin, Sydney.

Lambert, PA 2008, 'The comparative political economy of parental leave and child care: Evidence from twenty OECD countries', *Social Politics: International Studies in Gender, State & Society*, vol. 15, no. 3, pp. 315–344.

Landis, G 2007, 'Lateline Interview', Australian Broadcasting Corporation, 12 October, Sydney.

Lane, M and Henry, K 2001, 'Community development, crime and violence: A case study', *Community Development Journal*, vol. 36, no. 3, pp. 212–222.

Lane, S 2008, 'Abortion aid under review', ABC Radio, AM Program, 4 June, Transcript, Australian Broadcasting Commission, <www.abc.net.au/cgibin/common/printfriendly.pl?> <www.abc.net.au/am/content/2008/s2264631.htm>.

Law Society (Northern Territory) 2007, 'Australian Government Intervention in Northern Territory Indigenous communities', *Open Letter to the Prime Minister*, 29 June, Darwin.

Le Grand, J 1991, 'The theory of government failure', *British Journal of Political Science*, vol. 21, no. 4, pp. 423–442.

Le Grand, J 1993, 'Paying for or providing welfare?' in N. Deakin and R. Page (eds), The Costs of Welfare, Avebury Press, Aldershot.

Le Grand, J 1997, 'Knights, knaves or pawns? Human behaviour and social policy', *Journal of Social Policy*, vol. 26, no. 2, pp. 149–169.

Le Grand, J and Bartlett, W 1993, 'Introduction', in J. Le Grand and W. Bartlett (eds), *Quasi-Markets and Social Policy*, Macmillan, Basingstoke, pp. 1–12.

Leigh, A 2009, 'What evidence should social policymakers use?' *Economic Roundup Issue 1*, Australian Treasury, Canberra, pp. 27–43.

Levy, A and Kahan, B 1991, *The Pindown Experience and the Protection of Children*, Staffordshire County Council, Stafford, UK.

Lewis, J 1993, *Women and Social Policies in Europe: Work, Family and the State*, Edward Elgar, Aldershot.

Lewis, JM 2006, 'Health policy in Australia: Mind the growing gaps', in A. McLelland and P. Smyth (eds), *Social Policy in Australia: Understanding for Action*, Oxford University Press, Melbourne.

Lie, M and Baines, S 2007, 'Making sense of organizational change: Voices of older volunteers', *Voluntas International Journal of Voluntary and Nonprofit Organizations*, vol. 18, no. 3, pp. 225–240.

Lindert, P 2004, *Growing Public: Social Spending and Economic Growth since the Eighteenth Century*, Cambridge University Press, Cambridge.

Lipsky, M 1980, *Street-level Bureaucracy: Dilemmas of the Individual in Public Services*, Russell Sage Foundation, New York.

Lorentzen, T and Dahl, E 2005, 'Active labour market programmes in Norway: Are they helpful for social assistance recipients?' *Journal of European Social Policy*, vol. 15, no. 1, pp. 27–45.

Lowi, T 1966, 'Distribution, regulation, redistribution: The functions of government', in R.B. Ripley (ed), *Public Policies and Their Politics: Techniques of Government Control*, W.W. Norton, New York, pp. 27–40.

Lyons, M and Passey, A 2006, 'Need public policy ignore the Third Sector? Government policy in Australia and the United Kingdom', *Australian Journal of Public Administration,* vol. 65, no. 3, pp. 90–102.

Lyotard, JF 1994, *3e*, Manchester University Press, Manchester.

McAllister, I 2003, 'Border protection, the 2001 Australian election and the Coalition victory', *Australian Journal of Political Science*, vol. 38, no. 3, pp. 445–463.

McBeath, B and Meezan, W 2008, 'Market-based disparities in foster care service provision', *Research in Social Work Practice*, vol. 18, no. 1, pp. 27–41.

McClelland, A 2006, 'Values, concepts and social policy design', in A. McClelland and P. Smyth (eds), 2006, *Social Policy in Australia,* Oxford University Press, Melbourne, pp. 21–38.

McDonald, C 1999, 'Internal control and accountability in non-profit human service organisations', *Australian Journal of Public Administration*, vol. 58, no. 1, pp. 11–22.

McDonald, C 2003, 'Forward via the past? Evidence-based practice as a strategy in social work', *The Drawing Board: An Australian Review of Public Affairs,* vol. 3, no. 3, pp. 123–42.

Macdonald, G, Sheldon, B and Gillespie, J 1992, 'Contemporary studies of the effectiveness of social work', *British Journal of Social Work*, vol. 22, no. 6, pp. 615–43.

Macdonald, G 1998, 'Promoting evidence-based practice in child protection', *Clinical Child Psychology and Psychiatry*, vol. 3, no. 1, pp. 71–85.

Macdonald, K 1995, *Sociology of the Professions*, Sage, London.

McLeod, A 2007, 'Whose agenda? Issues of power and relationship when listening to looked-after young people', *Child and Family Social Work*, vol. 12, no. 3, pp. 278–286.

McLeod, A 2008, '"A friend and an equal": Do young people in care seek the impossible from their social workers?' *British Journal of Social Work*, Advanced Access, published 24 November, doi:10.1093/bjsw/bcn143.

McLeod, E, Bywaters, P, Tanner, D and Hirsch, M 2008, 'For the sake of their health: Older service users' requirements for social care to facilitate access to social networks following hospital discharge', *British Journal of Social Work*, vol. 38, no. 1, pp. 73–90.

Maddison, S, Denniss, R and Hamilton, C 2004, 'Silencing dissent: non-profit advocacy organisations and Australian democracy', *Discussion Paper 65*, The Australia Institute, Canberra.

Maddox, M 2005, *God Under Howard*, Allen & Unwin, Crows Nest, Australia.

Mahler, V and Jesuit, DK 2006, 'Fiscal redistribution in the developed countries: New insights from the Luxembourg Income Study', *Socio-Economic Review*, vol. 4, no. 3, pp. 483–511 by permission of Oxford University Press.

Mahler, V and Jesuit, DK 2008, *Fiscal redistribution data set, version 2*, February, viewed 10 November 2008, <www.lisproject.org/publications/fiscalredistdata/fiscred.htm>.

Mares, I 2007, 'The economic consequences of the welfare state', *International Social Security Review*, vol. 60, nos 2–3, pp. 65–81.

Mares, P 2001, *Borderline*, UNSW Press, Sydney.

Marques-Pereira, B and Siim, B 2002, 'Representation, agency and empowerment', in B. Hobson, J. Lewis and B. Siim (eds), *Contested Concepts in Gender and Social Politics*, Edward Elgar, Cheltenham.

Marsh, I 1994, 'Interest group analysis', in A. Parkin, J. Summers and D. Woodward (eds), *Government, Politics, Power and Policy in Australia,* Longman Cheshire, Melbourne.

Marston, G 2004, *Social Policy and Discourse Analysis: Policy Change in Public Housing*, Ashgate Publishing, Hampshire.

Martin, GP, Phelps, K and Katbamna, S 2004, 'Human motivation and professional practice: Of knights, knaves and social workers', *Social Policy and Administration*, vol. 38, no. 5, pp. 470–87.

Martiniello, J 2007, 'Howard's new tampa children overboard are our Aboriginal children', in Indigenous Law Centre *A Collection of Initial Responses to the Howard Government's Intervention in the Northern Territory*, June/July 2007, Darwin.

Mason, G 2002, *The Spectacle of Violence: Homophobia, Gender and Knowledge*, Routledge, New York.

Mathie, A and Cunningham, G 2003, 'Who is driving development? Reflections on the transformative potential of asset-based community development, *Occasional Paper*, Coady Institute, Antigonish, N.S.

Maynard-Moody, S and Mushena, M 2003, *Cops, Teachers, Counselors: Stories from the Front Lines of Public Service*, University of Michigan Press, Ann Arbor.

Meagher, G 2002, 'The politics of knowledge in social service evaluation', *UnitingCare Burnside Discussion Paper No. 1*, UnitingCare Burnside, North Parramatta.

Meagher, G 2006, 'What can we expect from paid carers?' *Politics and Society*, vol. 34, no. 1, pp. 33–53.

Meagher, G and Cortis, N 2009, 'The political economy of for-profit paid care: Theory and evidence', in D. King and G. Meagher (eds), *Paid Care in Australia: Politics, Profits, Practices*, Sydney University Press, Sydney, pp. 13–42.

Meagher, G and Parton, N 2004, 'Modernising social work and the ethics of care', *Social Work and Society*, vol. 2, no. 1, pp. 1–26.

Meagher, G and Healy, K 2006, *Who Cares? Volume 2: Employment Structure and Incomes in the Australian Care Workforce*, Paper 141, Australian Council of Social Service, Sydney, viewed 28 November 2008, <www.acoss.org.au/upload/publications/papers/389__Paper%20141%20care%20workers%20vol2%20for%20website.pdf>.

Meagher, G, Cortis, N and Healy, K 2009, 'Strategic challenges in child welfare services: A comparative study of Australia, England and Sweden', in K. Rummery, I. Greener and C. Holden (eds), *Social Policy Review 21*, The Policy Press, Bristol, pp. 217–244.

Melville, R 2003, *Changing Roles of Community-Sector Peak Bodies in a Neo- Liberal Policy Environment in Australia: Final Report*, University of Wollongong, Wollongong.

Mendes, P 2003, 'Australian neoliberal think tanks and the backlash against the welfare state', *Journal of Australian Political Economy*, vol. 51, June, pp. 29–56.

Mendes, P 2005, 'Welfare reform and mutual obligation', in C. Aulich and R. Wettenhall (eds), *Howard's Second and Third Governments*, UNSW Press, Sydney, pp. 135–151.

Mendes, P 2006, *Inside the Welfare Lobby, A History of the Australian Council of Social Service,* Sussex Academic Press, Eastbourne.

Mendes, P 2008a, 'Retrenching or renovating the Australian welfare state: The paradox of the Howard government's neoliberalism', *International Journal of Social Welfare*, vol. 17 pp. 1–9.

Mendes, P 2008b, *Australia's Welfare Wars Revisited,* 3rd edn, UNSW Press, Sydney.

Midgely, J 1999, 'Growth, redistribution and welfare: Toward social investment', *Social Services Review*, vol. 73, no. 1, pp. 3–21.

Minkoff, D, Aisenbrey, S and Agnone, J 2008, 'Organizational diversity in the US advocacy sector', *Social Problems*, vol. 55, no. 4, pp. 525–548.

Molyneux, M 2002, 'Gender and the silences of social capital: Lessons from Latin America', *Development and Change*, vol. 33, no. 2, pp. 167–188.

Moore, M, Beazley, S and Maelzer, J 1998, *Researching Disability Issues*, Open University Press, Buckingham.

Morris, J and Helburn, S 2000, 'Childcare centre quality differences: The role of profit status, client preferences, and trust', *Nonprofit and Voluntary Sector Quarterly*, vol. 29, no. 3, pp. 377–99.

Morrison, Z 2008, 'Place, social inclusion and "cultural justice"', in *Social Inclusion and Place Based Disadvantage Workshop Proceedings,* 13 June, Brotherhood of St Laurence and Department of Planning and Community Development, Victoria.

Mowbray, M 2005, 'Community capacity building or state opportunism?' *Community Development Journal*, vol. 40, no. 3, pp. 255–264.

Naldini, M 2003, *The Family in the Mediterranean Welfare States*, Frank Cass, London.

Nash, K 2000, *Contemporary Political Sociology, Globalisation, Politics and Power,* Blackwell, Malden.

Nathan, RP 2000, *Social Science in Government: The Role of Policy Researchers*, Rockefeller Institute Press, New York.

National Childhood Council on the Developing Child 2007, 'The science of early childhood development: Closing the gaps between what we know and what we do', *Report*, National Childhood Council on the Developing Child, Center for the Developing Child, Harvard University, <www.developingchild.net/pubs/persp/pdf/Science_Early_Childhood_Development.pdf>.

Nelson, JA and Folbre, N 2006, 'Why a well-paid nurse is a better nurse', *Nursing Economics*, vol. 24, no. 3, pp. 127–130.

Netten, A, Jones, K and Sandhu, S 2007, 'Provider and care workforce influences on quality of home care services in England', *Journal of Aging and Social Policy*, vol. 19, no. 3, pp. 81–97.

Newman, J 2001, *Modernising Governance: New Labour, Policy and Society,* Sage, London.

Newman, J 2002, 'Putting the "policy" back into social policy', *Social Policy and Society,* vol. 1, no. 4, pp. 347–354.

Newman, J 2005, *Remaking Governance: Peoples, Politics and the Public Sphere,* Polity, Cambridge.

NIPSSR (National Institute of Population and Social Security Research) 2000, 'Health insurance', *Health Insurance/Social Security in Japan,* National Institute of Population and Social Security Research, Tokyo, Japan.

Norton, A 2006, 'The CIS at thirty' [Executive director of the Centre for Independent Studies interviewed by Norton, Andrew], *Policy,* vol. 22, no. 1, pp. 44–49.

NSW Commission for Children and Young People 2004, *TAKING PARTicipation Seriously,* NSW Commission for Children and Young People, Surry Hills, New South Wales.

Nyberg, A 2007, 'Lessons from the Swedish experience', in E. Hill, B. Pocock and A. Elliott (eds), *Kids Count: Better Early Childhood Education and Care in Australia,* Sydney University Press, Sydney.

Nye, JS, Zelikow, PD and King, DC (eds) 2007, *Why People Don't Trust Government,* Harvard University Press, Cambridge.

Oakley, A 1974, *The Sociology of Housework,* Robertson, London.

Ocampo, JA 2006, 'Market, social cohesion, and democracy', *Working Papers 9,* United Nations, Department of Economics and Social Affairs.

O'Connor, I, Wilson, J, Setterlund, D and Hughes, M 2008, *Social Work and Human Service Practice,* 5th edn, Pearson/Longman, Frenchs Forest.

OECD, *The OECD Jobs Strategy: Enhancing the Effectiveness of Active Labour Market Policies,* OECD 1996, OECD Publications, Paris.

OECD, *Social Expenditure 1980–2003 Interpretive Guide of SOCX,* November 2007, OECD 2007, Organization for Economic Co-operation and Development, Paris, viewed 5 September 2008, <www.oecd.org/els/social/expenditure>.

OECD 2008a, *OECD Economic Surveys: United States,* Organization for Economic Co-operation and Development, Paris.

OECD 2008b, *Growing Unequal? Income Distribution and Poverty in OECD Countries,* Organization for Economic Co-operation and Development, Paris.

Office of Children and Young People 2004, *A Families First Guide to Implementing Sustainable and Effective Child and Family Service Networking in NSW, Sydney, New South Wales,* viewed 24 January 2009, <www.familiesfirst.nsw. gov.au>.

Ohmer, ML 2007, 'Citizen participation in neighborhood organizations and its relationship to volunteers' self- and collective efficacy and sense of community', *Social Work Research*, vol. 31, no. 2, pp. 109–120.

Okun, A 1975, *Equality and Efficiency: The Big Trade-Off*, The Brookings Institution, Washington DC.

Olsson, K 2008, 'Social inclusion: What would a truly inclusive society look like?' *Red*, Issue 2, Griffith University, Brisbane, pp. 4–9, viewed 25 March 2009, <www.griffith.edu.au/er/pdf/final-griun-redmag.pdf>.

Ong, A 2006, *Neoliberalism as Exception, Mutations in Citizenship and Sovereignty*, Duke University Press, Durham and London.

Osborn, M 2006, 'Changing the context of teachers' work and professional development: A European perspective', *International Journal of Educational Research*, vol. 45, no. 4–5, pp. 242–53.

Osbourne, D and Gabler, T 1992, *Re-inventing Government*, Addison-Wesley, Reading.

Painter, M 1992, 'Participation and power', in M. Munro-Clark (ed), *Citizen Participation in Government*, Hale and Iremonger, Sydney.

Parrott, L, Buchanan, J and Williams, D 2006, 'Volunteers, families and children in need: An evaluation of family friends', *Child and Family Social Work*, vol. 11, no. 2, pp. 147–155.

Parry, N and Parry, J 1979, 'Social work, professionalism and the state', in M. Parry, N. Rustin and C. Satyamurti (eds), *Social Work, Welfare and the State*, Edward Arnold, London, pp. 21–47.

Pawson, R and Tilley, N 1997, *Realistic Evaluation*, Sage, London and Thousand Oaks.

Paxton, P, Kunovich, S and Hughes, M 2007, 'Gender in politics', *Annual Review of Sociology*, vol. 33, pp. 263–284.

Pearson, N 2001, 'Re-building Indigenous communities', in P. Botsman and M. Latham (eds), 2001, *The Enabling State: People Before Bureaucracy*, Pluto Press, Sydney.

Peatling, S. 2008, 'Rudd's apology revealed', *Sydney Morning Herald*, 13 February.

Peel, M 2003, *The Lowest Rung: Voices of Australian Poverty*, Cambridge University Press, Melbourne.

Percy-Smith, J 2000, *Policy Responses to Social Exclusion*, McGraw Hill, London.

Phillips, R 2006a, 'Undoing an activist response: Feminism and the Australian Government's domestic violence policy', *Critical Social Policy*, vol. 26, no. 1, pp. 192–219.

Phillips, R 2006b, 'The role of nonprofit advocacy organizations in Australian democracy and policy governance', *Voluntas: International Journal of Voluntary and Nonprofit Organizations*, vol. 17, no. 1, pp. 57–75.

Phillips, R 2007, 'Tamed or trained? The co-option and capture of "favoured" NGOs', *Third Sector Review,* vol. 13, no. 2, pp. 27–48.

Pierre, J and Peters, GB 2000, *Governance, Politics and the State,* Macmillan, Basingstoke.

Pierson, C 2004, *The Modern State,* Routledge, London.

Pierson, P 1994, *Dismantling the Welfare State, Reagan, Thatcher and the Politics of Retrenchment,* Cambridge University Press, Cambridge.

Pilger, J 2008, 'Under cover of a racist myth, a new land grab in Australia', viewed 26 October 2008, <www.johnpilger.com/page.asp?partid=507>.

Polanyi, K 1944/2001, *The Great Transformation: The Political and Economic Origins of Our Time,* Beacon Press, Boston, Mass.

Popple, K 1995, *Analysing Community Work: Its Theory and Practice,* Open University Press, Buckingham.

Porter, D and Craig, D 2004, 'Third way and third world: Poverty and social inclusion in the rise of "inclusive" liberalism', *Review of International Political Economy,* vol. 11, no. 2, pp. 387–423.

Powell, F 2007, *The Politics of Civil Society: Neoliberalism or Social Left,* Polity Press, Cambridge.

Prescribed Area People's Alliance Delegation to Canberra 2009, *Open Letter to Jenny Macklin MP Regarding the Northern Territory Intervention* (circulated nationally in Australia via email on 13 February).

Putnam, R 2000, *Bowling Alone: The Collapse and Revival of American Community,* Simon and Schuster, New York.

Quiggin, J 2007, 'The risk society: Social democracy in an uncertain world', *Centre for Policy Development Occasional Paper Number 2,* Centre for Policy Development, viewed 5 November 2008, <http://cpd.org.au/sites/cpd/files/u2/JohnQuiggin_The_Risk_Society_CPD_July07.pdf>.

Radi, H 1990, *Jessie Street: Documents and Essays,* Women's Redress Press, Sydney.

Raeburn, J, Akerman, M, Komatra, C, Mejia, F and Oladimeji, P 2006, 'Community capacity building and health promotion in a globalized world', *Social Policy and Society,* vol. 7, no. 2, pp. 201–210.

Randolph, B 2003, 'Poverty and place: New thinking', in *Communities and Their Capacity to Tackle Disadvantage,* ACOSS Paper 130, Australian Council for Social Service, Sydney.

Randolph, B 2004, 'Social inclusion and place-focused initiatives in Western Sydney: A review of current practice', *Australian Journal of Social Issues,* vol. 39, no. 1, pp. 63–78.

Rawsthorne, M 2005 'Community development activities in the context of contracting', *Australian Journal of Social Issues,* vol. 40, no 2, pp. 227–240.

Rawsthorne, M and Shaver, S 2008, 'Government/non-government relations: The impact of department of family & community services contractual reporting and accountability requirements', *SPRC Report No. 2/08*, prepared for the Department of Families, Housing, Community Services and Indigenous Affairs, Social Policy Research Centre, University of New South Wales, Sydney.

Research Intelligence 2006, 'A new European racism', *Research Intelligence*, Issue 29, August, p. 3, viewed 10 February 2009, <www.liv.ac.uk/researchintelligence/issue29/europeanracism.html>.

Reuters 2007, 'Health in rural China worsening, costs rising—WHO', 1 November, viewed 1 July 2008, <www.reuters.com/article/latestCrisis/idUSPEK281625>.

Review of Government Services 2009, *Report on Government Services 2009*, Productivity Commission, Canberra.

Rhodes, R 1997, *Understanding Governance,* Open University Press, Philadelphia.

Richardson, L and Le Grand, J 2004, *Outsider and Insider Expertise: The Response of Residents of Deprived Neighbourhoods to an Academic Definition of Social Exclusion* CASE Paper, No 57.

Robinson, N and Rintoul, S 2008, 'Indigenous kids trampled in summit race for treaty', *The Australian*, 22 April.

Robson, C 2002, *Real World Research*, Blackwell, Oxford.

Rogers, C 2007, 'The impact of the Australian Government Job Network contracting on not-for-profit service providers', *Australian Journal of Public Administration*, vol. 66, no. 4, pp. 395–405.

Roman, C 2008, 'Academic discourse, social policy and the construction of new families', in K. Melby, A. Ravn and C. Wetterberg (eds), *Gender Equality and Welfare Politics in Scandinavia: The Limits of Political Ambition?* The Policy Press, Bristol.

Ronel, N 2006, 'When good overcomes bad: The impact of volunteers on those they help', *Human Relations*, vol. 59, no. 8, pp. 1133–1153.

Rothgang, H 2003, 'Description of the German long-term care projection model', in A. Comas-Herrera and R. Wittenberg (eds), European Study of Long-Term Care Expenditure, *Report to the European Commission, Employment and Social Affairs DG*, Grant number VS/2001/0272, *PSSRU Discussion Paper 1840*, viewed 13 December 2008, <http://ec.europa.eu/employment_social/spsi/docs/social_protection/ltc_study_en.pdf>.

Rothgang, H and Igl, G 2007, 'Long-term care', in *Social Security Systems in Germany—Status Quo and Recent Developments,* Max Planck Institute for Foreign and International Social Law Working Papers, vol. 2, August, viewed 16 February 2008, <www.mpisoc.mpg.de/shared/data/pdf/mpisoc_wp_2_2007.pdf>.

Rudd, K 2009, 'The global financial crisis', *The Monthly*, no. 42, February, viewed 24 November 2008, <www.themonthly.com.au/tm/node/1417>.

Ruming, K 2006, *MOSAIC Urban Renewal Evaluation Project: Urban Renewal Policy, Program and Evaluation Review*, City Futures Research Centre, Kensington, NSW.

Rummery, K and Glendinning, C 2000, 'Access to services as a civil and social rights issue: The role of welfare professionals in regulating access to and commissioning services for disabled and older people under New Labour', *Social Policy and Administration*, vol. 34, no. 5, pp. 529–50.

Said, EW 2003, *Orientalism*, Penguin Books, London.

Salamon, L and Sokolowski, W 2001, 'Volunteering in cross-national perspective: Evidence from 24 countries', *Working Papers of the Johns Hopkins Comparative Nonprofit Sector Project*, no. 40, The Johns Hopkins Center for Civil Society, Baltimore.

Salamon, L, Hems, L and Chinnock, K 2000, 'The nonprofit sector: For what and for whom?' *Working Papers of the Johns Hopkins Comparative Nonprofit Sector Project*, no. 37, The Johns Hopkins Center for Civil Society Studies, Baltimore.

Sallnäs, M 2005, 'Vårdmarknad med svårigheter – om privata aktörer inom institutionsvården för barn och ungdomar' [A care market with problems: On private entrepreneurs in residential care for children and youth], *Socialvetenskaplig Tidsskrift*, vol. 12, no. 2–3, pp. 226–245.

Sallnäs, M 2009, 'Swedish residential care in the landscape of out-of-home care', in M.E. Courtney and D. Iwaniec (eds), *Residential Care of Children: Comparative Perspectives*, Oxford University Press, Oxford.

Saunders, P 2002, *The Ends and Means of Welfare: Coping with Economic and Social Change in Australia*, Cambridge University Press, Cambridge.

Saunders, P 2003, 'Can social exclusion provide a new framework for measuring poverty?' *SPRC Discussion Paper*, No. 127, Social Policy Research Centre, Sydney.

Saunders, P 2004, *Lies, Damned Lies and the Senate Poverty Inquiry Report*, Issue Analysis No. 46, Centre for Independent Studies, Sydney.

Saunders, P 2005, *The Poverty Wars: Reconnecting Research With Reality*, UNSW Press, Sydney.

Saunders, P and Tsumori, K 2002, *Poverty in Australia, Beyond the Rhetoric*, Policy Monograph 57, Centre for Independent Studies, Sydney.

Saunders, P and Bradbury, B 2006, 'Monitoring trends in poverty and income distribution: Data, methodology and measurement', *Economic Record*, vol. 82, no. 258, pp. 341–364.

Saunders, P, Naidoo, Y and Griffiths, M 2007, *Towards New Indicators of Disadvantage: Deprivation and Social Exclusion in Australia*, Social Policy Research Centre, University of New South Wales, viewed 21 November 2008, <www.sprc.unsw.edu.au/reports/ARC_Exclusion_FinalReport.pdf>.

SCB 2006, *Skola, vård och omsorg i privat regi: en sammanställning av statistik 1995–2005* [*Schools, Care and Assistance in Private Control: A Compilation of Statistics 1995-2005*], Statistika Centralbyrån, Stockholm.

Schmid, H 2003, 'Rethinking the policy of contracting out social services to non-governmental organizations', *Public Management Review*, vol. 5, no. 3, pp. 307–323.

Schmidt, M 1996, 'When parties matter: A review of the possibilities and limits of partisan influence on public policy', *European Journal of Political Research*, vol. 30, pp. 155–183.

Schubert, M 2008, 'Church backs end to Howard ban on abortion aid', *The Age*, June 5.

Scourfield, P 2007a, 'Are there reasons to be worried about the "cartelization" of residential care?' *Critical Social Policy*, vol. 27, no. 2, pp 155–180.

Scourfield, P 2007b, 'Social care and the modern citizen: Client, consumer, service user, manager and entrepreneur', *British Journal of Social Work*, vol. 37, no. 1, pp. 107–122.

Sen, A 1997, *Social Exclusion: A Critical Assessment of the Concept and its Relevance*, Asian Development Bank, Geneva.

Sen, A 2000, 'Social exclusion, concept, application and scrutiny', *Social Development Papers No. 1*, Office of Environment and Social Development Asian Development Bank, Geneva.

Senanuch, P 2008, *Urban Poverty in Thailand*, VDM Verlag, Germany.

Shapiro, M 1992, *Reading the Postmodern Polity: Political Theory as Textual Practice*, University of Minnesota Press, Minneapolis, MN.

Sharp, R and Austen, S 2007, 'The 2006 Federal Budget: A gender analysis of the superannuation tax concessions', *Australian Journal of Labour Economics*, vol. 10, no. 2, pp. 61–77.

Silove, D, Steel, Z and Watters, C 2000, 'Policies of deterrence and the mental health of asylum seekers', *Journal of the American Medical Association*, vol. 284, no. 5, pp. 604–611.

Silver, H 1994, 'Social exclusion and social solidarity: Three paradigms', *Discussion Paper No. 69*, International Institute for Labour Studies, Geneva.

Simpson, L, Wood, L and Daws, L 2003, 'Community capacity building: Starting with people not projects', *Community Development Journal*, vol. 38, no 4, pp. 277–286.

Sipïla, J 1997, *Social Care Services: The Key to the Scandinavian Welfare Model*, Ashgate, Aldershot.

Skocpol, T 1992, *Protecting Soldiers and Mothers: The Political Origins of Social Policy in the US,* Belknap Press of Harvard University Press, Cambridge, Mass.

Small, V, Murdoch, L and Coorey, P with Peatling, S 2007, 'Howard racist, says Maori MP', *Sydney Morning Herald*, 10 July.

Smart, B 1993, *Postmodernity*, London, Routledge.

Smith, I, Lepine, E and Taylor, M 2007, *Disadvantaged by Where You Live? Neighbourhood Governance in Contemporary Urban Policy*, Polity Press, Cambridge.

Smith, J, Pagnucco, R and Lopez, G 1998, 'Globalizing human rights: The work of transnational human rights NGOs in the 1990s', *Human Rights Quarterly*, vol. 20, pp. 379–412.

Smith, N, Littlejohns, LB and Thompson, D 2001, 'Shaking out the cobwebs: Insights into community capacity and its relation to health outcomes', *Community Development Journal*, vol. 36, pp. 130–141.

Smith, SR 2005, 'NGOs and contracting', in E. Ferlie, L. Lynn Jr and C. Pollit (eds), *Oxford Handbook of Public Management*, Oxford University Press, Oxford, pp. 591–614.

Smyth, P 2006, 'The historical context for action', in A. McClelland and P. Smyth (eds), *Social Policy in Australia*, Oxford University Press, Melbourne, pp. 95–111.

Social Exclusion Task Force 2009, Cabinet Office Web Site, Social Exclusion Task Force, London, viewed 10 March 2009, <www.cabinetoffice.gov.uk/social_exclusion_task_force.aspx>.

Social Exclusion Unit 2000, *Social Exclusion Unit Website* (now defunct), for information see Social Exclusion Task Force, Cabinet Office, viewed 12 November 2007, <www.cabinetoffice.gov.uk/social_exclusion_task_force/context.aspx>.

Steel, Z, Momartin, S, Bateman, C, Hafshejani, A, Silove, D, Everson, N, Roy, K, Dudley, M, Newman, L, Blick, B and Mares, S 2007, 'Psychiatric status of asylum seeker families held for a protracted period in a remote detention centre in Australia', *Australian and New Zealand Journal of Public Health,* vol. 28, no. 6, pp. 527–536.

Stein, S 2004, *The Culture of Education Policy,* Teachers College Press, New York.

Stephens, J 1996, 'The Scandinavian welfare states: Achievements, crisis, and prospects', in G. Esping-Andersen (ed) *Welfare States in Transition, National Adaptations in Global Economies*, Sage Publications, London.

Stevens, A 2007, Survival of the ideas that fit: An evolutionary analogy for the use of evidence in policy, *Social Policy and Society,* vol. 6, no.1, pp. 25–35.

Stewart, R 1999, *Policy Analysis: Strategy and Accountability*, Macmillan, Melbourne.

Stiglitz, J 1993, *Economics*, W.W. Norton & Company, New York.

Stone, D 2000, 'Caring by the book', in M.H. Meyer (ed), *Care Work: Gender, Class and the Welfare State*, Routledge, New York, pp. 89–111.

Stone, R 2004, 'The direct care worker: A key dimension of home care policy', *Home Health Care Management & Practice*, vol. 6, no. 5, pp. 339–349.

Stott Despoja, N 2007, *Northern Territory Intervention Legislation—Second Reading Speech*, Federal Parliament, Canberra, viewed 2 September 2007, <www.democrats.org.au/speeches/index.htm?speech_id=2258>.

Summers, A 2003, *The End of Equality: Work, Babies and Women's Choices in 21st Century Australia*, Random House, Sydney.

SustainAbility, Global Compact, UNEP 2003, 'The 21st century NGO. In the market for change', December 2003, viewed 12 November 2007, <www.sustainability.com/>.

Swedish National Agency for Education 2007, *Children, Pupils and Staff— National level*, Report no. 298, Swedish National Agency for Education, Stockholm.

Szebehely, M and Trydegård, G-B 2007, 'Omsorgtjänster för alder och funktionshindrade: Skilda villkor, skilda trender?' [Care services for older people and people with disabilities: different conditions, different trends?], *Socialvetenskaplig Tidskrift*, vol. 14, no. 2-3, pp. 197–219.

Tangetere Council Press Release 29.6.2007, in *Indigenous Law Centre: A Collection of Initial Responses to the Howard Government's Intervention in the Northern Territory*, June/July 2007, Darwin, Indigenous Law Centre.

Taylor, C and White, S 2006, 'Knowledge and reasoning in social work: Educating for humane judgment', *British Journal of Social Work*, vol. 36, no. 6, pp. 937–954.

Taylor, S and Kelly, J 2006, 'Professionals, discretion and public sector reform in the UK: Revisiting Lipsky', *International Journal of Public Sector Management*, vol. 19, no. 7, pp. 629–642.

t'Hart, P and Vromen, A 2008, 'A new era for think tanks in public policy? International trends, Australian realities', *Australian Journal of Public Administration*, vol. 67, no. 2, pp. 135–148.

Thompson, N 2002, 'Social movements, social justice and social work', *British Journal of Social Work*, vol. 32, no. 6, pp. 711–722.

Thornley, C 2008, 'Efficiency and equity considerations in employment of health care assistants and support workers', *Social Policy and Society*, vol. 7, no. 2, pp.147–158.

Thorpe, R and Irwin, J 1996, *Women and Violence: Working for Change,* Hale and Iremonger, Sydney.

Trydegård, G-B 2001, 'Välfärdtjänster till salu – privatisering och alternativa driftformer under 1990-talet' [Welfare services for sale—privatization and alternative organizational forms in the 1990s], in M. Szebehely (ed), *Välfärdtjänster i omvandling* [*Welfare services under transformation*], SOU 2001, p. 52.

UN 2006, 'United Nations common understanding of a human rights based approach to development', *United Nations Development Group Policy Paper,* viewed 28 November 2008, <www.undg.org/?P=221>.

US Bureau of Labor Statistics 2007, *Women in the Labor Force: A Databook,* US Bureau of Labor Statistics, Washington DC.

Vabø, M 2006, 'Caring for people or caring for proxy consumers?' *European Societies,* vol. 8, no. 3, pp. 403–422.

Verity, F 2007, *Community Capacity Building—A Review of the Literature,* State Department of Health, South Australia.

Vinson, T 2007, *Dropping Off the Edge: The Distribution of Disadvantage in Australia,* Jesuit Social Services, Melbourne.

Vis, B 2007, 'States of welfare or states of workfare? Welfare state restructuring in 16 capitalist democracies, 1985–2002', *Policy & Politics,* vol. 35, no. 1, pp. 105–22.

Wallace, A 2007, '"We have had nothing for so long that we don't know what to ask for": New deal for communities and the regeneration of social excluded terrain', *Social Policy and Society,* vol. 6, no. 1, January, pp. 1–12.

Wallis, J and Dollery, B 2006, 'Revitalising the contribution that non-profit organizations can make to the provision of human services', *International Journal of Social Economics,* vol. 33, no. 7, pp. 491–511.

Walzer, M 1995, 'The concept of a civil society', in M. Walzer (ed), *Toward a Global Civil Society,* Berghahn Books, Providence, pp. 8–27.

Waterhouse, R 2000, *Lost in Care: Report of the Tribunal of Inquiry into the Abuse of Children in care in the Former County Council Areas of Gwynedd and Clwyd Since 1974,* The Stationery Office, London.

Webb, S 2001, 'Some considerations on the validity of evidence-based practice in social work', *British Journal of Social Work,* vol. 31, no. 1, pp. 57–79.

Weiss, CH 1979, 'The many meanings of research utilization', *Public Administration Review,* vol. 39, no. 5, pp. 426–431.

Weiss-Gal, I and Welbourne, P 2008, 'The professionalisation of social work: A cross-national exploration', *International Journal of Social Welfare,* vol. 17, no. 4, pp. 281–290.

Wells, P 2007, 'New Labour and evidence based policy making: 1997–2007', *People, Place & Policy Online* vol. 1, no. 1, pp. 22–29.

Western, M, Baxter, J, Pakulski, J, Tranter, B, Western, J, van Egmond, Chesters, J, Hosking, A, van Gellecum, M and O'Flaherty, Y 2007, 'Neoliberalism, inequality and politics: The changing face of Australia', *Australian Journal of Social Issues*, vol. 42, pp. 401–418.

Westhue, A 2006, *Canadian Social Policy: Issues and Perspectives,* 4th edn, Wilfred Laurier University Press, Ontario.

Whiteford, P 2001, 'Understanding poverty and social exclusion: Situating Australia internationally', in R. Fincher and P. Saunders (eds), *Creating Unequal Futures? Rethinking Poverty, Inequality and Disadvantage*, Allen & Unwin, Sydney, pp. 38–69.

WHO (World Health Organization) 2008, 'Country cooperation strategy at a glance', Human Development Report 2007/2008, viewed 12 November 2008, <www.who.int/countryfocus/cooperation_strategy/ccsbrief_china_en.pdf>.

Wiest, LR, Higgins, HJ and Frost, JH 2007, 'Quantitative literacy for social justice', *Equity & Excellence in Education*, vol. 40, no. 1, pp. 47–55.

Wilensky, H 2002, *Rich Democracies: Political Economy, Public Policy, and Performance*, University of California Press, Los Angeles.

Wilkes, L, Beale, B and Cole, R 2006, 'Aunties and Uncles Co-operative Family Project Ltd: Volunteers making a difference', *Contemporary Nurse*, vol. 23, no. 2, pp. 291–302.

Williams, F 1989, *Social Policy, A Critical Introduction*, Polity Press, Oxford and Malden.

Wilson, S, Meagher, G, Gibson, R, Denemark, D and Western, M 2005, *Australian Social Attitudes: The First Report*, UNSW Press, Sydney.

Women's Budget Group, n.d., viewed 3 March 2009, <www.wbg.org.uk/index.htm>.

Wong, K 2003, 'Empowerment as a panacea for poverty—old wine in new bottles? Reflections on the World Bank's conception of power', *Progress in Development Studies*, vol. 3, no. 4, pp. 307–322.

Wright, P, Turner, C, Clay, D and Mills, H 2006, 'The participation of children and young people in developing social care', *Social Care Institute for Excellence Participation Practice Guide 06*, Social Care Institute for Excellence, London.

Yeatman, A (ed) 1998, *Activism and the Policy Process,* Allen & Unwin, Sydney.

Yeend, P 2004, 'Mutual Obligation/Work for the Dole', *Current Issues E-brief*, Department of Parliamentary Services, Parliament of Australia, viewed 12 November 2008, <www.aph.gov.au/library/INTGUIDE/sp/dole.htm>.

Young, IM 2000, *Inclusion and Democracy,* Oxford University Press, Oxford and New York.

Yu, WC 2006, 'The reforms of health care finance in Hong Kong and urban China: A mixed attitude to social welfare', *Critical Social Policy*, vol. 26, no. 4, pp. 843–864.

Zetter, R, Griffiths, D, Ferretti, S and Pearl, M 2003, *An Assessment of the Impact of Asylum Policies in Europe 1990–2000*, Home Office Research Study 259, Home Office Research, Development and Statistics Directorate, London.

Ziguras, S 2006, 'Australian social security policy: Doing more with less?' in A. McClelland and P. Smyth, (eds), *Social Policy in Australia,* Oxford University Press, Melbourne, pp. 161–177.

Index